The Everything Guide to PHONICS

Instructional Routines, Word Lists, and More!

Word Lists Author
Shireen Pesez Rhoades, M.A.Ed.

Publishing Credits
Corinne Burton, M.A.Ed., *President* and *Publisher*
Aubrie Nielsen, M.S.Ed., *EVP of Content Development*
Emily Smith, M.Ed., *SVP of Content Development*
Véronique Bos, *Vice President of Creative*
Caroline Gasca, *Senior Content Manager*
Robin Erickson, *Senior Art Director*
Alyssa Lochner, *Senior Production Editor*

Image Credits: all images from iStock and/or Shutterstock

The classroom teacher may reproduce copies of materials in this book for classroom use only. The reproduction of any part for an entire school or school system is strictly prohibited. No part of this publication may be transmitted, stored, or recorded in any form without written permission from the publisher.

Website addresses included in this book are public domain and may be subject to changes or alterations of content after publication of this product. Shell Education does not take responsibility for the future accuracy or relevance and appropriateness of website addresses included in this book. Please contact the company if you come across any inappropriate or inaccurate website addresses, and they will be corrected in product reprints.

All companies, websites, and products mentioned in this book are registered trademarks of their respective owners or developers and are used in this book strictly for editorial purposes. No commercial claim to their use is made by the author(s) or the publisher.

A division of Teacher Created Materials
5482 Argosy Avenue
Huntington Beach, CA 92649-1039
www.tcmpub.com/shell-education
ISBN 979-8-7659-6497-2
© 2025 Shell Educational Publishing, Inc.
Printed by: 51497
Printed in: China

Table of Contents

Basics of Phonics 4
  Introduction 4
    What Is Phonics? 4
    What Is the Science of Reading? 4
    Phonics Instruction 4
    Why Is Phonemic Awareness Important? 5
    How Does Reviewing Phonics Skills
       Help with New Learning? 6
    How to Use This Book 7
  Teaching the Basics 8
    Articulation 8
    Basic Concepts 12
  Observation and Assessment 16
    The Importance of Assessing Phonics 16
    Key Elements of Assessments 16
  Phonics Terminology 17

Instructional Routines 23
  Introduction 24
    The Importance of Instructional Routines 24
    Instructional Routines Overview 24
  Routines 25
    Phonemic-Awareness Instruction 25
    Phonics Skills Instruction 32
    Phonics Skills Review 38
    High-Frequency Word Instruction 45

Word Lists 47
  Introduction 49
  Lists 51

References 330

Digital Learning Resources 332
  What's Included 332
  Accessing the Digital Resources 333

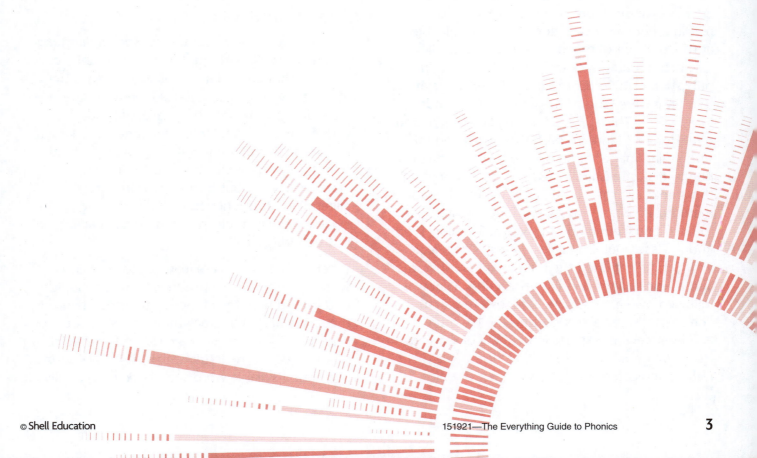

Introduction

What Is Phonics?

Phonics is the study of sounds and letters. It teaches learners the relationship between sounds, letters, and larger word parts and how to use those patterns to read and spell. It is a key strand of many models of reading.

Reading does not come naturally for most children. It is a complex process, and children need explicit, systematic instruction to "break the code" of written language (Moats 1999). "Since English is an alphabetic language, there is a fairly regular connection between the spelling of a word and its pronunciation" (Anderson et al. 1985, 10). Therefore, if we can help children acquire the phonetically accurate letter patterns that represent about 85 percent of the English language, we give them the first step toward literacy and access to a world of knowledge.

What Is the Science of Reading?

The Science of Reading refers to a collection of extensive research that guides teachers toward effective methods or practices for teaching reading. Phonics instruction has historically been at the forefront of much debate and scientific research. It dates back to *The New England Primer*, published in 1690 (Cothran 2014). Students at that time were taught that letters and sounds form words. This approach to reading dominated until Horace Mann, in the 1800s, proposed the "whole-language" approach. The Dick and Jane books, first published in 1836, were examples of this "look-say" method that depended on students memorizing whole words, without any attention to decoding (sounding out) words. Then, in 1955, Rudolf Flesch published *Why Johnny Can't Read*, in which he criticized the memorization of words and advocated for phonics instruction. That was followed by Jeanne Chall's extensive research. She spent three years analyzing the literature and interviewing experts in the field of reading. Her 1967 publication, *Learning to Read: The Great Debate*, indicated the need for direct phonics

instruction for beginning readers and older striving students as opposed to leaving students to rely on trial and error and the memorization of whole words.

In the 1990s, the debate continued, and the term *scientific research-based reading* was coined. From 1997 to 1999, the US National Reading Panel examined scientific literature with the intent of improving reading outcomes. The panel recommended systematic and explicit instruction in five areas: phonemic awareness, phonics, fluency, vocabulary, and comprehension. Research by cognitive scientists such as Tunmer and Hoover (2019) expanded this framework to understanding the cognitive capacities underlying learning to read, and work by Duke and Cartwright (2021) pointed out factors that impact students, including cultural knowledge, motivation and engagement, and executive functioning skills. Contributions from researchers from many fields continue to add to our understanding of the factors that contribute to success in reading and writing.

Phonics Instruction

For students to understand how spoken language is represented in writing, they must be able to identify phonemes. Phonemic awareness is the ability to hear, and by extension, manipulate, individual phonemes, the smallest sounds within words. Phonological awareness is a larger umbrella term that refers to a conscious attention to not only phonemes but also sentences, words, syllables, onsets, rimes, word stress, and alliteration. Both phonemic and phonological awareness play a role in foundational reading instruction.

When students who are learning to read and write begin to connect sounds with letters and understand how they function together in words, they have begun to crack the alphabetic code, or principle. For example, if a child knows that /d/ is represented by the letter *d*, that the vowel sound in a closed-syllable word such as *dog* is typically

Introduction *(cont.)*

short, and that /g/ is represented by *g*, then they demonstrate knowledge of the alphabetic principle. A meta-analysis of literacy research tells us that when students have strong phonological awareness and have grasped the alphabetic principle, they are more likely to become successful readers. When we teach children how to apply the skills of phonological awareness and the alphabetic principle, we are using phonics instruction.

Phonics should be explicitly taught to beginning readers using "systematic and direct instruction focused on the relation between subunits of words (e.g., graphemes, onsets, and rimes) and their corresponding sounds" (Henbest and Apel 2017, 304). What is explicit and systematic phonics instruction?

Explicit instruction models the use of phoneme-grapheme correspondences to decode words and overtly teaches each step through examples. It requires the teacher to have a clear purpose and to express that purpose to the learner. The lesson is directly taught: first through modeling or showing the student how to perform a task and then by engaging the student in guided practice. Finally, the student does independent practice with feedback from the teacher. When phonics is not overtly taught, students may try to identify new or difficult words by shape, picture clues, or context clues.

Explicit instruction need not be dull! Teachers should have students manipulate multisensory materials and incorporate movement whenever possible as that has been found to improve academic performance (Petrigna et al. 2022).

Systematic instruction is broken into logical, sequential steps that progress from simple to more complex patterns. With systematic instruction, skills build on and reinforce one another. They are not haphazardly taught or taught all at once. Use state standards or a research-based curriculum to determine an appropriate scope and sequence for your developing reader.

In time, with practice decoding increasingly complex word patterns, exposure to quality literature, and explicit instruction in high-frequency words, multisyllabic words, and morphemes, developing readers will be able to access complex texts. You will notice that they sound natural when they read aloud and that they understand what they are reading, rather than having to focus on sounding out words.

Why Is Phonemic Awareness Important?

Phonemic awareness is the ability to hear and manipulate individual sounds (phonemes) in the spoken language. There are 44 phonemes in the English language (Moats 2020). The National Reading Panel's (2000) analysis of hundreds of studies shows that phonemic awareness is a "critical foundational piece." It provides the basis on which the alphabetic principle can be built and increases children's ability to read and spell.

Imagine a child seeing an individual letter or a sequence of letters for the first time. What they see is abstract lines, curves, and dots that carry no meaning. For the alphabetic principle to be applied or for children to recognize that letter patterns represent sounds of the spoken language, children first need practice segmenting spoken words into individual phonemes or sounds (e.g., /r/ /ă/ /m/). They also need practice hearing individual sounds and blending those sounds to form a word (e.g., /r/ /ă/ /m/—*ram*). Furthermore, Anne Cunningham's (1990) research demonstrated that kindergarten and first grade children who were explicitly shown when, why, and where to apply blending and segmenting skills increased their reading proficiency levels over those who simply practiced the skills in isolation. Therefore, it is important for teachers to strategically link phonemic-awareness activities to both spoken and written language.

Phonemic awareness taught hand-in-hand with letter names and letter sounds is vital to the development of early reading skills. It helps

© Shell Education

151921—The Everything Guide to Phonics

5

Basics of Phonics

Introduction (cont.)

students see the valuable link between the abstract symbols on the page and the sounds they hear in words. When a child knows only a few letter sounds and is just beginning to grasp the grapheme-phoneme relationship, they might recognize and use only the initial or final sound to identify a word. "A child oblivious to the phonemic structure of speech, that is, for whom spoken words are indivisible wholes, will have no way of generating a candidate pronunciation for a novel word" (Share 1999). At the "full alphabetic stage," the student is able to analyze and decode whole words (Ehri 2020). Words and their meanings have been stored in long-term memory and can be retrieved quickly and effortlessly as sight words.

Phonemic awareness is also important for the development of spelling skills, or encoding. The child needs to be able to hear a word, hear the individual letter sounds in the word, and in turn attach written letter patterns to that word.

Since making speech sounds is natural for most children, phonemic awareness provides an anchor on which to attach subsequent skills. When a child learns that words are made up of individual sounds and that putting those sounds together results in the pronunciation of a word, the learning makes sense and is relevant. Furthermore, attaching a letter or sequence of letters to pronunciation, according to David Kilpatrick (2020), allows the brain to see the sequence of letters as a familiar unit, and in turn activates the word's pronunciation at lightning speed. This instant retrieval of what has now become a sight word is called *orthographic mapping*. It reduces the need for decoding and increases reading fluency and comprehension alike.

According to D. Ray Reutzel (2015), after the *Report of the National Reading Panel* was released in 2000, early childhood classrooms saw a new trend: many educators turned to rhyming and alliteration as ways of building phonemic awareness. Though working with larger segments of sound may be

necessary to get some students to the individual phoneme level, Reutzel cautions educators that using those strategies alone is not enough. "Focusing early phonemic awareness instruction on blending, segmenting, and manipulating phonemes has been shown to produce greater improvements in phonemic awareness and future reading achievement in young children than time spent on rhyming and alliteration" (2015, 16). This is an example of research that helps teachers focus on effective teaching strategies and better utilize instructional time.

How Does Reviewing Phonics Skills Help with New Learning?

Phonics instruction, in which the skills are presented sequentially from simple to more complex, helps children use their prior learning as a bridge to new learning. But the prior learning or prerequisite skills must be stored in long-term memory so they can be quickly retrieved with ease and manipulated in the short-term working memory when new skills are introduced. To achieve this, students need lots of repetition to stabilize learned skills, and the brain needs ample time to make meaningful connections to prior learning.

Short-term memory is what we pay attention to in the "now." Rapid manipulation of information in the short-term memory is called *working memory*. To learn information that you can retain and recall, you must transfer it from short-term to long-term memory. Skills or concepts get moved into long-term memory via what David Sousa (2011) refers to as "rehearsal." He explains that the learner must have adequate time and opportunities to process and reprocess new learning, as that is the critical component in the transference of information from working memory into long-term storage. With only one exposure to a learned concept, the brain will forget 50 to 80 percent of what it learned by day two and retain only 2 to 3 percent of it by day 30 (Murre and Dros 2015).

Introduction (cont.)

Eliciting previously learned information through review allows learners to attach new information to networks of stored memories. For example, the letter *s* might be part of a network that includes an image and the sound of a snake, the first letter in the *st* blend and in the word *stop*, and the emotions attached to those words. When students learn that *s* and *h* form a digraph that makes the *sh* sound in *ship*, they've linked another piece to the network. Then, when teachers review the previously stored *sh* digraph before teaching new digraphs such as *ch* or *th*, this ignites that entire neural network, thereby preventing these new abstract letter combinations from being processed as random pieces of information and being dumped by the short-term working memory as irrelevant.

Phonics programs that focus on the relationships between letters and sound patterns and allow for repeated and varied experiences with these patterns build automaticity or fluency in word recognition.

How to Use This Book

This book can be used to support an existing phonics curriculum, to address a stumbling block for striving readers, or to extend learning for accomplished readers.

On the following pages, you will find:

- **Teaching the Basics**—Includes articulation tips that explain how to pronounce individual sounds. Use the QR code or link below to access recordings of each phoneme, and display matching sound cards from the Digital Learning Resources (page 332). This section also shares tips on explaining basic phonics concepts to students.
- **Observation and Assessment**—Gives an overview of phonics assessments.
- **Phonics Terminology**—Defines key phonics terms.
- **Instructional Routines**—Shares effective ways to teach phonemic awareness, phonics, and high-frequency words.
- **Word Lists**—Includes thousands of words to support phonics and word-study lessons.
- **Digital Learning Resources**—Describes how to access the digital resources and shows what materials are included to support the instructional routines.

To access audio recordings of all the sounds, scan the QR code or visit this link:

tcmpub.digital/fp/soundwallaudio

Basics of Phonics

Teaching the Basics

Articulation

Note: The following descriptions of pronunciations reflect General American English. Learn about and take into account regional dialectic differences that your students may exhibit.

Short Vowel A: Say /ă/. Tell students that /ă/ is a vowel sound, and you say it with a wide, open smile. Say it again, holding the short *a* sound. Say a few words with short *a*: *hat*, *map*, *sad*, and *fan*.

Long Vowel A: Say /ā/. Point out that this vowel sound has a slight glide toward the end of the word, but it's considered one sound. Have students repeat the sound, which is found in the words *play* and *rain*.

Vowel Team AW: Ask students what they say when they see a cute puppy. (*Aww.*) Tell students that /aw/ is a vowel team. It represents one sound but is written with two letters: *au* or *aw*. Point out that /aw/ is formed farther back in the mouth than /ŏ/.

Consonant B: Say /b/. Tell students, "You start the /b/ sound with your lips pressed together and blow out air. You engage your voice. Place your hand on your neck to feel the vibration." Explain that it's easy to hear /b/ at the beginning of a word, such as *bus*. When a word ends in /b/, we elongate the preceding vowel sound, as in *cob*, and we don't emphasize the *b* as much.

Hard C: Say /k/. Point out that the /k/ sound is made at the back of the throat. It is pronounced with a puff of air at the beginning of a word. At the end of a word, it is not. Ask students to place their hands in front of their mouths to feel the puff of air as they say the /k/ in *cat*.

Digraph CH: The letters *ch* form a digraph. Tell students that the /ch/ sound is created by the tongue pressing against the ridge behind the top front teeth as if you are ready to pronounce /t/, the lips pursed, and an explosion of air, as in *chair*.

Digraph CK: The letters *ck* form a digraph. Tell students that when you hear /k/ at the end of a short-vowel word, such as *duck*, the sound is represented by the letters *ck*.

Consonant D: Say /d/. Point out that when you start the voiced sound, your lips are apart, you place your tongue on the ridge behind your top front teeth, and you blow out air. You also engage your voice. Have students place their hands on their necks to feel the vibration as they say *dot*. At the end of a word, the *d* is not emphasized. When a word ends in *d*, we elongate the preceding vowel sound, as in *mad*.

Short Vowel E: Say /ĕ/. Tell students that /ĕ/ is a vowel sound. Say it again, holding the short *e* sound. Point out that /ĕ/ is similar to the sound that short *i* makes, but with /ĕ/, the jaw drops lower. Say a few words with short *e*: *bed, hen,* and *red*.

Long Vowel E: Say /ē/. Point out that this vowel sound is made with a wide, smiley-mouth position. Have students repeat the sound, which is found in the words *bee* and *cheese*.

Consonant F: Say /f/. Explain that to form /f/, you rest your top teeth on your bottom lip and blow out air, as in *five*. Tell students the /f/ sound can be held for as long as you have air in your lungs.

Hard G: Say /g/. Say, "The /g/ sound is made at the back of the throat. You engage your voice. Place your hand on your neck to feel the vibration. It's easy to hear /g/ at the beginning of a word, such as *gum*. When a word ends in /g/, we elongate the preceding vowel sound, as in *big*, and we don't emphasize the *g* as much."

Consonant H: Say /h/. Tell students the /h/ sound starts with the lips apart. Point out that the puff of air for *h* is always followed by a vowel sound. The vowel sound affects the ending shape of the lips. Say a few words with *h*: *hat, head, hit, hot,* and *hut*.

8   151921— The Everything Guide to Phonics   © Shell Education

Basics of Phonics

Teaching the Basics *(cont.)*

Articulation *(cont.)*

Short Vowel I: Say /ĭ/. Tell students that /ĭ/ is a vowel sound. Say it again, holding the short *i* sound. Point out that this sound is made with a slight smile. Model producing the /ē/ sound but dropping the jaw a tiny bit to find /ĭ/. Say a few words with short *i*: *hit*, *hid*, *pin*, and *lid*.

Long Vowel I: Say /ī/. Point out that this vowel sound has a slight glide toward the end of the word, but it's considered one sound. Have students repeat the sound, which is found in the words *pie* and *kite*.

Consonant J: Say /j/. Point out that /j/ is made with the lips pursed, the tongue pressing against the ridge behind the top front teeth as if you are ready to pronounce /d/, and an explosion of air. The voice is engaged, as in *jar*.

Consonant K: Say /k/. Point out that the /k/ sound is made at the back of the throat. It is pronounced with a puff of air at the beginning of a word. At the end of a word, it is not. Ask students to place their hands in front of their mouths to feel the puff of air as they say *key* and less air as they say *lock*.

Consonant L: Make the /l/ sound. Point out that the tongue is pressed against the ridge behind the top front teeth, you blow air out, and the voice is engaged, as in *lip* and *lid*. Tell students the /l/ sound can be held for as long as you have air in your lungs. Note that /l/ is a later-developing, problematic sound for both English speakers and English learners.

Consonant M: Say /m/, holding the *m* sound. Point out that with /m/, you press your lips together, air comes out the nose, and you can feel a vibration in your throat, as in *moat*. Tell students the /m/ sound can be held for as long as you have air in your lungs.

Consonant N: Say /n/, holding the *n* sound. Point out that when /n/ is pronounced, the lips are apart, the tongue is pressed on the ridge behind the top front teeth, and air comes out the nose, as in *nose*. Tell students the /n/ sound can be held for as long as you have air in your lungs.

Digraph NG: The letters *ng* form a digraph. Tell students that the two letters represent the sound /ng/. It is a nasal sound, and air comes out of the nose. The mouth is open and relaxed. The *g* is not clearly heard. Practice extending the /ng/ sound in *ring*.

Short Vowel O: Say /ŏ/. Tell students that /ŏ/ is a vowel sound. Say it again, holding the short *o* sound. Point out that the jaw drops to its most open position when saying /ŏ/, as in *lock*.

Long Vowel O: Say /ō/. Point out that this vowel sound has a slight glide toward the end of the word, but it's considered one sound. Have students repeat the sound, which is found in the words *so* and *home*.

Phoneme /o͞o/: Say, "To pronounce /o͞o/, you can start with an /ū/ sound and lower your jaw slightly." Have students repeat the sound, which is found in the words *wood*, *took*, and *push*.

Diphthong OY: Say, "Diphthongs are vowels that glide from one sound to another. They are considered one sound, but they are written with two letters. The /oy/ sound starts in a back, rounded-lip position and glides to a front, smiley-mouth position. It can be spelled *oi* or *oy*, as in the words *join* and *boy*."

Diphthong OW: Say, "Diphthongs are vowels that glide from one sound to another. They are considered one sound, but they are written with two letters. The /ow/ sound glides from a front, open-mouth position to a back, closed-lip position. It can be spelled *ou* or *ow*, as in the words *out* and *cow*."

Basics of Phonics

Teaching the Basics (cont.)

Articulation (cont.)

Consonant P: Say /p/. Tell students that when *p* is pronounced, your lips are pressed together and you blow out a puff of air at the beginning of a word, as in *pad*. When *p* is at the end of a word, it does not have the puff of air. Ask students to place their hands in front of their mouths to feel the puff of air as they say *pad* and less air as they say *mop*.

Consonant Q (spelling QU): Tell students that consonant *q* represents the /k/ sound. The *u* makes the /w/ sound. Segment the *qu* blend into two sounds. Then blend /k/ /w/ into one unit. For example, for *queen*, say, "/k/ /w/. Blend." (/kw/) "/kw/ /ē/ /n/."

Consonant R: Say /r/, holding the sound. For initial /r/, tell students that the lips are pursed and the tongue forms a spoon shape in the middle of the mouth. Say a few words with *r*: *run*, *right*, and *read*. Tell students the /r/ sound can be held for as long as you have air in your lungs. Note that /r/ is a later-developing, problematic sound for both English speakers and English learners.

R-Controlled Vowel ER: Tell students that the lips are pursed and the tongue forms a spoon shape in the middle of the mouth. Say, "The /er/ sound is considered one sound. We call /er/ an *r*-controlled vowel because the *r* sound is strong and overpowers the *e* (or any of the vowels), as in *fern*, *turn*, *sir*, *work*, *earth*, and *myrtle*."

R-Controlled Vowel AR: Say, "The /ar/ sound is considered one sound, even though the mouth glides from an open /ŏ/ sound to a more closed /r/ sound, as when a pirate says, 'Arr, mateys.' We call /ar/ an *r*-controlled vowel because the *r* sound is strong and overlaps the vowel sound, as in *yard*, *barn*, and *march*."

R-Controlled Vowel OR: Tell students, "The /or/ sound is considered one sound, even though the mouth glides from a rounded, back /ō/ sound to an /r/ sound. We call /or/ an *r*-controlled vowel because the *r* sound is strong and overlaps the vowel sound, as in *fork*, *store*, and *chore*."

Consonant S: Say /s/, holding the sound. Point out that to make the /s/ sound, the lips are apart and you blow air over your tongue, as in *sip*. Tell students the /s/ sound can be held for as long as you have air in your lungs.

Digraph SH: The letters *sh* form a digraph. Tell students that /sh/ is a continuous sound, made with the lips pursed, the teeth close together, and the tongue shaped like a spoon, as in *ship*.

Consonant T: Say /t/. Tell students that to make this sound, your lips are apart, you place your tongue on the ridge behind your top front teeth, and you blow out a puff of air at the beginning of a word. When /t/ is at the end of a word, it does not have the puff of air. Ask students to place their hands in front of their mouths to feel the puff of air as they say *time* and less air as they say *eat*.

Digraph TH: Explain that there are two *th* sounds, one voiceless and one voiced. To make the first *th* sound, you press the tip of your tongue against the bottom edge of your top front teeth and blow air around your tongue, as in *teeth*. The second *th* sound requires you to activate your voice while blowing air around your tongue, as in *this*.

Short Vowel U: Say /ŭ/. Tell students that /ŭ/ is a relaxed vowel sound. Say a few words with short *u*: *fun*, *tub*, *cut*, and *sum*. Say them again, holding the short *u* sound. You may wish to have students say *um* or *umbrella* as a referent for producing the sound.

Long Vowel U: Point out that long *u* has two different sounds. The first sound is /ū/. Hold the /ū/ sound. Point out that the lips are rounded and the jaw is almost closed, as in the word *soon* or *dune*. The second sound is called the glided long *u*, which sounds like /yū/, as in *cube* or *phew*.

Teaching the Basics *(cont.)*

Articulation *(cont.)*

Consonant V: Say /v/. To form /v/, model resting your top teeth on your bottom lip and blowing out air with your voice activated as if you are humming. Tell students that *v* represents the /v/ sound, as in *van*. Tell students the /v/ sound can be held for as long as you have air in your lungs.

Consonant W: Say /w/. Model /w/ by pursing your lips as if to pronounce the /ū/ sound or by using the beginning of the word *why* as a referent for the *w* glide. Point out that the /w/ sound moves quickly to whatever vowel sound follows it (e.g., *way, we, why*).

Digraph WH: Tell students that digraph *wh* typically makes the same sound as *w*, though in some words you might hear a slight "hw" sound. In this guide, *wh* words will be classified as representing one sound: /w/. Many words that start with /w/ are spelled with *w*, but some words are spelled with *wh*.

Consonant X: The letter *x* represents the sound /ks/ as in *box*. The /k/ sound is made at the back of the throat, and the /s/ sound forces air out of the mouth. The letter *x* also represents the sound /gz/ as in *exam*. While technically a blend, *x* will be classified as representing one sound in the word lists.

Consonant Y: Make the /y/ sound, as in *yes*. Point out that the sides of the tongue rest against the roof of the mouth until the sound glides to whatever vowel sound follows the *y* (e.g., *yes, yip, yoke,* and *yum*).

Consonant Z: Say /z/, elongating the sound. Point out that your lips are apart and you blow air over your tongue with your voice engaged. Students should place their hands on their necks to feel the vibration as they say *zoo*. Tell students the /z/ sound can be held for as long as you have air in your lungs.

Short Vowels: Review the five short-vowel sounds. Start with /ĭ/, and gradually drop your jaw as you say /ĕ/, /ă/, and /ŏ/. Then, close your jaw slightly for /ŭ/. Show the letters or sound cards as you move from sound to sound. Point out that the duration of a "short" vowel sound can be long or short depending on the consonant that follows it.

Long Vowels: Review the six long-vowel sounds: /ā/, /ē/, /ī/, /ō/, /ū/, and /yū/. Review the long vowels by showing the letter or sound card as you say each sound.

Schwa (/ə/): Some people call schwa the "lazy sound" because your mouth and tongue are relaxed. It can sound like short *u* or short *i*. It is found in unstressed syllables, such as in the first syllable of *about* and the second syllable of *circus*.

Phoneme /zh/: Say, "The sound /zh/ is an infrequent sound in English that is often spelled with an *s*. It is a continuous sound, made with the lips pursed and the tongue shaped like a spoon. It is pronounced like /sh/ but with the voice engaged, such as in the words *vision* and *measure*."

Basics of Phonics

Teaching the Basics *(cont.)*

Basic Concepts

Blends, Initial: Tell students, "A *blend* is when two consonants are next to each other and you can hear the sound of both consonants. A blend can be found at the beginning of a word." Share the words *spot*, *grip*, and *pluck*. Segment each word, and point out the two consonant sounds at the beginning of each word. (Compare a blend to a *digraph*, where two consonants represent one sound.)

Blends, Final: Tell students, "A *blend* is when two consonants are next to each other and you can hear the sound of both consonants. A blend can be found at the end of a word." Share the words *left*, *best*, and *went*. Segment each word, and point out the two consonant sounds at the end of each word. (Compare a blend to a *digraph*, where two consonants represent one sound.)

Blend NK: The *n* represents the /ng/ sound and *k* represents /k/ in words like *sink* and *blink*. Be sure students are familiar with *ng* before introducing *nk*.

Compound Words: Tell students that words are sometimes made up of two smaller words put together, such as *moonlight* or *doghouse*.

Consonants: Consonants are sounds that are blocked or flow past the lips, teeth, tongue, or nose in different ways. Consonant sounds can be voiced or unvoiced, unlike vowels, which are always voiced.

Digraphs: Tell students that a digraph is two letters that represent one sound. Double consonants are types of digraphs.

Diphthongs OI and OY: Say, "Diphthongs are vowels that glide from sound to sound. They are considered one sound, but they are written with two letters. This diphthong can be spelled *oi* or *oy*." Point out that /oy/ is usually spelled *oi* in the middle of a word and *oy* at the end of a word, as in *boil* and *toy*.

Diphthongs OU and OW: Say, "Diphthongs are vowels that glide from sound to sound. They are considered one sound, but they are written with two letters. This diphthong can be spelled *ou* or *ow*, as in *pout* and *pow*." Point out that the *ou* spelling typically occurs at the beginning or in the middle of a word, whereas the *ow* spelling typically occurs in the middle or at the end of one-syllable words.

Final Y as Long Vowel E: Say, "Final *y* represents the long *e* sound in two-syllable words." Write and model blending the word *lady*. Say, "The *y* at the end of *lady* represents /ē/."

Final Y as Long Vowel I: Say, "In one-syllable words, when you hear /ī/ at the end of a word, the letter *y* often represents this sound." Display and discuss the words *try*, *shy*, and *by*.

Letters: Tell students that letters represent sounds. Use the first letter of a student's name to demonstrate this. Add that letters help form words.

Long Vowel A (AI): Write the letters *ai*, and tell students that together the letters *ai* represent the /ā/ sound. Tell students this spelling is generally found in the middle of words, such as in *paint*, *braid*, and *wait*.

Long Vowel A (AY): Write the letters *ay*, and tell students that together the letters *ay* represent the /ā/ sound. Tell students this spelling is generally found at the end of words, such as in *may*, *clay*, and *way*.

Long Vowel E (EA): Write the letters *ea*, and tell students, "The *ea* spelling for the long *e* sound is used at the beginning, middle, or end of a word, such as in *eat*, *least*, and *sea*."

Long Vowel E (EE): Write the letters *ee*, and tell students, "The *ee* spelling for the long *e* sound is generally found in the middle or at the end of a word, such as in *beep*, *seen*, or *three*."

Basics of Phonics

Teaching the Basics *(cont.)*

Basic Concepts *(cont.)*

Long Vowel I (IE): Write the letters *ie*, and tell students that together the letters *ie* make the /ī/ sound at the end of a one-syllable word, such as in *lie*, *die*, and *tie*.

Long Vowel I (IGH): Write the letters *igh*, and tell students that together the letters *igh* make the long *i* sound. Tell students this spelling is generally found in the middle or at the end of a word, such as in *high*, *thigh*, and *right*.

Long Vowel O (OA): Write the letters *oa*, and tell students, "The *oa* spelling for the long *o* sound is generally found at the beginning or in the middle of a one-syllable word, such as in *oat* or *coat*."

Long Vowel O (OE): Write the letters *oe*, and tell students, "The *oe* spelling for the long *o* sound is generally found at the end of a one-syllable word, such as in *toe* or *woe*."

Long Vowel O (OW): Write the letters *ow*, and tell students, "The *ow* spelling for the long *o* sound is generally found at the end of a word, such as in *snow* or *glow*."

Long Vowel U (EW): Tell students, "The *ew* spelling for the long *u* sound or the glided long *u* sound can be found at the end of a one-syllable word, such as in *grew*, *flew*, and *few*."

Long Vowel U (OO): Tell students, "The *oo* spelling for the long *u* sound can be found in the middle or at the end of a word, such as in *food*, *hoop*, and *zoo*."

Long Vowel U (UE): Tell students, "The *ue* spelling for the long *u* sound or the glided long *u* sound can be found in the middle or at the end of a word, such as in *blue*, *duel*, or *fuel*."

Long Vowels: Tell students that the long-vowel sounds /ā/, /ē/, /ī/, /ō/, /ū/, and /yū/ appear in open syllables, VC*e* words, and words with vowel teams.

Multisyllabic Words: Tell students that many "long" words are made up of syllables and each syllable has a vowel sound. Of those vowel sounds, stressed-syllable vowels have clearer sounds than unstressed-syllable vowels, which often sound like schwa.

Sentences: Tell students that most sentences tell or ask something. Sentences are made up of words. Sentences are separated from other sentences by a period (or other mark) and a space.

Short Vowels: Tell students that the short-vowel sounds /ă/, /ĕ/, /ĭ/, /ŏ/, and /ŭ/ appear in closed syllables, such as CVC or CVCC words.

Silent E: Teach students that silent *e* in a VC*e* word tells readers that the preceding vowel generally represents a long vowel. The two vowels form a vowel team separated by a consonant. Display words with the VC*e* pattern (e.g., *lane*, *Pete*, *like*, *note*, and *June*). Say, "The *e* is silent, but it gives the first vowel courage to say its letter name."

Soft C: Remind students about the "hard" /k/ sound of *c*. Tell students that the letter *c* has another sound, /s/, which is called the "soft" sound. The letter *c* often represents the /s/ sound when it's in front of *e*, *i*, or *y*. Display and discuss the words *cell*, *city*, and *spicy*.

Soft G: Remind students about the "hard" /g/ sound of *g*. Tell students that the letter *g* has another sound, /j/, which is called the "soft" sound. The letter *g* often represents the /j/ sound when it's in front of *e*, *i*, or *y*. Display and discuss the words *huge*, *giant*, and *gym*.

Stress: Tell students that if a word or a syllable is stressed, it means it is said louder, held longer, or said with a higher pitch. One way to detect which syllable is stressed is to pretend you are calling a dog whose name is the word.

Teaching the Basics *(cont.)*

Basic Concepts *(cont.)*

Suffixes: Say, "A suffix comes at the end of a word. It can change the meaning of a word, or it can change the part of speech."

Plural Suffixes: Tell students that when we talk about two or more objects, we add –s or –es to the end of the word to make the word plural (unless the word has an irregular plural, such as *knives* or *oxen*).

Plural Suffix ES: Tell students that when changing a word that ends with *s, x, z, ch, tch, sh, ge,* or *dge* to plural, you have to add a syllable. Say, "To make a word like *bus* plural, you can't just add an *s* sound and say, 'busss.' You have to add an *es* syllable and say, 'buses.'" (bŭs•əz) Repeat with *fox, buzz, bench, patch,* and *dish.* To words that end in *ge* or *dge,* such as *garage* and *judge,* just add *s* to create the *es* syllable.

Plural Suffix S: Tell students that the suffix –s means "more than one." It can sound like /s/ or /z/. Tell students that if a noun ends with a voiceless sound, such as the /t/ in *pet,* the plural will use the voiceless ending sound /s/. If the noun ends with a voiced sound, such as the /l/ in *eel,* the plural will use the voiced ending sound /z/.

Past-Tense Suffix: Tell students that the suffix –ed means "it happened in the past." Say, "You can change a verb to past tense by adding –ed, and it can sound like /d/, /t/, or /əd/ (unless the word has an irregular past tense form, such as *taught* or *put*)."

Past-Tense Suffix ED (/d/): Tell students that if an action verb ends with a voiced sound, they will write –ed and use the voiced /d/ to signal past tense, as in *mailed, climbed,* and *played.*

Past-Tense Suffix ED (/əd/): Tell students that if an action verb ends with a /t/ or /d/ sound, they have to add a syllable that sounds like /əd/ and add a *d* or an *ed,* as in *traded* or *dented.*

Past-Tense Suffix ED (/t/): Tell students that if an action verb ends in a voiceless sound, they will write –ed and use the voiceless /t/ to signal past tense, as in *kicked, fished,* and *mopped.*

Suffix ING: Say, "The suffix –ing is made up of two sounds, /ĭ/ and /ng/. Together, they sound like –ing." (Note: The short *i* is raised before *ng,* so it almost sounds like a long *e.*) Ask students to stand. Say, "The –ing in *standing* lets us know the action is in progress because we are continuing to stand."

Trigraphs: Tell students that trigraphs are three letters that represent one sound.

Trigraph DGE: Tell students the letters *dge* form a trigraph. When the /j/ sound comes after a one-syllable short-vowel word, it can sometimes be spelled *dge,* as in *edge.*

Trigraph TCH: Tell students the letters *tch* form a trigraph. When the /ch/ sound comes after a one-syllable short-vowel word, it can sometimes be spelled *tch,* as in *itch.*

Vowel Teams: Tell students that two vowels can represent one sound. (They can also represent glided diphthong sounds.)

Vowel Team OO: Tell students that *oo* is a vowel team. It can represent the /o͝o/ sound, as in *book,* or the /ū/ sound, as in *food.*

Vowel Teams AU and AW: Tell students that *au* and *aw* are vowel teams. Point out that /aw/ is formed farther back in the mouth than /ŏ/. Point out the two spellings of /aw/: *au* and *aw.* Au can be found at the beginning or in the middle of a word, as in *author* or *fault,* whereas *aw* can be found anywhere in a word, as in *awl, bawl,* or *saw.*

Basics of Phonics

Teaching the Basics *(cont.)*

Basic Concepts *(cont.)*

Vowels: Tell students that vowels are not inherently short or long; those are just convenient labels. How long you hold the vowel depends on the consonant that follows the vowel and whether the vowel is tense or lax (how much tension is in the tongue). Tell students that vowels are voiced, uninterrupted sounds.

Words: Tell students that words identify things, people, actions, and ideas, e.g., *pencil*, *student*, *stretch*, and *recess*. Words are separated by spaces from other words on a page. Words are made up of letters. Talk about the different places you see letters and words (e.g., signs or books).

Basics of Phonics

Observation and Assessment

The Importance of Assessing Phonics

Frequent, cumulative assessment and observation are the key to understanding what students know, what they still need to learn, and how to tailor an instructional plan that achieves goals for each student.

If you work with students at home, take note of the words they struggle to read. Use the instructional routines and personalize word lists to help your reader review concepts, gain confidence, and show mastery.

At school, phonics screeners and benchmark assessments establish a baseline for the phonics knowledge that students possess.

Formative and summative assessments offer information about students' responses to instruction. Formative assessments reveal how students apply newly taught skills during day-to-day instructional time. Summative assessments provide insight into how students are generalizing their skills.

A deep understanding of student progression toward curricular objectives allows teachers to maximize their whole-group instruction and provide targeted reteaching of specific skills (Blevins 2017).

Key Elements of Assessments

Type of Assessment	Notes about Phonics Assessments
Benchmark Assessment *Determines entry performance and serves as a benchmark from which progress is measured*	• Should include the following: 　» Alphabet recognition (naming capital letters, lowercase letters, and letter sounds) 　» Reading decodable words 　» Reading sight words (or high-frequency words) 　» Spelling (given mid-year and end-of-year)
Formative Assessment *Measures day-to-day application of skills*	• Can occur daily and be noted in checklists or anecdotal records • Includes students' answers to questions posed, their ability to read aloud or whisper-read fluently, and their work on dictations • Allows for on-the-spot redirection, additional practice, modeling, or small-group reteaching • Confirms whether moderate or intensive reteaching is needed
Summative Assessment *Measures mastery of specified content*	• Should be given after each unit (or every couple of weeks) to be able to form differentiated instructional groups • Includes reading inventories and dictations • Should include words and patterns from the current week and the previous five weeks • Should include a score for accuracy and speed/fluency

Phonics Terminology

Term	Definition
affix	any word part that attaches to the beginning or end of a word; an umbrella term for prefixes and suffixes
base	a word part or a standalone word that carries the basic meaning of the word Examples: The base word in *running* is *run*, and the base word in *unfriendly* is *friend*.
to blend	to put separate sounds together to form a spoken word Types of blending include continuous, cumulative, vowel-first, letter-team, onset-rime, and more.
closed syllable	a syllable with a short vowel followed by one or more consonants
compound words	words that are created when two or more individual words are joined together to make a new word with a new meaning
consonant	the following 21 letters of the alphabet: *b, c, d, f, g, h, j, k, l, m, n, p, q, r, s, t, v, w, x, y, z* These letters represent sounds that are made when air is partially blocked by the tongue, teeth, nose, or lips. English has 25 consonant phonemes (Moats 2020).
consonant blend	two or more adjacent consonants (graphemes) before or after a vowel within a syllable The sounds "blend" together, but each sound can be heard individually, such as in *bl* or *sw*. Blends should not be described as one sound because the consonants retain their identity in a blend (Moats 2020).
consonant cluster	two or more consonant sounds (phonemes) before or after a vowel sound within a syllable Technically, this is the oral language equivalent of the term *consonant blend* (Moats 2020).
continuous blending	vocalizing the sounds of a word in order until you reach the end of the word; used for most blending instruction
continuous sounds	sounds that can be extended until you run out of breath (as compared to stops, which are of a short duration) Examples: consonant sounds, such as /f/, /v/, /s/, /z/, /th/, /<u>th</u>/, /sh/, /zh/, /h/, /m/, /n/, /ng/, /l/, /r/, and vowel sounds

Basics of Phonics

Phonics Terminology *(cont.)*

Term	Definition
cumulative blending	vocalizing the first sound, vocalizing the second sound, returning to the beginning to blend those sounds, adding the third sound, returning to the beginning to blend all three sounds; can be used to identify a specific sound-spelling issue
decodable text	text that contains a large percentage of words that incorporate the letter-sound relationships students have already been taught
to decode	to use sound-letter correspondences to read words
dictation	saying words and sentences to be written by students, often guided by the teacher
digraph	two letters that form a new sound when they appear side by side and do not retain their individual sounds; often assumed to refer to consonants Examples: *ch, sh, ph, wh, ng, ck, dd,* and *ll*
diphthong	a vowel that glides in the middle to a new position and sounds as if it has two parts Examples: the /ow/ sound in *house* or the /oy/ sound in *boil*
to encode	to write words using sound-spelling correspondences
explicit	stated clearly, accurately, and succinctly Explicit instruction is where skills are taught and modeled clearly and directly to students through lessons with clear objectives and scaffolded support. The three parts of instruction are teacher modeling (I do), guided teacher-student practice (We do together), and student independent practice (You do).
Fry's instant word list	a list of 1,000 high-frequency words compiled by Dr. Edward Fry in 1957 and updated in 1980 This list contains all parts of speech, and the words are arranged in order of frequency of occurrence in reading materials, with about 100 words per grade level.
grapheme	the smallest unit in a writing system; a letter and/or letter combination that represents a phoneme
high-frequency words	words that are most used in the English language and student texts
implicit	suggested but not directly expressed or stated Implicit instruction is the exposure to concepts through books or materials as compared with teacher-led instruction.

Basics of Phonics

Phonics Terminology *(cont.)*

Term	Definition
irregular words	words that do not follow common sound-letter correspondences and are not easily decodable Words can be temporarily irregular if a pattern has not yet been studied or can be permanently irregular.
letter	a written symbol that represents one or more speech sounds English has 26 letters that singly or in combination represent 44 speech sounds.
letter-team blending	identifying a team of letters in a word before blending the sounds in order
long vowel	a vowel sound that sounds like the letter name, often symbolized with an accent called a macron: /ā/, /ē/, /ī/, /ō/, /ū/, and /yū/ The duration of a long-vowel sound can be long or short depending on the consonant that follows it. The letter *y* acts as a long vowel in some words, such as *fly, hype, and foggy.*
to map sounds	to associate sounds and spellings
to map words	to break a word into sounds (phonemes) and then match the sounds with letters (graphemes)
morpheme	the smallest unit of meaning that cannot be further divided; the smallest meaningful part of a word Example types: prefix, suffix, base, root
morphology	the study of words and morphemes and how words are formed Derivational morphemes are prefixes or suffixes that often change a word's part of speech. Inflectional morphemes are suffixes that often alter a part of speech.
multisyllabic words	words with more than one syllable
onset	the part of a syllable that comes before the vowel An onset can be a consonant, digraph, or blend; some syllables do not have an onset. Example: In the word *slide*, *sl* is the onset and *ide* is the rime.
open syllable	a syllable ending in a long vowel, spelled with one vowel letter

Phonics Terminology *(cont.)*

Term	Definition
orthographic mapping	the process used to store words and word patterns in long-term memory; a cognitive task whereby readers quickly connect sounds (phonemes) and letters (graphemes) and recall the pronunciation, meaning, and spelling of words
phoneme	the smallest unit of sound in a spoken word, usually rendered in symbols and surrounded by virgules: / / There are 44 phonemes in English (Moats 2020).
phoneme deletion	the ability to remove sounds at different positions within a word, such as initial, medial, and final position
phoneme isolation	the ability to identify sounds at different positions within a word, such as initial, medial, and final position Example: In *dog*, identifying that /d/ is the initial sound, /ŏ/ is the middle sound, and /g/ is the final sound shows the ability to isolate phonemes.
phoneme manipulation	the ability to add, delete, or substitute sounds in spoken words
phonemic awareness	the awareness of the smallest units of sound (phonemes) and the ability to manipulate those sounds
phonics	reading instruction that teaches sound-letter correspondences
phonological awareness	the awareness of (attention to and manipulation of) the sounds of spoken language, including phonemes, onset-rime units, syllables, word boundaries, stress, rhyme, and alliteration
prefix	an affix attached to the beginning of a word; generally, a prefix changes a word's meaning Example: the prefix *re–*
r-controlled vowels	vowels that are followed by *r* and whose sounds combine or weld to a great degree: /er/, /ar/, and /or/
rhyme	two or more words with matching ending sounds (starting with the last stressed vowel sound)
rime	the last part of a one-syllable word that includes the vowel and any consonants that follow it All syllables have a rime because all syllables have a vowel sound. Example: In the word *bat*, *b* is the onset and *at* is the rime.

Basics of Phonics

Phonics Terminology *(cont.)*

Term	Definition
root	a word part or morpheme that cannot stand alone but is used to form a family of words with related meanings Example: *brev* is a root that means short or brief
schwa	a neutral/undefined vowel sound found in unstressed syllables; it can sound like short *u*, short *i*, or short *e* depending on the speaker The phoneme is written like an upside-down *e*: /ə/. Example: The *a* in the word *about* makes more of a short *u* sound and the *e* in *carpet* makes more of a short *i* sound than is indicated by the vowel.
to segment	to separate a spoken word into its separate sounds
short vowel	a vowel sound often symbolized with an accent called a breve: /ă/, /ĕ/, /ĭ/, /ŏ/, /ŭ/; featured in closed syllables The duration of a short-vowel sound can be long or short depending on the consonant that follows it. The letter *y* acts as a short vowel in some words, such as *myth*.
sight words	words that can be read automatically, quickly, and with little effort because they have been stored in long-term memory These words may or may not contain irregular sound-spelling patterns.
sound boxes	consecutive boxes into which students place counters or letter tiles to represent the sounds in a word; also known as Elkonin boxes
suffix	an affix attached to the end of a word; generally, a suffix changes a word's meaning or part of speech. Examples: the derivational suffix *–ly* and the inflectional suffix *–s*
syllable	a unit of pronunciation that contains one vowel sound and may or may not include consonants before or after the vowel Commonly taught syllable types include closed, open, vowel-team, VC*e*, vowel-*r*, consonant-*le*, and unstressed. Note: Syllable boundaries are often different in speech and in print.
systematic	organized and carefully planned Systematic instruction means intentionally sequenced lessons and activities ranging from basic to more complex to ensure skill mastery.

© Shell Education

151921—The Everything Guide to Phonics

Basics of Phonics

Phonics Terminology *(cont.)*

Term	Definition
trigraph	a three-letter combination that represents one sound Trigraphs can consist of all consonants or a mixture of vowels and consonants. Examples: *tch*, *dge*, and *igh*
unvoiced sounds	sounds that are produced without activating the vocal cords (whispered): /p/, /t/, /k/, /f/, /th/, /s/, /sh/, /h/, and /ch/
voiced sounds	sounds that are produced by activating the vocal cords (sung): /b/, /d/, /g/, /m/, /n/, /ng/, /v/, /th/, /z/, /zh/, /j/, /w/, /y/, /l/, /r/, and all vowels
vowel	the following letters: *a, e, i, o, u,* and sometimes *y* These letters represent sounds made when air flows freely from the mouth while speaking. Included in the broad vowel category are the glided version of *u* (/yū/), the diphthongs /ow/ and /oy/, and the *r*-controlled vowels /er/, /ar/, and /or/.
vowel flexing	a strategy for adjusting the pronunciation of a vowel sound in a word, particularly with regard to an unstressed syllable and schwa.
vowel-*r* combinations	vowels that are followed by *r* and whose sound is shaped by *r* to a greater or lesser degree; the first three are often referred to as *r*-controlled vowels: /er/, /ar/, /or/, *air, eer,* and *oor. Ire* words have the clearest division between the vowel sound and the /r/ sound.
vowel teams	spellings of two or more adjacent letters that produce one vowel sound (e.g., *oa, ay, ai, ea, oo, igh, ough*) In a broad sense, a VC*e* syllable includes a vowel team comprised of the first vowel and the silent *e*.
word	a combination of letters or sounds that communicates a meaning; typically shown in writing with a space on either side

Instructional Routines
Table of Contents

Introduction 24

Routines 25

Phonemic-Awareness Instruction 25
Blend Word Parts 25
Listen for Sounds. 26
Listen for Rhyming Words. 27
Manipulate Word Parts. 28
Segment Word Parts. 29
Use Sound Boxes to Blend/Segment 30
Use the Sound Wall. 31

Phonics Skills Instruction. 32
Continuous Blending. 32
Cumulative Blending. 33
Dictation 34
Letter-Team Blending 35
Syllable Division 1 36
Syllable Division 2 37

Phonics Skills Review 38
Build a Word Chain. 38
Isolate Sounds to Spell 39
Read Multisyllabic Words. 40
Sort Words/Pictures 41
Try Another Sound 42
Word Hunt. 43
Word Riddles 44

High-Frequency Word Instruction 45
Introduce High-Frequency Words 45
Read and Write High-Frequency Words. 46

Instructional Routines

Introduction

The Importance of Instructional Routines

In the classroom, routines are crucial for creating effective learning environments. Routines provide students with guidelines for coming to school, lining up, getting materials, working with others, and being mindful classroom participants. Instructional routines provide students with dependable steps for learning new information. Routines allow more time to be spent on student participation and less time spent on explaining procedural steps. With that in mind, we have selected 22 research-based routines to guide your explicit phonics instruction.

Instructional Routines Overview

Use these 22 research-based routines to guide your explicit phonics instruction throughout the year. The routines are grouped alphabetically in each of the following categories:

- Phonemic-Awareness Instruction
- Phonics Skills Instruction
- Phonics Skills Review
- High-Frequency Word Instruction

Together, these instructional routines form a core of essential routines to support a firm foundation in reading skills. All the routines can be used to good effect at more than one grade level. The objective at the top of each page identifies the purpose of the routine.

Most of the key materials are provided digitally (see page 332) and can be used with multiple routines. Select words from the word lists (pages 51–329) and refer to Teaching the Basics (pages 8–15) to provide your readers with targeted phonics and phonemic awareness practice, high-frequency word instruction, and spelling practice.

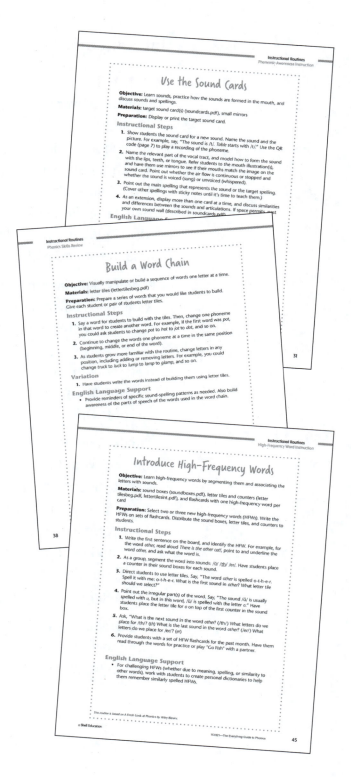

Instructional Routines
Phonemic-Awareness Instruction

Blend Word Parts

Objective: Orally blend word parts (phonemes, onsets and rimes, syllables, or words) to create a whole word.

Preparation: Prepare a list of words for students to blend.

Instructional Steps

1. If blending phonemes, say, "Words are made up of different sounds called *phonemes*. Today we will blend phonemes together to make whole words. I will give you the different parts of a word. You will put the pieces together like a puzzle."

For Words with Two Parts

2. Extend your right arm out in front of you, with your hand cupped, as if you are holding a word part. Simultaneously, say the first word part. For example, if blending the phonemes in *zoo*, say, "/z/." Repeat the motion with your left hand for the second part of the word. Say, "/ū/." Have students repeat what you say and make the same motions, first with their left hands and then their right hands.

3. Join your hands together while you blend the two word parts. Have students make the same motion. Ask, "What's the word?" (*zoo*)

For Words with Three or More Parts

2. Hold your left arm out to the side, and model tapping your shoulder, elbow, and wrist (for three-part words) or your shoulder, upper arm, forearm, and wrist (for four-part words) as you say each word part. Have students repeat what you say and make the same motions with their right hands and left arms.

3. Sweep your hand down your arm to represent blending the sounds into the word. Have students make the same motion. Ask, "What's the word?"

English Language Support

- Some students' native languages are heavily based on consonant-vowel syllables. Build blending success with these students by having them blend syllables before blending discrete sounds.

This routine is based on What the Science of Reading Says: Literacy Strategies for Early Childhood *by Jodene L. Smith.*

Instructional Routines
Phonemic-Awareness Instruction

Listen for Sounds

Objective: Listen for sounds or the positions of sounds in words and demonstrate understanding with movement.

Preparation: Prepare a list of words to demonstrate a phonics concept.

Instructional Steps

1. Direct students to listen carefully for specific sounds or the positions of sounds in words that you say aloud. Pronounce the words slowly and clearly, but try not to add an extraneous "uh" sound to stops or exaggerate ending sounds that are not normally exaggerated.

2. Select one of these student responses, or create your own:

Listen for Sounds

Stomp If You Hear It: Ask students to stomp once if they hear the target sound and sit quietly if they do not. For example, say, "Stomp if you hear the /p/ sound: *pen, bat, top.*" Allow time for students to return to their starting positions.

Tap If You Hear It: Tell students to tap their chins if they hear the target sound and keep their hands in their laps if they do not. For example, say, "Tap your chins if you hear the /ar/ sound: /h/ /ar/ /d/." Students should tap their chins when they hear /ar/ and keep their hands in their laps for the other sounds.

Identify the Position of Sounds

Step Forward: Say a word with the target sound either in the initial, middle, or final position. Have students step forward if the sound is at the beginning of the word and step backwards if the sound is at the end of the word. Have them hop if the sound is in the middle.

English Language Support

- Hold continuous sounds for two beats so students can clearly hear and process the individual sounds.

This routine is based on What the Science of Reading Says: Literacy Strategies for Early Childhood *by Jodene L. Smith.*

Instructional Routines
Phonemic-Awareness Instruction

Listen for Rhyming Words

Objective: Listen for words that have similar ending patterns.

Materials: sets of pictures depicting the words

Preparation: Prepare a list of rhyming words and distractors. Prepare sets of pictures (as long as this scaffold is needed).

Instructional Steps

1. Orally provide an example of words that rhyme. For example, say, "*Hat* and *mat* rhyme because they end with the same /ăt/ sound." Provide additional examples as needed.

2. Say pairs of words, and ask students to identify whether the words rhyme.

3. After students are comfortable identifying rhyming words, say a sequence of three words, and ask students to identify either the two words that rhyme or the one that does not. For example, for the sequence *sit*, *fit*, and *tub*, ask, "Which of these words rhyme?" or "Which word does not rhyme with the others?"

4. As students become comfortable identifying rhyming words, ask them to produce rhymes. For example, ask, "What word rhymes with *not*?"

Collaborative

1. Provide partners with pictures.

2. Have students match the pictures that rhyme.

3. Ask partners to produce other words that rhyme with each set of pictures.

English Language Support

- Post a list of rhyming words and pictures for students to read and reference.

This routine is based on A Fresh Look at Phonics *by Wiley Blevins.*

© Shell Education
151921—The Everything Guide to Phonics
27

Instructional Routines

Phonemic-Awareness Instruction

Manipulate Word Parts

Objective: Orally substitute word parts (phonemes, onset-rime, words in compound words)

Preparation: Prepare a list of words for students to manipulate.

Instructional Steps

1. Say a word to students, sketch it, and ask them to repeat it. Model segmenting it into parts, e.g., *bat*, /b/ /ă/ /t/.

2. Tell students the sound, syllable, or word part that they should substitute in the segmented word. For example, say, "Change the /b/ in *bat* to /h/. (pause) What is the new word?" or "Change the *bow* in *rainbow* to *coat*. What is the new word?" Sketch the new word.

Extra Support

Materials: sound boxes (soundboxes.pdf), different-color counters or cubes

Preparation: Print sound boxes, and gather sets of different-color counters.

One-Syllable Words

1. Provide each student with a three- or four-box sound box and different-color counters. Give them three (or four) blue counters and one white counter.

2. Say a one-syllable word. Ask students to repeat it. Have students segment the word into sounds, moving one blue counter into each sound box as they identify the sounds.

3. Direct students to manipulate the specified sound. Have students place their white counter on top of the sound that is being manipulated. Have students share the new word.

Two-Syllable Words

1. Provide each student with a two-box sound box and different-color counters. Give them two blue counters and one white counter.

2. Say a two-syllable word. Ask students to repeat it. Have students segment the word into syllables, moving one blue counter into each sound box as they identify the syllables.

3. Direct students to manipulate the specified syllable. Have students place the white counter on top of the syllable that is being manipulated. Have students share the new word.

English Language Support

- Define each word for students, and have them create a hand gesture for it.

This routine is based on A Fresh Look at Phonics *by Wiley Blevins.*

28   151921— The Everything Guide to Phonics   © Shell Education

Instructional Routines
Phonemic-Awareness Instruction

Segment Word Parts

Objective: Segment words into parts (phonemes, onset and rime, syllables, morphemes, or compound words).

Preparation: Prepare a list of 8–10 words for students to segment.

Segment Words

For Words with Two Parts

1. Say, "Words are made up of different parts. Today we will segment, or break apart, words into onset and rime. I will say a word. You will break it into parts."

2. Say a word aloud, such as *fish*. Have students repeat the word. With your right hand, gesture as if you are pulling apart the onset block—the consonant, consonant digraph, or consonant blend that comes before the vowel—and say, "/f/."

3. With your left hand, gesture as if you are pulling apart the rime block—the vowel and everything after it in the syllable—and say, "/ĭsh/."

4. Ask, "What two parts make up the word *fish*?" (/f/, /ĭsh/) Repeat the onset and rime as you gesture pulling the two pieces apart. Then, say the word.

For Words with Two or More Parts

1. Say, "Words are made up of different parts. Today we will segment words into syllables, like robots. I will say a word. You will break it into parts."

2. Model placing the flat back of your hand under your chin with your mouth closed, and ask students to look closely at your chin to see how many times it drops as you slowly say a word. Have students use this technique to count the number of syllables in words.

Segment Sentences

1. Say a sentence aloud. Take a step forward for each word in the sentence, having students count the number of words. Emphasize that you are looking for whole words, not parts of words.

2. Say another sentence, and have students step forward, hop in place, or hold up a finger for each word they hear. Continue segmenting sentences, having students count the number of words in each sentence.

English Language Support

- Have pairs of students contribute words or sentences for segmenting practice.

This routine is based on What the Science of Reading Says: Literacy Strategies for Early Childhood *by Jodene L. Smith.*

© Shell Education

Instructional Routines
Phonemic-Awareness Instruction

Use Sound Boxes to Blend/Segment

Objective: Orally blend sounds to make words or segment words into sounds or syllables by manipulating counters.

Materials: sound boxes (soundboxes.pdf), counters (lettertilesint.pdf)

Preparation: Prepare a list of words for students to blend or segment. Print sound boxes and 2–6 counters for each student. Ask students to place one counter underneath each box.

Blend Sounds

1. Say the phonemes of a word. For example, say, "/m/ /ǎ/ /ch/." Have students push a counter into each box as you say each sound. For added support, repeat the sounds while tapping under each box.

2. Model sliding your finger under the sound boxes. Ask students, "What is the word?" Have students run their fingers under the sound boxes as they blend the sounds and say the word *match*.

Blend Syllables

1. Say the syllables of a word. Have students push a counter into each box as you say each syllable. For added support, repeat the syllables while tapping under each box. Slide your finger under the sound boxes as students blend the syllables. Note: When we speak, we sometimes divide words into syllables differently than when we write. Don't worry about written syllable division for this activity.

Segment Words into Sounds

1. Say a word for students to segment into sounds. Have students repeat the word. For example, say, "match." For added support, elongate the word. (/mmmǎǎǎch/). Have students push a counter into each box as they say each sound. For example, they would say, "/m/ /ǎ/ /ch/."

Segment Words into Syllables

1. Say a word for students to segment into syllables. For example, say, "after." Have students repeat the word. Have students push a counter into each box as they say each syllable. For example, they would say, "af•ter," and identify that the word has two syllables.

English Language Support

- Have students place their hands under their chins to count the jaw drops/syllables more easily.

This routine is based on A Fresh Look at Phonics *by Wiley Blevins and* Letter Lessons and First Words *by Heidi A. Mesmer.*

Instructional Routines
Phonemic-Awareness Instruction

Use the Sound Cards

Objective: Learn sounds, practice how the sounds are formed in the mouth, and discuss sounds and spellings.

Materials: target sound card (soundcards.pdf), small mirrors

Preparation: Display or print the target sound card.

Instructional Steps

1. Show students the sound card for a new sound. Name the sound and the picture. For example, for the /t/ card, say, "The sound is /t/. *Table* starts with /t/." Use the QR code (page 7) to play a recording of the phoneme.

2. Name the relevant part of the vocal tract, and model how to form the sound with the lips, teeth, or tongue. Refer students to the mouth illustration(s), and have them use mirrors to see if their mouths match the image on the sound card. Point out whether the air flow is continuous or stopped and whether the sound is voiced (sung) or unvoiced (whispered).

3. Point out the main spelling that represents the sound or the target spelling. (Cover other spellings with sticky notes until it's time to teach them.)

4. As an extension, display more than one card at a time, and discuss similarities and differences between the sounds and articulations. If space permits, post your own sound wall (described in soundcards.pdf).

English Language Support

- Model articulating sounds rather than calling on students to pronounce sounds, which may embarrass them. Be encouraging of students' attempts to form sounds, which may not exist in their home languages.

This routine is based on What the Science of Reading Says about Word Recognition *by Jennifer Jump and Robin D. Johnson and* Speech to Print *by Louisa Cook Moats.*

Instructional Routines
Phonics Skills Instruction

Continuous Blending

Objective: Read words by blending the sounds in order from left to right.

Preparation: Prepare a list of these types of words: CVC words, words with two-consonant blends, or one-syllable words with open syllables (e.g., *top*, *mist*, or *so*).

Instructional Steps

1. Post a word for students to read. For example, write the word *sun*.

2. Point to the beginning of the word, and say, "Watch as I blend." Slowly slide your finger under each letter, and say the sounds. For example, say, "/sssŭŭŭnnn/."

3. Return to the beginning of the word. Say, "Blend." Slide your finger under the word at a slow pace, and have students blend the sounds in order from the first letter to the last letter.

4. Say, "Word." Have students say the word at normal speed.

Independent

1. Distribute word lists to students, and have them use the routine to decode words.

2. Check in with students, and have them blend words as you listen. Provide corrective feedback as necessary.

English Language Support

- After blending several words, define them or use them in sentences to build students' vocabulary. Don't assume that students know the words used for blending practice just because they are "simple" words.

This routine is based on Shifting the Balance *by Jan Burkins and Kari Yates and* Cultivating Readers, Literacy Routine Map *by Lexie Domaradzki.*

Instructional Routines
Phonics Skills Instruction

Cumulative Blending

Objective: Read words by blending the sounds in a cumulative pattern, returning to the first letters each time a new sound is added.

Materials: letter cards (lettercards.pdf), letter tiles (lettertilesbeg.pdf), pocket chart

Preparation: Prepare a list of these types of words: CVC words, words with two-consonant blends, or one-syllable words with open syllables (e.g., *den*, *step*, or *we*).

Instructional Steps

1. Post a word for students to read. For example, write the word *plot*.

2. Tap under the *p*, and ask, "Sound?" (/p/) Tap under the second letter, and ask, "Sound?" (/l/) Say, "Blend," as you slowly slide your finger under the first two letters. (/pl/)

3. Tap under the third letter, and ask, "Sound?" (/ŏ/) Then, say, "Blend," as you slide your finger under the first three letters. (/plŏ/)

4. Tap under the last letter, and ask, "Sound?" (/t/) Then, say, "Blend," as you slide your finger under the entire word. (/plŏt/)

5. Say, "Word." Have students say the word at normal speed.

Collaborative

1. Model the activity with letter cards and a pocket chart.

2. For the word *plot*, display the four letter cards, slightly spread out. Ask for the sound of the first letter. Then, ask for the second sound. Push the first two cards together, and ask students to blend the two sounds.

3. Ask for the third sound. Then, push the third card to touch the first two cards, and ask students to blend the sounds.

4. Ask for the ending sound. Then, push the last card to touch the first three cards, and ask students to blend the whole word.

5. Provide partners with letter tiles. Have students blend words in pairs, manipulating the letter tiles as if they were letter cards, as in steps 2–4.

English Language Support

- After blending, draw pictures of the words and define them to help build students' schemata.

This routine is based on Shifting the Balance *by Jan Burkins and Kari Yates and* Cultivating Readers, Literacy Routine Map *by Lexie Domaradzki.*

© Shell Education

Instructional Routines
Phonics Skills Instruction

Dictation

Objective: Spell sounds and words with learned sound patterns through guided practice.

Materials: sound cards (soundcards.pdf) (*optional*), chart paper

Preparation: Prepare a list of sounds, words, or sentences for students to write. The sounds and words should have been previously taught.

Spell Sounds

1. Clearly say, "The sound is _____." Ask students to repeat the sound and then write it. Help students by showing them the correct letter-formation technique—narrating your movements as you write.

2. Affirm students' answers by writing the letter(s) so students can check and correct their work.

Spell Words

1. Clearly say, "The word is _____." For example, say, "nudge." Ask students to repeat it.

2. Say, "Sound out *nudge.*" Elongate the word (/nnnŭŭŭj/) while simultaneously moving your hand to mark the initial, middle, and final sounds. You may need to guide students further (e.g., "What is the beginning sound?" (/nnn/) "Write /nnn/. What is the next sound?...")

3. Have students independently write the word and reread it to themselves. Write the word so students can check their work.

Write Sentences

1. Say, "Now, you will write a sentence with _____ words. The sentence is _____." Repeat the sentence. Then say, "What is the first word? Sound it out," and so on. As students are working, you may wish to point out a particular spelling on a sound card.

2. Display the sentence so students can check their work, or collect the dictation as a sample of student writing.

English Language Support

- Model doing dictations on chart paper while students do them on their individual papers so they can see what is expected of them. Explain each decision you make so that students can internalize these discussions and eventually describe to you their thought processes.

This routine is based on Cultivating Readers, Literacy Routine Map *by Lexie Domaradzki and* A Fresh Look at Phonics *by Wiley Blevins.*

Instructional Routines
Phonics Skills Instruction

Letter-Team Blending

Objective: Before students blend, draw their attention to new phonics patterns in the words.

Preparation: Prepare a list of words to demonstrate a phonics concept. Determine what markings you will use throughout the year as you call attention to each letter team (e.g., underline vowel teams, use breves and macrons to indicate short and long vowels, box digraphs and trigraphs, and circle affixes).

Vowel Teams

Follow this routine for words with vowel teams, diphthongs, *r*-controlled vowels, and vowel-*r* combinations.

1. Post a word for students to read, for example, the word *note*. Point out the vowel pattern *o_e*. Say, "I see a vowel team." (Tap under the two vowels and underline them.) Say, "The sound is /ō/. The *e* is silent."

2. Point to the beginning of the word, and ask, "What is the word?" Slide your finger under the word, and have students blend the sounds to read *note*.

Consonant Teams

Follow this routine for words with digraphs and trigraphs.

1. Post a word for students to read, for example, *bench*. Point to the digraph *ch*. Say, "I see a digraph." (Point to the *ch* and box it.) Say, "The sound is /ch/."

2. Point to the beginning of the word, and ask, "What is the word?" Slide your finger under the word, and have students blend the sounds to read *bench*.

Affixes

Follow this routine for words with prefixes and suffixes.

1. Post a word for students to read, for example, *swinging*. Point to the suffix *–ing,* and explicitly call out the meaning. Say, "I see a suffix." (Circle it.) Say, "The sound is /ĭng/. This suffix tells us it's an ongoing action. Someone is swinging or was swinging for a period of time."

2. Point to the beginning of the word, and ask, "What is the word?" Slide your finger under the word, and have students blend the sounds to read *swinging*.

English Language Support

- Preview the sound-spelling patterns to draw attention to the letters that work together to produce a sound.

This routine is based on Cultivating Readers, Literacy Routine Map *by Lexie Domaradzki and* Word Identification Strategies *by Barbara J. Fox.*

Instructional Routines
Phonics Skills Instruction

Syllable Division 1

Objective: Segment words into syllables to practice reading two-syllable words.

Materials: letter cards (lettercards.pdf), pocket chart, letter tiles (lettertilesbeg.pdf)

Preparation: Prepare a list of words to demonstrate one of these syllable patterns:

- V/CV produces an open first syllable with a long vowel (ro•bot).
- VC/V produces a closed first syllable with a short vowel (rob•in).
- VCCV words are typically syllabicated between the middle consonants: VC/CV (e.g., mag•net or con•test). Note the exceptions:
  - If the middle consonants form an *r* or *l* blend, divide the word before the blend. (se•cret)
  - If the middle consonants form a digraph, divide the word after the digraph. (rock•et)

Instructional Steps

1. Explain that every syllable has a vowel sound and a written vowel.

2. Display a multisyllabic word using letter cards and a pocket chart. Teach students to look for the vowels first. Spread the vowels apart from the middle consonant(s). Count the number of consonants between the two vowels, and look for known patterns (VCV or VCCV). Demonstrate syllable division by moving the consonants to join the left or right vowel. Check that the syllable division produces the desired pronunciation.

3. Share the applicable rule as you model reading each syllable. Discuss the unstressed-syllable schwa sound if relevant.

4. Support students as they syllabicate words using letter tiles. If you ask them to divide *final* into syllables and they erroneously display fin•al, remind them that the first syllable is closed and produces a short *i*. Guide them to divide the word as fi•nal so they can pronounce the word with long *i*.

English Language Support

- Clearly explain each decision you make. Encourage students to repeat the steps after you so they can internalize the steps. Have students help make anchor charts listing the syllable-division steps.

This routine is based on Speech to Print *by Louisa Cook Moats and* A Fresh Look at Phonics *by Wiley Blevins.*

Instructional Routines
Phonics Skills Instruction

Syllable Division 2

Objective: Segment words into syllables to practice reading two-syllable words.

Materials: letter cards (lettercards.pdf), pocket chart, letter tiles (lettertilesbeg.pdf)

Preparation: Prepare a list of words to demonstrate one of these syllable patterns:

- VCCCV words are generally divided after the first consonant that appears between the vowels (e.g., mon•ster). However, keep digraphs and blends together (e.g., bath•tub, bank•rupt).
- C + *le*—Words that end in a consonant + *le* are divided before that consonant (e.g., pur•ple, ta•ble).

Instructional Steps

1. Explain that every syllable has a vowel sound and a written vowel.

2. Display a multisyllabic word using letter cards and a pocket chart. Teach students to look for the vowels first and to look for an *–le* ending.

3. If there is no *–le* ending, spread the vowels apart from the middle consonants. If there are no digraphs or blends, divide the word as VC/CCV. If there is a digraph or blend, keep those letters together. Move the consonant cards to join the left or right vowel.

4. If the word ends in consonant + *le*, have students syllabicate by counting back to divide the word before that consonant. Separate the letter cards to show the syllable division.

5. Share the applicable rule as you model reading each syllable. Discuss the unstressed-syllable schwa sound if relevant.

6. Support students as they syllabicate words using letter tiles. Remind students to look for the vowels first.

7. Have students read the segmented syllables. Then, listen to them blend the syllables to read the words.

English Language Support

- Ask students to catch you making a mistake when you divide words into syllables. Have them explain what you did wrong.

This routine is based on Speech to Print *by Louisa Cook Moats.*

Instructional Routines
Phonics Skills Review

Build a Word Chain

Objective: Visually manipulate or build a sequence of words one letter at a time.

Materials: letter tiles (lettertilesbeg.pdf)

Preparation: Prepare a series of words that you would like students to build. Give each student or pair of students letter tiles.

Instructional Steps

1. Say a word for students to build with the tiles. Then, change one phoneme in that word to create another word. For example, if the first word was *pot*, you could ask students to change *pot* to *hot* to *jot* to *dot*, and so on.

2. Continue to change the words one phoneme at a time in the same position (beginning, middle, or end of the word).

3. As students grow more familiar with the routine, change letters in any position, including adding or removing letters. For example, you could change *truck* to *luck* to *lump* to *lamp* to *glamp*, and so on.

Variation

1. Have students write the words instead of building them using letter tiles.

English Language Support

- Provide reminders of specific sound-spelling patterns as needed. Also build awareness of the parts of speech of the words used in the word chain.

This routine is based on Letter Lessons and First Words *by Heidi A. Mesmer.*

Instructional Routines
Phonics Skills Review

Isolate Sounds to Spell

Objective: Prior to spelling, segment words into individual sounds using kinesthetic movements.

Materials: sound boxes (soundboxes.pdf), counters and letter tiles (lettertilesbeg.pdf)

Preparation: Prepare a list of words to demonstrate a phonics concept. Distribute materials to each student.

Instructional Steps

1. Say a word for students to segment and spell. For example, say, "chip." Model segmenting the word into sounds using your preferred kinesthetic gesture. Have students perform the gesture mirroring you. For example, to segment *chip*, you could tap a finger on a surface, tap your right hand down your left arm, or make a rainbow gesture with your arms from right to left while you isolate the sounds in the word: /ch/ /ĭĭĭ/ /p/.

2. To reinforce segmenting, have each student move one counter into their sound boxes for each sound they hear.

3. Have students replace the counters with letter tiles to match phonemes to graphemes and practice spelling.

4. Reinforce spelling by having students write the words. Remind students to use a kinesthetic strategy as support when they write new words.

Independent

1. Assess student use of kinesthetic strategies in independent practice. Note if students are using the strategies independently as they spell new words.

English Language Support

- Encourage students to compare sounds in their home languages with sounds in English. Discuss whether the consonants are pronounced with more air or less air or whether the vowels glide in the middle or remain stable.

This routine is based on Letter Lessons and First Words *by Heidi A. Mesmer.*

© Shell Education

Instructional Routines
Phonics Skills Review

Read Multisyllabic Words

Objective: Learn a word-attack strategy to make reading a long word less intimidating.

Preparation: Prepare a list of two to four words you would like students to break apart and decode. Determine how you want students to annotate each word part, e.g., underline vowel teams, box digraphs and trigraphs, and circle affixes.

Strategy for Reading Long Words

1. Locate and underline each vowel or vowel team.

2. Circle any familiar endings or suffixes (e.g., –ing, –ed, –ment)

3. Circle any familiar prefixes (e.g., re–, un–)

4. Segment the word into syllables (see routines pages 36–37) to help determine the vowel sounds.

5. Blend the sounds in each syllable from left to right.

6. Say the whole word, and see if it makes sense. If not, try stressing the word in different ways.

Instructional Steps

1. Display the first word, leaving a little space between each letter. Model following the strategy above. For example, write the word *harnesses*. Say, "This is a long word. I'm going to use our strategy for reading long words to help me decode it. Step 1 is to locate and underline each vowel or vowel team." Apply step 1 and each relevant step in the strategy.

2. Have student volunteers mark up the second word.

3. Have students work in pairs to mark up the third word.

4. Have each student mark up the fourth word individually and share their experience using this strategy to read multisyllabic words with partners.

English Language Support

- Help students shift stress from one syllable to the next, and point out any cognates (words with the same root).

This routine is based on Speech to Print *by Louisa Cook Moats.*

40   151921— The Everything Guide to Phonics   © Shell Education

Instructional Routines
Phonics Skills Review

Sort Words/Pictures

Objective: Identify similarities and differences in phonics patterns by sorting.

Materials: pictures depicting the target words or target words written on strips of paper (wordsort.pdf), word-sort charts (wordsort.pdf)

Preparation: Prepare a list of words to demonstrate a phonics concept. If using word cards, display and read aloud the words to be sure students know the words. If using picture cards, display the pictures, and name them.

Instructional Steps

1. Give pairs of students sets of words or pictures and a word-sort chart.

2. Have partners sort the words/pictures based on similar letters or sounds. You may choose to tell partners how to do the sort by introducing categories and sorting one or two examples, or you may have partners determine the categories on their own.

3. Have partners share how they sorted the words/pictures and explain why they put specific cards in each category. Model the sorts for the whole group. Have the group explicitly discuss the different categories partners used to sort their words.

Independent

1. Have students independently sort words/pictures and explain to you their rationale for sorting words/pictures the way they did.

2. Use this independent sort to assess student understanding of phonics patterns.

English Language Support

- At the beginning of the activity, spend more time reviewing the pictures or words. Name the first word, and pass it to the first student. That student should name the word, and pass it to the next student, and so on.

This routine is based on A Fresh Look at Phonics *by Wiley Blevins.*

Instructional Routines
Phonics Skills Review

Try Another Sound

Objective: Practice reading words, self-correcting when you don't hear a recognizable word.

Preparation: Prepare a list of words with vowel-team spellings that can be pronounced in different ways (e.g., *ea, oo, or, ow*).

Instructional Steps

1. Write a sentence with the target word underlined: *The box is <u>heavy</u>*. Begin to use letter-team blending to read the word. For example, say, "I see a vowel team, but I don't know which sound of *ea* to use. I will say the word using different options for the vowel sound and listen for when the word sounds right."

2. Model. Say, "I see an *e* and an *a*, so I'm going to try long *e* first. If that doesn't sound right, I'm going to try short *e*." Model sounding out the word with /ē/ (/h/ /ē/ /v/ /ē/) and then /ĕ/ (/h/ /ĕ/ /v/ /ē/).

3. Encourage students to use this strategy when they get stuck reading a word.

Extension

1. Apply the activity to spelling. Say a word, for example, *raisin*.

2. Have students identify the possible spellings for long *a* (e.g., *a_e, ai, ay*). Write the word using these spellings: *rasein, raisin, raysin*.

3. Give partners time to determine the correct spelling for the long *a* sound and discuss why the other spellings are not typical of English (e.g., silent *e* and *ay* are found at the ends of words).

English Language Support

- Have students help make anchor charts with phonics concepts, a short sentence about the phonics pattern, and example words for reference.

This routine is based on We're Not in Kansas Anymore: The TOTO Strategy for Decoding Vowel Pairs *by Ruth Lyn Meese.*

Instructional Routines
Phonics Skills Review

Word Hunt

Objective: Search decodable texts for words with a target spelling pattern or affix.

Materials: decodable texts

Preparation: Prepare a list with spelling patterns or words that appear in a decodable text.

Instructional Steps

1. Give students copies of decodable texts. Have students search for the spelling patterns or words you prepared. Ask students to share the words they find.

2. Create a class list, and review the list of words together. As students share, discuss the sound-spelling patterns, the positions of the spellings in the words, exceptions, and overarching phonics rules.

Collaborative

1. Have students work in small groups to find words with a target spelling pattern. This could include words posted in the room.

2. Have students share the words they find with others.

3. Follow step 2 of the Instructional Steps above.

English Language Support

- Allow time for students to verbalize their growing understanding of phonics patterns in words. Rehearse with students phrases to help them express their learning.
  - The _____ pattern normally sounds like _____, but here it _____.
  - The prefix _____ means _____.
  - The spelling _____ is only found at the end of a word.
  - _____ can be found at the beginning or in the middle of a word.

This routine is based on A Fresh Look at Phonics *by Wiley Blevins.*

© Shell Education

Instructional Routines
Phonics Skills Review

Word Riddles

Objective: Create or use clues to identify which word is being described from a list of words.

Preparation: Prepare a list of known decodable words or high-frequency words that have similar patterns.

Instructional Steps

1. Display three words at a time, for example, *those*, *there*, and *share*. Read the words aloud. Tell students that they are going to solve word riddles. Explain that a riddle is a series of questions designed to give clues about a topic.

2. Provide students with two phonics clues and one meaning clue about one of the three words, one clue at a time, until they are able to guess the word. For example, you might say, "Which word am I thinking of? It has a silent *e*. The word has a /th/ sound. It is the opposite of *here*." (*there*)

3. Repeat the steps with each set of three words you display for students.

Independent

1. Encourage students to come up with word riddles of their own. Remind them that the first two clues must be phonics related. Then, encourage students to take their riddles home for family members to solve.

2. Combine students' word riddles into a class riddle book.

English Language Support

- Before beginning the activity, go through examples of phonics-related clues and meaning clues with students. Support students in expressing their thoughts by displaying sentence frames.

This routine is based on The Games Children Play *by Nancy Padak and Timothy Rasinski.*

Instructional Routines
High-Frequency Word Instruction

Introduce High-Frequency Words

Objective: Learn high-frequency words by segmenting them and associating the letters with sounds.

Materials: sound boxes (soundboxes.pdf), letter tiles and counters (lettertilesbeg. pdf, lettertilesint.pdf), and flashcards with one high-frequency word per card

Preparation: Select two or three new high-frequency words (HFWs). Write the HFWs on sets of flashcards. Distribute the sound boxes, letter tiles, and counters to students.

Instructional Steps

1. Write the first sentence on the board, and identify the HFW. For example, for the word *other*, read aloud *There is the other cat!*, point to and underline the word *other*, and ask what the word is.

2. As a group, segment the word into sounds: /ŭ/ /th/ /er/. Have students place a counter in their sound boxes for each sound.

3. Direct students to use letter tiles. Say, "The word *other* is spelled o-t-h-e-r. Spell it with me: o-t-h-e-r. What is the first sound in *other*? What letter tile should we select?"

4. Point out the irregular part(s) of the word. Say, "The sound /ŭ/ is usually spelled with *u*, but in this word, /ŭ/ is spelled with the letter *o*." Have students place the letter tile for *o* on top of the first counter in the sound box.

5. Ask, "What is the next sound in the word *other*?" (/th/) "What letters do we place for /th/?" (*th*) "What is the last sound in the word *other*?" (/er/) "What letters do we place for /er/?" (*er*)

6. Provide students with a set of HFW flashcards for the past month. Have them read through the words for practice or play "Go Fish" with a partner.

English Language Support

- For challenging HFWs (whether due to meaning, spelling, or similarity to other words), work with students to create personal dictionaries to help them remember similarly spelled HFWs.

This routine is based on A Fresh Look at Phonics *by Wiley Blevins.*

© Shell Education

Instructional Routines
High-Frequency Word Instruction

Read and Write High-Frequency Words

Objective: Practice and reinforce high-frequency words by reading, writing, and spelling the words.

Materials: multisensory resources (whiteboards, desktops, shaving cream, or gel bags), sentence strips

Preparation: Select two or three high-frequency words (HFWs). Prepare sets of sentence strips by writing the HFW on the front and a sentence using the word on the back. Distribute the multisensory resources.

Instructional Steps

1. Model writing a high-frequency word (HFW). Say, "The word is _____. Watch as I write the word and spell it. Now, it's your turn. Write the word three times. Say each letter each time you write it." (Students can skywrite the word, write it on whiteboards, trace it on their desks with a finger, or write the word using multisensory writing resources.)

2. For each HFW, display a sentence strip. Read the sentence. Ask students to signal when the HFW is read. Discuss the meaning of the word within the sentence.

Collaborative

1. Distribute the sentence strips to partners.

2. For each strip, have partners read the sentence. Ask them to identify the HFW in each sentence.

3. Challenge students to expand the sentences by adding meaningful adjectives or prepositional phrases. Support students as needed.

English Language Support

- Have students read their HFW sentences to three different partners to build their fluency.

This routine is based on A Fresh Look at Phonics *by Wiley Blevins.*

Word Lists Table of Contents

Introduction 49

   How to Use the Word Lists 49

Lists 51

   Short Vowels 51
   Short A Words 52
   Short E Words 59
   Short I Words 66
   Short O Words 73
   Short U Words 78

   Long Vowels 85
   Long A Words 87
   Long E Words 93
   Long I Words 100
   Long O Words 106
   Long U Words 112
   Glided Long U Words 118

   Advanced Vowel Teams 121
   /aw/ Words 122
   /oo / Words 128
   /ow/ Words 131
   /oy/ Words 135

   R-Controlled Vowels 139
   /ar/ Words 140
   /er/ Words 143
   /or/ Words 148
   "AIR" Words 153
   "EER" Words 157
   "IRE" Words 161
   "OOR" Words 164

   Consonant Patterns 167
   Initial Blends 168
   Final Blends 176
   Final Double-Letter Digraphs 186
   Consonant-*le* Words 187

Consonant Digraphs 189
CH Digraph 190
CK Digraph 196
GH Digraph 199
NG Digraph 204
PH Digraph 207
SH Digraph 209
TH Digraph 211
WH Digraph 217

Soft Consonants 221
Soft C Patterns 222
Soft G Patterns 228

Silent Letters 235
Silent Letter: B 236
Silent Letter: C 237
Silent Letter: D 238
Silent Letter: G 239
Silent Letters: GH 240
Silent Letter: H 241
Silent Letter K 242
Silent Letter: L 243
Silent Letter: M 244
Silent Letter: N 245
Silent Letter: P 246
Silent Letter: S 247
Silent Letter: T 248
Silent Letter: U 249
Silent Letter: W 250

Contractions 251

Prefixes 255
Common Prefixes 257
Common Assimilated Prefixes 261
Advanced Prefixes 269
Advanced Assimilated Prefixes 272

Roots 277

© Shell Education   151921—The Everything Guide to Phonics   **47**

Word Lists Table of Contents *(cont.)*

Suffixes 307
Derivational Suffixes 310
Inflectional Suffixes 321

Word Lists

Introduction

How to Use the Word Lists

The word lists in this guide give access to hundreds of examples of word patterns to support phonemic awareness, decoding, spelling, and word-study practice. However, it is important to follow a foundational reading-skills or morphology curriculum and to select only those words that include the sound-letter patterns or word parts that have been (or will be) taught. With that in mind, words can be pulled from the word lists for use with the instructional routines found on pages 23–46, and more.

Some ways to use the words in these lists include the following:

- for blending or segmenting
- to create blending lines
- for fluency practice
- for word sorts
- for word lists
- for anchor charts
- to create decodable text*
- for high-frequency word instruction
- for activity pages
- for assessments
- for dictation or spelling practice
- for home reading practice

In this guide, one-syllable words that can be considered advanced words are <u>underlined</u>. These include unusual words, such as words borrowed from other languages, words with uncommon spelling patterns, or words that are infrequently used by English speakers.

*Note: It may be tempting to generate decodable passages through AI apps, but there is an art to creating controlled, decodable texts that meet the criteria of being instructive, comprehensible, and engaging. Decodables should be based on phonics skills students have been taught but not sacrifice comprehensibility or engagement for the sake of high-decodability percentages. Blevins (2017) recommends analyzing classroom decodable texts for the following seven issues, and if they're found, either rewriting problematic sentences or purchasing better texts.

1. the overuse of low-utility words
2. the use of nonstandard English sentence structures
3. the use of tongue twisters
4. the use of too many abstract pronouns
5. the use of simplistic language that skews the accuracy of scientific concepts
6. the overuse of odd character names
7. the avoidance of the word *the*

The Everything Guide to Phonics

Short Vowels Table of Contents

Short A Words 52

Short A Patterns 52
Closed Syllables with A 52
Closed Syllables with AM or AN 54
Closed Syllables with ANG or ANK 56

Rhyming Sets 57

Homophones and Compound Words 58

Short E Words 59

Short E Patterns 59
Closed Syllables with E 59
Closed Syllables with ENG 62
Closed Syllables with EA 62
Closed Syllables with A or AI 63

Rhyming Sets 64

Homophones and Compound Words 65

Short I Words 66

Short I Patterns 66
Closed Syllables with I 66
Closed Syllables with ING, INK, or YNC 69
Closed Syllables with U or UI 70
Closed Syllables with Y 70

Rhyming Sets 71

Homophones and Compound Words 72

Short O Words 73

Short O Patterns 73
Closed Syllables with O 73
Closed Syllables with A 75

Rhyming Sets 76

Homophones and Compound Words 77

Short U Words 78

Short U Patterns 78
Closed Syllables with U 78
Closed Syllables with O, OE, or OO 81
Syllables with O_E 81
Closed Syllables with OU or OUGH 82
Closed Syllables with A 82

Rhyming Sets 83

Homophones and Compound Words 84

Notes: High-frequency words only include Fry's first 300 words. Rule breakers are only one-syllable words. For most patterns, words are listed only if their stressed syllable follows the focus pattern.

Short A Patterns

Closed Syllables with A

High-Frequency Words

add	at	have
after	back	last
as	had	that
asked	has	

Rule Breakers

quad	wad	watch
swab	was	
swat	wash	

Words with Two Sounds

ab	app	at
ad	as	ax
add	ash	

Words with Three Sounds

act	has	rack
ask	hash	rag
back	hat	rap
bad	hatch	rash
badge	have	rat
bag	jab	sack
bash	jazz	sad
bass	knack	sag
bat	lab	sap
batch	lack	sash
bath	lad	sass
cab	lag	sat
cap	lap	sax
cash	lash	shack
cat	lass	shall
catch	latch	tab
chap	lax	tack
chat	mad	tad
dab	map	tag
dad	mash	tap
dash	mass	tax
fad	mat	that
fat	match	thatch
fax	math	vat
gab	nab	wag
gag	nag	wax
gal	nap	whack
gap	pack	wrap
gas	pad	wrath
gash	pal	yak
gnash	pass	yap
gnat	pat	zap
hack	patch	
had	path	

Short Vowels
Short A Words

Short A Patterns

Closed Syllables with A *(cont.)*

Words with Four Sounds

bask	flag	slap
blab	flap	slash
black	flash	slat
brad	flat	smack
brag	frat	smash
brash	glad	snack
brass	glass	snag
brat	grab	snap
cask	grad	snatch
cast	graph	spat
clad	grass	stab
clap	last	stack
clash	mask	staff
class	mast	stag
crab	pact	stash
crack	past	swag
crag	quack	tact
crash	raft	task
crass	rapt	thrash
drab	scab	track
drag	scat	trap
fact	shaft	trash
fast	slab	vast
flab	slack	

Words with Five Sounds

blast	grasp	strap
clasp	scalp	tract
craft	scrap	
draft	scratch	
flask	splash	
graft	splat	

Words with a Stressed First Syllable

absent	fabric	practice
access	factor	rabbit
action	falcon	radish
actor	fashion	rapid
actress	faster	rascal
after	fastest	rattle
album	fraction	saddle
apple	fracture	sadly
aspect	gadget	salad
athlete	gallon	salvage
attic	gallop	satchel
babble	gavel	satin
badly	gravel	savage
balance	habit	scatter
ballad	happen	scrabble
ballot	happy	shadow
basket	hatchet	shallow
battle	jacket	splatter
cabbage	ladder	statue
cabin	magnet	status
cackle	malice	tablet
cactus	massive	tackle
caption	master	tactful
capture	matter	tactic
cashew	napkin	talent
casket	package	talon
castle	packet	taxi
cattle	paddle	tractor
cavern	palace	traffic
chapel	passage	travel
chapter	passion	vacuum
classic	pasture	valley
cracker	patent	value
dragon	pattern	wagon
drastic	plastic	wrapper

© Shell Education

151921—The Everything Guide to Phonics

53

Short Vowels
Short A Words

Short A Patterns

Closed Syllables with A *(cont.)*

Words with a Stressed Second Syllable

adapt	distract	retract
attach	enact	rewrap
attract	exact	subtract
collapse	extract	surpass
canal	perhaps	unlatch
contract	protract	unpack
contrast	react	unsnag
detract	retag	unwrap

Words with Three or More Syllables

abdicate	balcony	habitat
abdomen	cabinet	happiness
acrobat	calculate	latitude
acronym	calendar	maximum
Africa	capital	national
agony	casual	navigate
Alaska	chaperone	Nebraska
altitude	collaborate	Nevada
appetite	congratulate	procrastinate
aptitude	contraction	rational
aqueduct	disaster	reaction
astronaut	evaporate	sacrifice
attitude	exaggerate	spatula
attractive	gratitude	subtraction
avenue	gymnastics	

Closed Syllables with AM or AN

High-Frequency Words

am	began	land
an	can	man
and	example	plants
animals	family	than
answer	hand	

Rule Breakers

any	swamp	wand
many	swan	want

Words with Two Sounds

am	an

Words with Three Sounds

amp	ham	ran
and	jam	sham
ant	lamb	tan
can	man	than
dam	pan	van
fan	ram	yam

Words with Four Sounds

band	gram	scam
bran	hand	scan
camp	lamp	slam
champ	lance	spam
chance	pant	span
chant	plan	swam
clam	pram	tamp
clan	ramp	tram
cram	ranch	
damp	rant	
dance	sand	

Short A Patterns

Closed Syllables with AM or AN (cont.)

Words with Five Sounds

blanch	glance	scant
bland	gland	scram
branch	grand	slant
brand	grant	stamp
clamp	pants	stance
cramp	plant	stand
France	prance	trance

Words with Six Sounds

strand

Words with a Stressed First Syllable

ambush	famine	rancher
ample	fancy	random
answer	flannel	ransom
anthem	grammar	sample
bandage	hammer	sandal
bandit	hamper	sander
banner	handle	sandwich
camel	handsome	sandy
campus	handy	scammer
candle	lantern	scandal
candor	mammal	scanner
candy	manage	scramble
cannon	mansion	Spanish
canvas	pamphlet	stammer
canyon	panel	trample
channel	panic	transfer
damage	planet	translate
dampen	planner	vandal
dandy	rampage	vanish

Words with a Stressed Second Syllable

command	expand
demand	implant
enchant	transplant

Words with Three or More Syllables

abandon	financial
Alabama	Indiana
ancestor	janitor
animal	Kansas
annual	Louisiana
antonym	manager
banana	manicure
camera	Montana
Canada	New Hampshire
candidate	stamina
canopy	substantial
champion	understand
companion	
contaminate	
example	
family	

Short Vowels
Short A Words

Short A Patterns

Closed Syllables with ANG or ANK

Words with Three Sounds

bang	pang	tang
fang	rang	wrang
gang	sang	yang
hang	shag	

Words with Four Sounds

bank	rank	tank
clang	sank	thank
dank	shank	twang
hank	slang	yank
lank	swang	

Words with Five Sounds

blank	frank	sprang
clank	plank	stank
crank	prank	swank
drank	shrank	
flank	spank	

Words with a Stressed First Syllable

anger	cranky	spanking
angle	dangle	tangle
angry	hanger	tangy
ankle	language	thankful
baggage	lanky	thankless
bangle	mangle	wrangle
blanket	prankster	wrangler

Words with a Stressed Second Syllable

defang	preshrank	shebang
embank	rehang	unhang

Words with Three or More Syllables

antigang	rectangle
boomerang	rectangular
cryobank	thanksgiving
detangle	triangle
embankment	triangular
entangle	

Short Vowels
Short A Words

Rhyming Sets

- ab, cab, crab, dab, drab, flab, gab, grab, jab, lab, nab, scab, slab, stab, tab

- back, black, crack, hack, jack, knack, lack, pack, plaque, quack, rack, sac, sack, shack, slack, smack, snack, stack, tack, track, whack, yak

- act, attract, contract, detract, distract, enact, exact, extract, fact, pact, protract, react, retract, subtract, tact, tract

- ad, add, bad, brad, clad, dad, fad, glad, grad, had, lad, mad, pad, plaid, sad, tad

- calf, gaffe, giraffe, graph, half, laugh, staff

- aft, craft, daft, draft, graft, graphed, laughed, raft, shaft

- bag, brag, crag, drag, flag, gag, hag, lag, nag, rag, sag, shag, snag, stag, swag, tag, wag

- gal, pal, shall

- am, clam, cram, dam, dram, glam, gram, ham, jam, lam, lamb, pram, ram, scam, scram, sham, slam, spam, swam, tram, yam

- amp, camp, champ, clamp, cramp, damp, lamp, ramp, stamp, tamp

- an, ban, bran, can, clan, fan, man, pan, plan, ran, scan, span, tan, than, van

- chance, dance, France, glance, lance, prance, stance, trance

- blanch, branch, ranch

- and, band, bland, brand, canned, command, demand, expand, fanned, gland, grand, hand, land, planned, sand, scanned, stand, strand, tanned

- bang, clang, fang, gang, hang, pang, rang, sang, slang, sprang, tang, twang

- bank, blank, crank, dank, drank, flank, frank, lank, plank, prank, rank, sank, shrank, spank, stank, tank, thank, yank

- ant, aunt, can't, chant, grant, pant, plant, rant, scant, slant

- app, cap, chap, clap, flap, frappe, gap, lap, map, nap, rap, sap, scrap, slap, snap, strap, tap, trap, wrap, yap, zap

- bass, brass, class, crass, gas, glass, grass, lass, mass, pass, sass, surpass

- ash, bash, brash, cash, clash, crash, dash, flash, gash, gnash, hash, lash, mash, rash, sash, slash, smash, splash, stash, trash

- ask, bask, cask, flask, mask, task

- blast, cast, fast, last, mast, passed, past, vast

- at, bat, brat, cat, chat, fat, flat, frat, gnat, hat, mat, pat, rat, sat, scat, slat, spat, splat, that, vat

- batch, catch, hatch, latch, match, patch, scratch, snatch, thatch

- bath, math, path, wrath

- ax, backs, cracks, fax, lax, max, packs, quacks, racks, sacks, sax, tacks, tax, whacks, wax

- has, jazz

© Shell Education

151921—The Everything Guide to Phonics

57

Short Vowels
Short A Words

Homophones and Compound Words

Homophones

ad/add
ant/aunt
capital/capitol
chance/chants
graft/graphed
lam/lamb
laps/lapse
manner/manor
packed/pact
palate/palette/pallet
passed/past
rap/wrap
rapped/rapt/wrapped
sac/sack
sacks/sax
tacks/tax
tracked/tract
wax/whacks

Compound Words

afternoon	classroom	landform
aftershock	databank	landlord
airbag	dishrag	landmark
applesauce	dustrag	landscape
backbone	flagpole	landslide
background	flagship	laptop
backpack	flashback	masterpiece
backstop	flashlight	matchstick
backtrack	fleabag	outflank
backyard	gangplank	outrank
basketball	grandchild	outsang
bathroom	granddaughter	overhang
bathtub	grandfather	pancake
battleship	grandmother	patchwork
beanbag	grandparents	ragtag
blackberry	grandson	ragweed
blackbird	hamburger	riverbank
blackboard	hamstring	sandbank
blacksmith	handbag	sandbar
blacktop	handcuffs	sandbox
campfire	handshake	sandpaper
campground	handspring	sandstone
campsite	handstand	scrapbook
candlestick	hatchback	snowbank
cannot	jetlag	washrag
catfish	lamppost	whizbang
catnap	lampshade	windbag
clambake	landfall	zigzag
classmate	landfill	

Short Vowels
Short E Words

Short E Patterns

Closed Syllables with E

High-Frequency Words

end	men	tell
every	never	them
get	next	then
help	second	together
left	sentence	well
let	set	went
letters	spell	when

Words with Two Sounds

edge	egg	etch

Words with Three Sounds

bed	gem	net	vex
beg	get	peck	web
bell	guess	peg	wed
bet	hedge	pen	wedge
cell	hem	pep	well
check	hen	pet	wet
chef	hex	red	when
chess	jet	retch	whet
debt	led	sedge	wreck
deck	ledge	sell	wren
den	leg	set	wretch
elf	less	shed	yell
elk	let	shell	yen
end	men	tell	yes
fed	mesh	ten	yet
fell	mess	them	
fetch	met	then	
gel	neck	vet	

Words with Four Sounds

belch	guest	shred
belt	heft	sketch
bench	held	sled
bend	helm	smell
bent	help	speck
best	hemp	sped
bled	jest	spell
bless	kelp	stem
bred	kept	step
cent	knelt	swell
chest	left	tend
clef	lend	tense
deft	melt	tent
delve	mend	test
dense	nest	text
dent	next	theft
depth	pelt	thresh
desk	pent	trek
dredge	pest	tress
dress	pledge	vend
felt	prep	vent
fence	press	vest
fend	quell	weld
fest	rent	welt
fleck	rest	went
fled	scent	wept
flesh	self	west
flex	send	wrench
fresh	sense	wrest
fret	sent	zest
glen	shelf	

© Shell Education

151921—The Everything Guide to Phonics

59

Short Vowels
Short E Words

Short E Patterns

Closed Syllables with E (cont.)

Words with Five Sounds

blend	friend	strep
cleft	quest	stress
clench	slept	stretch
crept	smelt	swept
crest	spend	tempt
drench	spent	trench
French	stench	trend

Words with Six Sounds

squelch	strength

Words with a Stressed First Syllable

beggar	empty	lesson
better	engine	letter
blender	enter	lettuce
census	envy	level
center	epic	lever
cheddar	essay	medal
clever	exit	meddle
credit	expert	medic
crescent	extra	melon
debit	fellow	member
denim	felon	memo
dental	fennel	menace
dentist	freckle	mental
dentures	friendly	mention
desert	friendship	mentor
dresser	gesture	message
dwelling	helmet	metal
edit	kettle	method
effort	lecture	necklace
elbow	legend	
emblem	lemon	

Words with a Stressed First Syllable (cont.)

nectar	rescue	tenor
nephew	restless	tension
nestle	schedule	tenure
never	second	Texas
pebble	segment	texture
pedal	seldom	tremor
peddle	selfish	twenty
pencil	senate	velvet
penguin	sentence	vendor
penny	session	venture
pension	settle	venue
petal	seven	vessel
pregnant	shelter	wedding
present	special	welcome
pressure	spelling	western
pretzel	splendid	whether
question	splendor	wreckage
reckless	stellar	wrestle
relic	temper	yellow
relish	temple	
reptile	tennis	

Short Vowels
Short E Words

Short E Patterns

Closed Syllables with E *(cont.)*

Words with a Stressed Second Syllable

address	direct	offense
affect	dissent	percent
amend	distress	perfect
arrest	duet	possess
ascent	effect	pretend
assent	eject	prevent
assess	elect	profess
attempt	erect	progress
attend	event	project
caress	exempt	protect
cement	expect	reflect
collect	expel	refresh
commence	expense	regress
commend	express	reject
condense	extend	repel
confess	hotel	request
connect	immense	respect
consent	impress	revenge
contempt	inject	select
content	inspect	subject
correct	intense	success
defend	intent	suggest
defense	invent	suspect
depend	lament	suspend
depress	lapel	suspense
descend	motel	undress
descent	neglect	unless
detect	object	
digress	offend	

Words with Three or More Syllables

adventure	elephant	potential
affection	elevate	precipice
apprentice	emptiness	prejudice
attention	envelope	president
benefit	episode	protection
celebrate	escalate	reception
chemical	essential	recommend
collection	every	reflection
Connecticut	excavate	regular
connection	exercise	remember
convention	expensive	represent
correction	general	residue
decimal	generous	respectful
decorate	gentleman	revenue
dedicate	hesitate	selection
defective	infection	sensitive
deficit	injection	several
Delaware	inspection	specimen
demonstrate	investigate	stethoscope
develop	lemonade	successful
directions	melody	surrender
director	Mexico	synthetic
educate	New Mexico	telescope
effective	offensive	televise
election	parentheses	together
electric	pedestrian	yesterday
elegant	pedicure	
element	penalty	

© Shell Education   151921—The Everything Guide to Phonics   **61**

Short Vowels
Short E Words

Short E Patterns

Closed Syllables with ENG

Rule Breakers

English

Words with Four Sounds

length

Words with Five Sounds

dregs

Words with Six Sounds

strength

Words with a Stressed First Syllable

English	penguin
lengthen	strengthen
lengthy	

Closed Syllables with EA

High-Frequency Words

| head | read |

Words with Three Sounds

dead	head
deaf	lead
death	read

Words with Four Sounds

bread	stead
breath	sweat
dealt	thread
dread	threat
health	tread
meant	wealth
realm	

Words with Five Sounds

| breadth | spread |
| breast | stealth |

Short E Patterns

Closed Syllables with EA (cont.)

Words with a Stressed First Syllable

breakfast	pheasant
breathless	pleasant
deadly	pleasure
deafen	ready
dreadful	steady
feather	stealthy
healthy	sweater
heather	sweaty
heaven	threaten
heavy	treasure
jealous	wealthy
leather	weapon
meadow	weather
measure	zealous

Words with a Stressed Second Syllable

ahead	instead

Words with Three or More Syllables

already	jealousy
heavenly	treacherous

Closed Syllables with A or AI

High-Frequency Words

again	many
any	said

Words with Three Sounds

said

Words with a Stressed First Syllable

any	many

Words with a Stressed Second Syllable

again	against

Short Vowels
Short E Words

Rhyming Sets

- check, deck, fleck, neck, peck, speck, trek, wreck

- affect, checked, collect, connect, correct, detect, direct, effect, eject, elect, expect, inject, inspect, neglect, object, pecked, perfect, project, protect, reflect, reject, respect, select, subject, suspect, wrecked

- ahead, bed, bled, bread, dead, dread, fed, fled, head, instead, lead, led, read, red, said, shed, shred, sled, sped, spread, stead, thread, tread, wed

- chef, clef, deaf

- cleft, deft, heft, left, theft

- beg, egg, leg, peg

- dredge, edge, hedge, ledge, pledge, sedge, wedge

- bell, cell, dell, fell, gel, quell, sell, shell, smell, spell, swell, tell, well, yell

- felled, held, smelled, spelled, weld, yelled

- elf, self, shelf

- health, stealth, wealth

- belt, dealt, felt, knelt, melt, pelt, smelt, welt

- elves, selves, shelves

- help, yelp

- gem, hem, stem, them

- attempt, contempt, exempt, tempt, unkempt

- again, den, glen, hen, men, pen, ten, then, when, wren, yen

- commence, condense, defense, dense, fence, hence, immense, sense, tense

- bench, clench, drench, French, stench, trench, wrench

- amend, bend, blend, defend, depend, end, extend, fend, friend, lend, mend, rend, send, spend, suspend, tend, trend, vend

- length, strength

- ascent, bent, cement, cent, consent, content, dent, descent, dissent, event, gent, invent, meant, pent, prevent, rent, scent, sent, spent, tent, vent, went

- prep, rep, step, strep

- crept, kept, slept, swept, wept

- address, assess, bless, caress, chess, digress, dress, express, guess, impress, less, mess, press, progress, regress, stress, success, tress, yes

- flesh, fresh, mesh, thresh

- arrest, best, blessed, breast, chest, crest, dressed, fest, guest, jest, lest, messed, nest, pest, quest, rest, test, vest, west, wrest, zest

- breath, death

- bet, debt, fete, fret, get, jet, let, met, net, pet, set, sweat, threat, vet, wet, whet, yet

- etch, fetch, retch, sketch, stretch, wretch

- checks, decks, flecks, flex, hex, necks, pecks, specks, vex, wrecks

- next, text

- feather, heather, leather, weather, whether

Short Vowels
Short E Words

Homophones and Compound Words

Homophones

accept/except
affect/effect
ascent/assent
bread/bred
cell/sell
cellar/seller
censor/sensor
cent/scent/sent
cents/sense
dense/dents
descent/dissent
flecks/flex
guessed/guest
lead/led
levee/levy
medal/meddle/metal
pedal/peddle/petal
presence/presents
read/red
residence/residents
rest/wrest
retch/wretch
tense/tents
weather/whether
wet/whet

Compound Words

anybody
anyone
anything
anywhere
bedbug
bedrock
bedroom
bedtime
bedspread
bedsprings
breakfast
checkbook
deadline
dressmaker
eggplant
eggroll
eggshell
everybody
everyone
everything
everywhere
forever
gentleman
headache

headfirst
headlights
headphones
headstand
heavyweight
herself
himself
leatherback
lengthwise
myself
necklace
network
nevertheless
northwest
southwest
sweatshirt
textbook
themselves
treadmill
wavelength
weathervane
website
yourself

© Shell Education

151921—The Everything Guide to Phonics

65

Short Vowels
Short I Words

Short I Patterns

Closed Syllables with I

High-Frequency Words

beginning	Indian	river
big	into	still
children	is	thing
city	it	think
did	it's	this
different	its	until
give	list	which
him	little	will
his	live	with
if	miss	
in	picture	

Rule Breakers

bind	guild	pint
blind	guilt	rind
build	hind	wild
child	kind	wind
find	mild	
grind	mind	

Words with Two Sounds

if	in	it
ill	is	itch

Words with Three Sounds

bib	give	mitt	sit
bid	hid	mix	six
big	hill	nib	thick
bill	him	nick	thin
bin	hip	nip	this
bit	his	pick	tick
chick	hiss	pig	tiff
chill	hit	pill	till
chin	hitch	pin	tin
chip	imp	pit	tip
did	inch	pitch	vim
dig	jig	pith	which
dill	kick	rib	whim
dim	kid	rich	whip
din	kill	rid	whiz
dip	kin	ridge	wick
dish	kiss	riff	wig
ditch	kit	rig	will
fib	knit	rim	win
fifth	lick	rip	wish
fill	lid	shin	wit
fin	limb	ship	with
fish	lip	sick	witch
fit	lit	sieve	zip
fix	live	sill	zit
fizz	miff	sin	
gig	mill	sip	
gill	miss	sis	

Short I Patterns

Closed Syllables with I *(cont.)*

Words with Four Sounds

binge	glitch	rift	spit
blip	grid	rinse	stick
bliss	grill	risk	stiff
brick	grim	shift	still
bridge	grin	shrill	stitch
brim	grip	sift	swig
chimp	grit	silk	swill
cinch	hilt	silt	swim
click	hinge	since	swish
cliff	hint	singe	Swiss
clip	kiln	skid	switch
crib	kilt	skiff	thrill
crick	lift	skill	tilt
disk	lilt	skim	tinge
drill	limp	skin	tint
drip	lint	skip	trick
film	lisp	skit	trill
filth	list	slick	trim
finch	milk	slid	trip
fist	mince	slim	twig
flick	mint	slip	twill
flip	mist	slit	twin
flit	pinch	smidge	twitch
fridge	prick	smith	whisk
frill	prim	sniff	wilt
frizz	quick	snip	wince
gift	quill	snit	winch
gilt	quip	snitch	wind
gist	quit	spill	wisp
glib	quiz	spin	wrist

Word with Five Sounds

blimp	flint	prince	squish
brisk	fringe	prism	stint
clinch	frisk	quilt	strip
crimp	glint	shrimp	swift
cringe	grist	skimp	thrift
crisp	Grinch	split	twinge
drift	primp	sprig	twist
flinch	print	squid	

Words with Six Sounds

glimpse	script	sprint	squint
scrimp	splint	spritz	strict

Short Vowels
Short I Words

Short I Patterns

Closed Syllables with I *(cont.)*

Words with a Stressed First Syllable

bigger	fixes	little
biggest	fixture	middle
biscuit	flicker	midnight
bitter	frigid	mildew
blister	giggle	mimic
blizzard	ginger	mischief
brittle	given	mission
chicken	glisten	mitten
children	griddle	mixes
chilly	grimace	mixture
chimney	guilty	nickel
chipmunk	Hindu	picket
citrus	igloo	pickle
civic	illness	picky
civil	image	picnic
cricket	impact	picture
crimson	index	pigeon
digit	infant	pilgrim
dimple	injure	pillage
dinner	inning	pillar
dipper	insect	pillow
distant	instance	pistol
district	instant	pivot
dizzy	instinct	pricker
driven	issue	princess
fickle	isthmus	prison
fiction	kidnap	quiver
fiddle	kitchen	ribbon
fidget	kitten	riddle
fifty	lily	rigor
figure	limit	river
filter	linen	rivet
finish	liquid	scissors
fissure	listen	

Words with a Stressed First Syllable *(cont.)*

scribble	spillage	vision
scrimmage	spinach	visit
shimmer	splinter	vivid
shiver	sticker	whimper
signal	sticky	whisper
silly	stingy	whistle
silver	stringent	wicked
simmer	thicken	wiggle
simple	thicket	willow
sinew	thimble	windy
sister	ticket	winter
sixty	tickle	wisdom
sizzle	timid	witness
skillet	tissue	wizard
skinny	victim	wriggle
slipper	victor	written
sliver	village	
sniffle	vintage	

Words with a Stressed Second Syllable

admit	enlist	remit
assist	equip	resist
commit	exist	restrict
conflict	forbid	submit
constrict	insist	unfit
convince	instill	until
dismiss	permit	unzip
eclipse	persist	
emit	predict	

68   151921— The Everything Guide to Phonics

© Shell Education

Short Vowels
Short I Words

Short I Patterns

Closed Syllables with I *(cont.)*

Words with Three or More Syllables

anticipate	division	peninsula
audition	eliminate	position
cinnamon	exhibit	principal
citizen	exquisite	principle
committee	illustrate	prohibit
condition	imitate	reminisce
configure	immigrate	restrictions
continue	indicate	ritual
contradict	industry	signature
criminal	initial	similar
critical	intellect	subscription
criticize	interest	Thanksgiving
curriculum	Michigan	victory
deliver	minimum	vinegar
description	Mississippi	Virginia
different	nutrition	visitor
difficult	official	West Virginia
diminish	original	
disintegrate	participate	

Closed Syllables with ING, INK, or YNC

Words with Three Sounds

ding	ring	wring
ink	sing	zing
king	thing	
ping	wing	

Words with Four Sounds

bling	link	swing
bring	mink	sync
chink	pink	think
cling	rink	wink
fling	sink	
kink	sling	

Word with Five Sounds

blink	drink	slink
brink	shrink	stink
clink	skink	string

Words with a Stressed First Syllable

blinker	mingle	sprinkle
crinkle	pinkie	tinker
jingle	ringer	trinket
kingdom	shingle	twinkle
linger	single	wrinkle

Words with Three or More Syllables

singular	synchronize

© Shell Education

151921—The Everything Guide to Phonics

69

Short Vowels
Short I Words

Short I Patterns

Closed Syllables with U or UI

Words with Four Sounds

build	guild
built	guilt

Words with a Stressed First Syllable

builder	guilty
building	
business	
busy	

Closed Syllables with Y

Words with Three Sounds

gym	myth

Words with Four Sounds

cyst	lynch
hymn	nymph

Words with Five Sounds

crypt

Words with a Stressed First Syllable

cryptic	rhythm
crystal	symbol
cymbals	symptom
cynic	syndrome
gymnast	syntax
gypsy	system
physics	

Words with a Stressed Second Syllable

abyss	encrypt

Words with Three or More Syllables

chrysalis	symmetry
cylinder	sympathy
cynical	synonym
mystery	synthesize
mystify	typical
physical	
sycamore	

Short Vowels
Short I Words

Rhyming Sets

- bib, crib, fib, glib, nib, rib

- brick, chick, click, crick, flick, kick, lick, nick, pick, prick, quick, sick, slick, stick, thick, tic, tick, trick, wick

- clicked, conflict, constrict, flicked, licked, nicked, picked, predict, pricked, restrict, strict, ticked, tricked

- bid, did, grid, hid, kid, lid, rid, skid, slid, squid

- bridge, fridge, ridge, smidge

- if, cliff, miff, riff, skiff, sniff, stiff, tiff, whiff

- drift, gift, lift, rift, shift, sift, swift, thrift

- big, dig, fig, gig, jig, pig, rig, sprig, swig, twig, wig

- bill, chill, dill, drill, fill, frill, gill, grill, hill, ill, kill, mill, pill, quill, shrill, sill, skill, spill, still, swill, thrill, till, trill, twill, until, will

- billed, build, chilled, filled, grilled, guild, killed

- milk, silk

- built, gilt, guilt, hilt, lilt, quilt, silt, tilt, wilt

- brim, dim, grim, gym, him, hymn, limb, prim, rim, skim, slim, swim, trim, vim, whim

- blimp, chimp, crimp, imp, limp, primp, scrimp, shrimp, skimp

- bin, chin, din, fin, grin, in, inn, kin, pin, shin, sin, skin, spin, thin, tin, twin, win

- convince, mince, prince, rinse, since, wince

- grinned, pinned, sinned, wind

- bling, bring, cling, ding, fling, king, ping, ring, sing, sling, spring, sting, string, swing, thing, wing, wring, zing

- blink, brink, chink, clink, drink, ink, kink, link, mink, pink, rink, shrink, sink, slink, stink, sync, think, wink

- cinch, clinch, finch, flinch, Grinch, inch, lynch, pinch, winch

- binge, cringe, fringe, hinge, singe, syringe, tinge, twinge

- flint, glint, hint, lint, mint, print, splint, sprint, squint, stint, tint

- blip, chip, clip, dip, drip, flip, grip, hip, lip, nip, quip, rip, ship, sip, skip, slip, snip, strip, tip, trip, whip, zip

- chipped, clipped, crypt, dipped, dripped, flipped, gripped, nipped, script, sipped, skipped, slipped, snipped, tipped, zipped

- bliss, dismiss, hiss, kiss, miss, sis, Swiss, this

- dish, fish, squish, swish, wish

- bisque, brisk, disk, frisk, risk, whisk

- crisp, lisp, wisp

- assist, consist, cyst, exist, fist, gist, grist, hissed, insist, kissed, list, missed, mist, persist, resist, twist, wrist

- admit, bit, commit, emit, fit, flit, grit, hit, it, kit, knit, lit, mitt, permit, pit, quit, remit, sit, skit, slit, snit, spit, split, submit, wit, zit

- ditch, glitch, hitch, itch, pitch, rich, snitch, stitch, switch, twitch, which, witch

- fifth, myth, pith, smith

- give, live, sieve

- bricks, clicks, fix, flicks, kicks, licks, mix, nix, picks, six, sticks, ticks, wicks

- fizz, frizz, his, is, quiz, whiz, whizz

Short Vowels
Short I Words

Homophones and Compound Words

Homophones

been/bin
billed/build
chili/chilly
gilt/guilt
gorilla/guerilla
him/hymn
in/inn
incite/insight
it's/its
knit/nit
mince/mints
missed/mist
principal/principle
prints/prince
ring/wring
sink/sync
tic/tick
which/witch

Compound Words

bittersweet
driftwood
fisherman
gingerbread
hillside
inchworm
infield
input
inside
jigsaw
kickball
kickstand
milkshake
piggyback
pigtails
pinhead
pitchfork
ringmaster
ringtone
riptide
shipwreck
springboard
springtime
stingray
swimsuit
tinfoil
windmill
windpipe
windshield
witchcraft
within

Short Vowels
Short O Words

Short O Patterns

Closed Syllables with O

High-Frequency Words

got	on
not	stop

Rule Breakers

comb	tomb	won
Monday	ton	
son	womb	

Words with Two Sounds

odd	on

Words with Three Sounds

bob	fob	lock	pot
bog	fog	lodge	rob
bomb	fox	log	rock
botch	gob	lop	rod
box	god	lot	rot
chock	got	mob	shock
chop	hock	mock	shod
cob	hog	mom	shop
cog	hot	mop	shot
con	job	nod	sob
cop	jock	not	sock
cot	jog	notch	sod
dock	jot	opt	sop
dodge	knob	pock	top
dog	knock	pod	tot
doll	knot	pop	wok
dot	lob	posh	

Words with Four Sounds

blob	flop	slob
block	fond	slog
blot	font	slop
blotch	frock	slosh
bond	frog	slot
chomp	glob	smock
clock	plod	smog
clod	plop	snob
clog	plot	snot
clot	pomp	spot
conch	pond	stock
crock	prod	stop
crop	prom	throb
crotch	prop	trod
drop	romp	trot
flock	Scot	

Words with Five Sounds

blond	splotch
frond	stomp

Words with Six Sounds

prompt

Short Vowels
Short O Words

Short O Patterns

Closed Syllables with O *(cont.)*

Words with a Stressed First Syllable

blossom	foggy	pollen
body	follow	possum
bonfire	fossil	posture
bonnet	gobble	problem
bother	goblet	product
bottle	goggles	profit
bottom	gossip	project
boxes	hobble	promise
closet	hobby	prophet
cobble	hockey	rhombus
collar	hollow	robber
college	honest	robin
comet	honor	rocket
comic	hostel	rotten
comma	hostile	scholar
comment	jogger	sloppy
common	knowledge	soccer
complex	lobby	socket
concert	lobster	solid
conduct	locker	sonic
congress	model	sonnet
conquer	modern	sponsor
constant	monster	tonsils
contact	nonsense	topic
content	nostril	topple
contest	novel	toxic
copper	novice	tropic
copy	nozzle	volume
costume	olive	vomit
cottage	optic	wobble
cotton	option	yonder
doctor	oxen	
dollar	pocket	
dollop	polish	

Words with a Stressed Second Syllable

adopt	forgot	unknot
beyond	respond	upon
concoct	response	Vermont

Words with Three or More Syllables

abolish	cooperate	policy
accommodate	deposit	politics
accomplish	dominate	popular
astonish	economy	possible
colony	hippopotamus	poverty
colossal	holiday	probably
comedy	honesty	property
compensate	hospital	prosecute
complicate	misconduct	synopsis
comprehend	modernize	thermometer
compromise	modify	volatile
concentrate	molecule	Wisconsin
concoction	nominate	
confiscate	obstacle	
consolidate	omnivore	
constantly	operate	
controversy	oxygen	

Short O Patterns

Closed Syllables with A

High-Frequency Words

want

Words with Three Sounds

spa · wash
wad · watt
wan

Words with Four Sounds

quad · swat
swab · wand
swan · want

Words with Five Sounds

squad · squat
squash

Words with a Stressed First Syllable

quadrant · waddle
squadron · wattage

Words with Three or More Sylables

Hawai'i · Islamist
Islamic

Short Vowels
Short O Words

Rhyming Sets

- blob, bob, cob, fob, glob, gob, job, knob, lob, mob, rob, slob, snob, sob, swab, throb
- block, chock, clock, crock, dock, flock, frock, hock, jock, knock, lock, mock, pock, rock, shock, smock, sock, stock, wok
- clod, cod, god, nod, odd, plod, pod, prod, quad, rod, shod, sod, squad, trod, wad
- bog, clog, cog, dog, fog, frog, hog, jog, log, nog, slog, smog
- dodge, garage, lodge
- bomb, mom, prom
- chomp, pomp, romp, stomp
- con, don, on, upon
- beyond, blond, bond, fond, frond, pond, respond, wand
- long, prong, song, strong, throng, tong, wrong
- chop, cop, crop, drop, flop, hop, lop, mop, plop, pop, prop, shop, slop, sop, stop, top
- adopt, chopped, cropped, dropped, flopped, hopped, lopped, mopped, opt, popped, shopped, stopped, topped
- posh, slosh, squash, wash
- blot, clot, cot, dot, forgot, got, hot, jot, knot, lot, not, plot, pot, rot, Scot, shot, slot, snot, spot, squat, swat, tot, trot, watt
- blotch, botch, crotch, notch, splotch

Short Vowels
Short O Words

Homophones and Compound Words

Homophones

complement/compliment
hostel/hostile
knot/not
locks/lox
profit/prophet

Compound Words

bottleneck
cannot
chopstick
clockwork
cobweb
copycat
copyright
dockside
dodgeball
doghouse
dollhouse
hotdog
popcorn
potluck
shopkeeper
spotlight
stockroom
topsoil
upon

Short U Patterns

Closed Syllables with U

High-Frequency Words

but	must	such
cut	number	under
just	run	up
much	study	us

Rule Breakers

| bull | full | push |
| bush | pull | put |

Words with Two Sounds

| up | us |

Words with Three Sounds

buck	gum	nun
bud	gun	nut
budge	gush	pub
buff	gut	puck
bug	hub	puff
bum	huff	pug
bun	hug	pun
bus	hull	pup
but	hum	putt
butt	hung	rub
buzz	hush	rug
chuck	hut	run
chug	hutch	rung
chum	judge	rush
cub	jug	rut
cud	jut	shuck
cuff	luck	shun
cull	lug	shush
cup	lull	shut
cuss	lung	sub
cut	lush	such
dub	much	suck
duck	muck	sum
dud	mud	sun
dug	mug	sung
dull	mull	sup
dumb	mum	thug
dung	mush	thumb
Dutch	muss	tub
fudge	mutt	tuck
fun	nub	tug
fuss	nudge	ump
fuzz	null	yuck
gull	numb	yum

Short Vowels
Short U Words

Short U Patterns

Closed Syllables with U *(cont.)*

Words with Four Sounds

bluff	fluff	munch	snuck
blush	flung	must	snuff
brush	flush	pluck	snug
bulb	funk	plug	spud
bulge	fund	plum	spun
bulk	flux	plus	stub
bump	glum	plush	stuck
bunch	glut	pulp	stud
bunk	grub	pulse	stuff
bunt	grudge	pump	stun
bust	gruff	punch	stung
chunk	gulch	punk	sulk
club	gulf	punt	sunk
cluck	gulp	rump	swum
clutch	gunk	runt	swung
crud	gust	rust	thrum
crumb	hulk	scuff	thrush
crush	hump	scum	thump
crutch	hunch	shrub	trudge
crux	hunk	shrug	tuft
drug	hunt	skull	tusk
drum	husk	sludge	
duct	jump	slug	
dump	junk	slum	
dunk	just	slush	
dusk	lump	smudge	
dust	lunch	smug	
flub	mulch	snub	

Words with Five Sounds

blunt	grunt	struck
brunch	plump	strum
brunt	plunge	strut
clump	scrub	stump
clunk	scruff	stunk
crunch	shrunk	stunt
crust	skulk	trump
drunk	skunk	trunk
flunk	slump	thrust
grump	spunk	trust

Words with Six Sounds

scrunch	sculpt

© Shell Education

151921—The Everything Guide to Phonics

79

Short Vowels
Short U Words

Short U Patterns

Closed Syllables with U *(cont.)*

Words with a Stressed First Syllable

bubble	justice	sculptor
bucket	knuckle	sculpture
buddy	lumber	snuggle
budget	luggage	structure
bulky	muffin	struggle
bundle	mumble	study
bunny	muscle	stumble
button	mushroom	subject
buzzer	mushy	subway
chuckle	musket	sudden
clumsy	mustang	sulky
cluster	mustard	sullen
crumble	nugget	summit
culture	number	summon
custom	public	Sunday
dungeon	publish	suspect
flutter	pucker	thunder
fumble	puddle	trumpet
funnel	pumpkin	tumble
funny	punish	tunnel
glutton	puppet	ugly
grumpy	puppy	umpire
gullet	puzzle	uncle
gulley	rubber	under
huddle	rubbish	vulture
humble	rugged	
hundred	rumble	
hungry	rummage	
husband	rupture	
jungle	rustle	

Words with a Stressed Second Syllable

abrupt	deduct	exult
adjust	destruct	induct
adult	disgust	indulge
begun	disrupt	instruct
conduct	distrust	insult
construct	divulge	obstruct
consult	engulf	result
corrupt	erupt	

Words with Three or More Syllables

compulsive	eruption	muscular
conductor	gullible	production
construction	impulsive	productive
constructive	indulgent	repulsive
customer	instructions	substitute
destruction	interrupt	supplement
destructive	Kentucky	ultimate
disgusting	lullaby	
disruption	mulberry	

Short U Patterns

Closed Syllables with O, OE, or OO

High-Frequency Words

another	mother	other
does	of	
from	once	

Words with Two Sounds

of

Words with Three Sounds

does	ton	won
son	tongue	

Words with Four Sounds

blood	from	month
flood	monk	once

Words with Five Sounds

front	sponge

Words with a Stressed First Syllable

bloody	dozen	other
brother	govern	oven
color	honey	shovel
comfort	lovely	smother
compass	money	stomach
cover	monkey	wonder
doesn't	mother	

Words with a Stressed Second Syllable

among

Closed Syllables with O, OE, or OO (cont.)

Words with Three or More Syllables

another	discover	somersault
colorful	government	wonderful
comfortable	governor	
company	recover	

Syllables with O_E

High-Frequency Words

above	some
come	something
one	sometimes

Words with Three Sounds

come	none
done	one
dove	shove
love	some

Words with Four Sounds

glove

Words with a Stressed Second Syllable

above

Short Vowels
Short U Words

Short U Patterns

Closed Syllables with OU or OUGH

High-Frequency Words

country   young
enough

Words with Three Sounds

rough   tough
touch   young

Words with Four Sounds

<u>slough</u>

Words with a Stressed First Syllable

country   southern
couple   touching
cousin   tougher
double   toughest
rougher   toughness
roughest   trouble
roughly   younger

Words with a Stressed Second Syllable

enough

Closed Syllables with A

High-Frequency Words

was   what

Words with Three Sounds

was   what

Short Vowels
Short U Words

Rhyming Sets

- club, cub, dub, flub, grub, hub, nub, pub, rub, scrub, shrub, snub, stub, sub, tub

- buck, chuck, cluck, duck, luck, muck, pluck, puck, shuck, snuck, struck, stuck, suck, truck, tuck, yuck

- chucked, clucked, conduct, construct, deduct, destruct, ducked, duct, induct, instruct, obstruct, plucked, sucked

- blood, bud, crud, cud, dud, flood, mud, spud, stud

- budge, fudge, grudge, judge, nudge, sludge, smudge, trudge

- bluff, buff, cuff, enough, fluff, gruff, huff, puff, rough, scruff, scuff, slough, snuff, stuff, tough

- buffed, fluffed, huffed, puffed, scuffed, stuffed, tuft

- bug, chug, drug, dug, hug, jug, lug, mug, plug, pug, rug, shrug, slug, smug, snug, thug, tug

- engulf, gulf

- bulge, divulge, indulge

- bulk, hulk, skulk, sulk

- cull, dull, gull, hull, lull, mull, null, skull

- adult, consult, cult, exult, insult, result

- bum, chum, come, crumb, drum, dumb, from, glum, gum, hum, mum, numb, plum, rum, scum, slum, some, strum, sum, swum, thrum, thumb, yum

- bump, clump, dump, grump, hump, jump, lump, plump, pump, rump, slump, stump, thump, trump

- begun, bun, done, fun, gun, none, nun, one, pun, run, shun, son, spun, stun, sun, ton, won

- brunch, bunch, crunch, hunch, lunch, munch, punch, scrunch

- fund, shunned, stunned

- clung, dung, flung, hung, lung, rung, slung, strung, stung, sung, swung, tongue, wrung, young

- expunge, grunge, lunge, plunge, sponge

- bunk, chunk, clunk, drunk, dunk, flunk, funk, gunk, hunk, junk, monk, punk, shrunk, skunk, spunk, stunk, sunk, trunk

- dunce, once

- blunt, brunt, bunt, front, grunt, hunt, punt, runt, stunt

- cup, pup, scup, sup, up

- abrupt, corrupt, disrupt, erupt, interrupt

- bus, cuss, fuss, muss, plus

- blush, brush, crush, flush, gush, hush, lush, plush, rush, slush

- dusk, husk, musk, tusk

- adjust, bussed, bust, crust, cussed, disgust, distrust, dust, fussed, gust, just, mussed, must, rust, thrust, trust

- but, butt, cut, glut, gut, hut, jut, mutt, nut, putt, rut, shut, strut, what

- clutch, crutch, Dutch, hutch, much, such, touch

- above, dove, glove, love, of, shove

- bucks, crux, ducks, flux, plucks, pucks, trucks, tucks

- buzz, does, fuzz, was

© Shell Education

151921—The Everything Guide to Phonics

83

Short Vowels
Short U Words

Homophones and Compound Words

Homophones

bundt/bunt
bussed/bust
but/butt
ducked/duct
muscle/mussel
mussed/must
mustard/mustered
none/nun
one/won
plumb/plum
some/sum
son/sun

Compound Words

bumblebee	sometimes
buttercup	somewhere
butterfly	subway
buttermilk	sunblock
clubhouse	sunburn
cupcake	Sunday
drugstore	sundown
drumbeat	sunlight
drumstick	sunshine
dumbstruck	thumbtack
lumberjack	touchdown
lunchbox	touchscreen
lunchroom	underground
nothing	underline
punchbowl	underpants
runaway	undershirt
runoff	underwear
runway	uproar
someone	upstairs
something	upstream

Long Vowels Table of Contents

Long A Words ... 87

Long A Patterns ... 87
VCe and VCCe Syllables ... 87
Open Syllables with AY ... 88
Closed Syllables with AI ... 88
Open Syllables with A ... 89
Closed Syllables with EA ... 90
EI and EIGH Words ... 90
Open Syllables with EY ... 90
Open Syllables with ET ... 90

Rhyming Sets ... 91

Homophones and Compound Words ... 92

Long E Words ... 93

Long E Patterns ... 93
VCe Syllables ... 93
EA Words ... 93
EE Words ... 95
Open Syllables with E ... 96
EI Words ... 96
EY Words ... 96
IE Words ... 97
ICE and INE endings ... 97
IGUE and IQUE endings ... 97

Rhyming Sets ... 98

Homophones and Compound Words ... 99

Long I Words ... 100

Long I Patterns ... 100
VCe Syllables with I ... 100
VCe Syllables with Y ... 101
IE Words ... 101
IGH Words ... 101
ILD and IND ... 102
Open Syllables with Y or YE ... 102
Open Syllables with I ... 103

Rhyming Sets ... 104

Homophones and Compound Words ... 105

Long O Words ... 106

Long O Patterns ... 106
VCe Syllables ... 106
OA Words ... 106
OE Words ... 107
OW Words ... 107
OLD, OLK, OLL, OLT, OST, and OTH Words ... 108
OUGH and OUL Words ... 109
ON Words ... 109
Open Syllables with O ... 109

Rhyming Sets ... 110

Homophones and Compound Words ... 111

Long Vowels Table of Contents *(cont.)*

Long U Words 112

Long U Patterns 112
VCe Syllables with U 112
VCe Syllables with O or OO 112
EU or EW Words 112
O Words 113
OO Words 113
UE Words 114
U and UI Words 114
OU and OUGH Words 115
Open Syllables with U 115

Rhyming Sets 116

Homophones and Compound Words 117

Glided Long U Words 118

Glided Long U Patterns 118
VCe Syllables with Glided U 118
Glided EU and Glided EW Words 118
Glided UE Words 118
Open Syllables with Glided U 118

Rhyming Sets and Homophones 119

Notes: High-frequency words only include Fry's first 300 words. Rule breakers are only one-syllable words. For most patterns, words are listed only if their stressed syllable follows the focus pattern.

Long Vowels
Long A Words

Long A Patterns

VCe and VCCe Syllables

High-Frequency Words

came	made	page	state
change	make	place	take
face	name	same	

Rule Breakers

have

Words with Two Sounds

ace	age	ape
ache	ale	ate

Words with Three Sounds

bade	fame	male	same
bake	fate	mane	sane
bale	faze	mate	sate
bane	gale	maze	save
base	game	name	shade
bathe	gape	nape	shake
cage	gate	pace	shale
cake	gave	page	shame
came	gaze	pale	shape
cane	hale	pane	shave
cape	hate	pave	take
case	haze	phase	tale
cave	jade	race	tame
chafe	kale	rage	tape
chase	knave	rake	vane
dale	lace	rate	vase
dame	lake	rave	wade
date	lame	raze	wage
daze	lane	safe	wake
face	late	sage	whale
fade	made	sake	wane
fake	make	sale	wave

Words with Four Sounds

baste	drape	paste	space
blade	flake	phrase	spade
blame	flame	place	stage
blaze	frame	plane	stake
brace	glade	plate	stale
brake	glaze	quake	state
brave	grace	range	stave
change	grade	scale	taste
crane	grape	scathe	trace
crate	grate	skate	trade
crave	grave	slate	waste
craze	graze	slave	
drake	haste	snake	

Words with Five Sounds

grange	scrape

Words with Six Sounds

strange

Words with a Stressed First Syllable

basement	graceful	pavement	statement
bracelet	grateful	safety	

Words with a Stressed Second Syllable

amaze	charade	engrave	mistake
arrange	create	erase	parade
ashamed	crusade	escape	persuade
awake	debate	estate	replace
became	disgrace	exchange	
behave	embrace	impale	
cascade	engage	inhale	

© Shell Education

151921—The Everything Guide to Phonics

Long Vowels
Long A Words

Long A Patterns

Open Syllables with AY

High-Frequency Words

always	day	play	way
away	may	say	

Rule Breakers

says

Words with Two Sounds

bay	jay	pay	yay
day	lay	ray	
gay	may	say	
hay	nay	way	

Words with Three Sounds

bray	fray	pray	stay
clay	gray	slay	sway
flay	play	spay	tray

Words with Four Sounds

splay	spray	stray

Words with a Stressed First Syllable

crayon	mayor	playful
grayish	payment	prayer
layer	player	sayings

Words with a Stressed Second Syllable

allay	betray	display	relay
array	decay	hooray	today
astray	delay	okay	
away	dismay	portray	

Words with Three or More Syllables

betrayal	repayment
portrayal	

Closed Syllables with AI

High-Frequency Words

air

Rule Breakers

aisle	plaid	said

Words with Two Sounds

aid	ail	air
aide	aim	

Words with Three Sounds

bail	hair	maize	sail
bait	jail	nail	tail
chain	laid	paid	vain
chair	lain	pail	waif
fail	lair	pain	wail
fair	maid	pair	wait
faith	mail	raid	waive
gain	maim	rail	
gait	main	rain	
hail	Maine	raise	

Words with Four Sounds

braid	frail	saint	trail
brain	grain	slain	train
claim	paint	snail	trait
drain	plain	Spain	waist
faint	plait	staid	
flail	praise	stain	
flair	quail	taint	

88   151921— The Everything Guide to Phonics   © Shell Education

Long A Patterns

Closed Syllables with AI (cont.)

Words with Five Sounds

quaint	stairs	strain	traipse
sprain	straight	strait	

Words with a Stressed First Syllable

ailment	drainage	raisin	traitor
daily	failure	sailor	waiter
dainty	fairy	strainer	waitress
dairy	painter	tailor	
daisy	prairie	trainer	

Words with a Stressed Second Syllable

acquaint	complain	exclaim	refrain
affair	contain	explain	remain
afraid	despair	impair	repair
attain	detain	maintain	retain
await	disdain	obtain	
avail	domain	ordain	
campaign	entail	pertain	

Words with Three or More Syllables

acquaintance	entertainment	retainer
available	impairment	
container	maintenance	
entertain	remainder	

Open Syllables with A

High-Frequency Words

a   later   paper

Word with One Syllable

a

Words with a Stressed First Syllable

able	crater	labor	patron
acorn	crazy	ladle	radar
agent	data	lady	raven
April	fable	latent	razor
apron	famous	later	sacred
Asian	fatal	lazy	savior
baby	favor	major	savor
bacon	flaky	maple	shaky
bagel	flavor	mason	skater
baker	gable	nasal	stable
basic	glacier	nation	staple
basil	gravy	naval	station
basin	hatred	navel	table
basis	hazel	navy	vacant
cable	hazy	paper	vapor
cradle	label	patient	wafer

Words with Three or More Syllables

agency	invasion	stationery
craziness	laziness	vacancy
donation	location	vacation
drapery	mania	
equation	outrageous	
equator	Pennsylvania	
frustration	radio	
impatient	stationary	

Long Vowels
Long A Words

Long A Patterns

Closed Syllables with EA

High-Frequency Words

great

Words with Four Sounds

break   great   steak

Words with a Stressed First Syllable

greatly   greatness

Words with Three or More Syllables

breakable   unbreakable

EI or EIGH Words

Rule Breakers

sleight

Words with Two Sounds

eight   lei   weigh
heir   neigh

Words with Three Sounds

beige   reign   their   weight
eighth   rein   veil
feign   sleigh   vein

Words with Four Sounds

freight   skein

Words with a Stressed First Syllable

eighty   neighbor   weightless

EI or EIGH Words (cont.)

Words with a Stressed Second Syllable

devein   eighteen   unveil

Words with Three or More Syllables

neighborhood

Open Syllables with EY

High-Frequency Words

they

Words with Two Sounds

hey   they   whey

Words with Three Sounds

grey   prey

Words with a Stressed First Syllable

greyhound

Words with a Stressed Second Syllable

convey   obey   survey

Words with Three or More Syllables

disobey   surveyor

Open Syllables with ET

Words with a Stressed Second Syllable

ballet   croquet   sachet
bouquet   duvet   sorbet
buffet   filet   valet
chalet   gourmet

Long Vowels
Long A Words

Rhyming Sets

- array, away, bay, bray, betray, clay, day, decay, delay, dismay, display, flay, fray, gay, gray, grey, hay, hey, hooray, jay, lay, may, nay, neigh, obey, okay, pay, play, portray, pray, prey, ray, relay, say, slay, sleigh, spay, splay, spray, stay, stray, sway, they, today, tray, way, weigh, whey

- afraid, aid, aide, bade, blade, braid, decayed, fade, frayed, glade, grade, jade, laid, made, maid, paid, parade, persuade, played, prayed, raid, shade, spade, sprayed, stayed, swayed, trade, wade, weighed

- chafe, safe, waif

- cage, gauge, page, rage, sage, stage, wage

- ache, awake, bake, brake, break, cake, drake, fake, flake, lake, make, mistake, quake, rake, sake, shake, snake, stake, steak, take, wake

- ail, ale, bail, bale, dale, exhale, fail, flail, frail, gale, hail, hale, impale, inhale, jail, kale, mail, male, nail, pail, pale, quail, rail, sail, sale, scale, shale, snail, stale, tail, tale, trail, veil, wail, whale

- aim, became, blame, came, claim, dame, exclaim, fame, flame, frame, game, lame, maim, name, reclaim, same, shame, tame

- bane, brain, cane, chain, complain, contain, crane, drain, explain, feign, gain, grain, lain, lane, main, Maine, maintain, mane, obtain, pain, pane, plain, plane, rain, reign, rein, remain, sane, skein, slain, Spain, sprain, stain, strain, train, vain, vane, vein, wane

- arrange, change, exchange, grange, range, strange

- acquaint, faint, paint, quaint, saint, taint

- ape, cape, crepe, drape, escape, grape, nape, scrape, shape, tape

- affair, air, aware, bare, bear, blare, care, chair, dare, despair, fair, fare, flair, flare, glare, hair, hare, heir, impair, lair, mare, pair, pare, pear, prayer, rare, repair, scare, share, snare, spare, square, stair, stare, swear, tear, their, there, they're, ware, wear

- ace, base, brace, case, chase, erase, face, grace, lace, pace, place, race, replace, space, trace, vase

- baste, haste, taste, waist, waste

- ate, await, bait, crate, create, date, eight, estate, fate, freight, gait, gate, grate, great, hate, late, mate, plait, plate, rate, sate, skate, slate, state, straight, strait, trait, wait, weight

- behave, brave, cave, crave, gave, grave, knave, pave, rave, save, shave, slave, stave, waive, wave

- amaze, blaze, craze, days, daze, faze, gaze, glaze, graze, haze, lays, laze, maize, maze, phase, phrase, plays, praise, prays, raise, rays, raze, stays, ways, weighs

© Shell Education

Long Vowels
Long A Words

Homophones and Compound Words

Homophones

aid/aide	pair/pare/pear
ail/ale	patience/patients
air/heir	plain/plane
ate/eight	plait/plate
bail/bale	praise/prays
bare/bear	pray/prey
base/bass	rain/reign/rein
based/baste	raise/rays/raze
braid/brayed	sail/sale
brake/break	saver/savor
days/daze	slay/sleigh
fair/fare	spade/spayed
flair/flare	staid/stayed
gait/gate	stake/steak
grate/great	stair/stare
hail/hale	stationary/stationery
hair/hare	straight/strait
hangar/hanger	tail/tale
hay/hey	taper/tapir
lain/lane	their/there/they're
lays/laze	vain/vane/vein
made/maid	wade/weighed
mail/male	wail/whale
main/Maine/mane	waist/waste
maize/maze	wait/weight
nay/neigh	waive/wave
paced/paste	ware/wear/where
pail/pale	way/weigh/whey
pain/pane	

Compound Words

airplane	mainland
airport	maybe
baseball	namesake
baseboard	painkiller
breakdown	paintbrush
breakthrough	paperback
caveman	paycheck
chairlift	payday
chairman	playdate
daybreak	playground
daydream	playmate
daylight	playpen
fairground	playroom
fairway	racetrack
gangplank	railroad
gatekeeper	rainbow
gateway	raincoat
grapefruit	raindrop
grapevine	rainfall
gravestone	rainstorm
graveyard	sailboat
greyhound	salesperson
hairbrush	scarecrow
haircut	skateboard
hairspray	spacecraft
haystack	stagecoach
lakefront	staircase
lakeshore	stairwell
layout	stakeholder
mailbox	tablespoon
mailman	wasteland

Long E Patterns

Long Vowels
Long E Words

VCe Syllables

High-Frequency Words

these

Rule Breakers

ewe   eye

Words with Two Sounds

eke   eve

Words with Three Sounds

cede	meme	theme
gene	mete	these
here	scene	

Words with Four Sounds

scheme   Swede

Words with a Stressed Second Syllable

compete	extreme	secrete
complete	impede	serene
concede	precede	severe
delete	recede	sincere
deplete	replete	stampede
discrete	revere	supreme
excrete	secede	trapeze

Words with Three or More Syllables

completely   intercede

EA Words

High-Frequency Words

each	leave	read	year
eat	mean	really	
hear	near	sea	

Rule Breakers

bear	great	pear	tear
break	heart	steak	wear
earth	learn	swear	

Words with Two Sounds

each	ease	eave	sea
ear	eat	pea	tea

Words with Three Sounds

beach	hear	near	sheaf
bead	heat	neat	shear
beak	heave	peace	teach
beam	jean	peach	teak
bean	knead	peak	teal
beat	leach	peal	team
cease	lead	peas	tear
cheap	leaf	peat	tease
cheat	league	plea	veal
deal	leak	reach	weak
dean	lean	read	wean
dear	leap	real	weave
east	lease	ream	wheat
fear	leash	reap	wreak
feat	leave	rear	wreath
flea	mead	seal	year
gear	meal	seam	zeal
heal	mean	sear	
heap	meat	seat	

© Shell Education

Long E Patterns

EA Words (cont.)

Words with Four Sounds

beard	cleat	glean	sneak
beast	cleave	grease	speak
bleach	creak	jeans	spear
bleak	cream	least	steal
bleat	crease	plead	steam
breach	dream	please	treat
breathe	feast	pleat	tweak
clean	freak	preach	yeast
clear	gleam	smear	

Words with Five Sounds

scream	squeal	stream
squeak	streak	

Words with a Stressed First Syllable

beacon	eagle	meaning	spearmint
beagle	easel	nearly	teacher
beaver	eastern	neatly	tearful
bleachers	easy	neatness	teary
cheaper	fearful	peaceful	treason
cheapest	fearless	preacher	treatment
clearly	feature	queasy	unclear
creature	greasy	really	weaken
deacon	leader	reason	weary
dearest	leafy	seamless	weasel
dearly	leakage	season	yearly
dreamer	leaky	sneakers	
eager	meager	sneaky	

Words with a Stressed Second Syllable

appeal	disease	ordeal	reveal
appear	endear	preheat	unclean
conceal	ideal	reheat	unclear
deceased	increase	release	unleash
decrease	mislead	repeal	unreal
defeat	misread	repeat	

Words with Three or More Syllables

appearance   disappear

Long Vowels
Long E Words

Long E Patterns

EE Words

High-Frequency Words

between	keep	see	three
feet	need	seem	tree

Rule Breakers

been

Words with Two Sounds

bee	gee	see	wee
eel	knee	tee	
fee	pee	thee	

Words with Three Sounds

beech	geek	reef	weed
beef	glee	reek	week
beep	heed	reel	weep
beet	heel	seed	wheel
cheek	keel	seek	wheeze
cheep	keen	seem	
cheer	keep	seen	
cheese	kneel	seep	
deed	leech	sheen	
deem	leek	sheep	
deep	meek	sheet	
deer	meet	teem	
feed	need	teen	
feel	peek	teeth	
feet	peel	teethe	
flee	peep	three	
free	reed	tree	

Words with Four Sounds

bleed	fleet	sleep	steel
bleep	freeze	sleet	steep
breech	greed	sleeve	steer
breed	Greek	sneer	sweep
breeze	green	sneeze	sweet
creed	greet	speech	tweed
creek	preen	speed	tweet
creep	queen	spree	
fleece	sleek	steed	

Words with Five Sounds

screech	spleen	street
screen	squeeze	

Words with a Stressed First Syllable

beetle	freely	seedling
breezy	freezer	seesaw
cheesy	gleeful	sleeveless
cheetah	greedy	steeple
deepen	greenish	sweeten
deeply	needle	tweezers
feeble	needless	weekly
freedom	needy	wheedle

Words with a Stressed Second Syllable

agree	degree	proceed
asleep	discreet	redeem
beseech	esteem	succeed
between	exceed	
canteen	indeed	

Words with Three or More Syllables

disagree	Tennessee

Long Vowels
Long E Words

Long E Patterns

Open Syllables with E

High-Frequency Words

be	he	people
being	idea	she
even	me	we

Rule Breakers

the

Words with Two Sounds

be	me	we
he	she	

Words with a Stressed First Syllable

cedar	female	regal
decent	fever	scenic
defect	frequent	senior
depot	legal	sequel
detour	meter	sequence
Egypt	prefix	species
even	preview	tepee
equal	recent	
evil	recess	

Words with Three or More Syllables

convenient	frequently	recently
decency	illegal	scenery
equally	indecent	uneven
evenly	meteor	
feverish	procedure	

EI Words

Rule Breakers

beige	lei	veil
feign	reign	vein
heir	rein	
heist	their	

Words with Three Sounds

seize	sheik

Words with Four Sounds

weird

Words with a Stressed First Syllable

ceiling	leisure	seizure
either	neither	

Words with a Stressed Second Syllable

caffeine	deceit	receipt
conceit	deceive	receive
conceive	perceive	

EY Words

Rule Breakers

grey	obey	they
hey	prey	

Words with Two Sounds

key

Long E Patterns

IE Words

Rule Breakers

sieve

Words with Three Sounds

chief	niece	siege
lien	piece	thief
mien	pier	tier

Words with Four Sounds

brief	grief	shriek
field	grieve	thieves
fiend	pierce	wield
fierce	shield	yield

Words with Five Sounds

priest

Words with a Stressed First Syllable

briefly	fiendish	hygiene
brownie	fiercely	movie
cookie	genie	pixie
diesel	goalie	rookie
eerie	grievance	series

Words with a Stressed Second Syllable

achieve	cashier	reprieve
apiece	debrief	retrieve
belief	relief	
believe	relieved	

Words with Three or More Syllables

achievement	retrieval
believable	unbelievable
calorie	unwieldy

ICE and INE Endings

Words with a Stressed First Syllable

chlorine	saline

Words with a Stressed Second Syllable

latrine	police	sardine
machine	ravine	vaccine
marine	routine	

Words with Three or More Syllables

gasoline	magazine	tangerine

IGUE and IQUE Endings

Words with a Stressed Second Syllable

antique	intrigue
boutique	oblique
critique	technique
fatigue	unique

Long Vowels
Long E Words

Rhyming Sets

- agree, be, bee, degree, fee, flea, flee, foresee, free, gee, glee, he, key, knee, lea, me, pea, pee, plea, sea, see, she, ski, spree, tea, tee, thee, three, tree, we, wee

- beach, beech, beseech, bleach, breach, breech, each, leach, leech, peach, preach, reach, screech, speech, teach

- bead, bleed, breed, cede, concede, creed, deed, exceed, feed, freed, greed, heed, keyed, knead, lead, mead, need, peed, plead, proceed, read, recede, reed, seed, she'd, speed, stampede, steed, succeed, Swede, tweed, we'd, weed

- beef, belief, brief, chief, grief, leaf, reef, relief, sheaf, thief

- beak, bleak, cheek, chic, creak, creek, freak, geek, Greek, leak, leek, meek, peak, peek, pique, reek, seek, sheik, shriek, sleek, sneak, speak, squeak, streak, teak, tweak, weak, week, wreak

- appeal, conceal, deal, feel, heal, heel, ideal, keel, kneel, meal, peal, peel, real, reel, reveal, seal, squeal, steal, steel, teal, veal, wheel, zeal

- field, shield, wield, yield

- beam, cream, deem, dream, gleam, meme, ream, scheme, scream, seam, seem, steam, stream, team, teem, theme

- bean, between, clean, dean, gene, glean, green, jean, keen, latrine, lean, lien, machine, marine, mean, mien, preen, queen, ravine, routine, scene, screen, seen, sheen, spleen, teen, vaccine, wean

- asleep, beep, bleep, cheap, cheep, creep, deep, heap, Jeep, keep, leap, peep, reap, seep, sheep, sleep, sweep, steep, weep

- adhere, appear, beer, career, cheer, clear, dear, deer, ear, fear, gear, hear, here, jeer, mere, near, peer, pier, queer, rear, sear, severe, shear, sheer, sincere, smear, sneer, spear, sphere, steer, tear, tier, veer, year

- fierce, pierce

- beard, cleared, seared, sheared, smeared, speared, weird

- apiece, cease, crease, decrease, fleece, grease, Greece, increase, lease, niece, peace, piece

- leash, quiche

- beast, ceased, creased, east, feast, least, priest, yeast

- beat, beet, bleat, cheat, cleat, compete, complete, conceit, defeat, delete, deplete, eat, feat, feet, fleet, greet, heat, meat, meet, mete, neat, peat, pleat, receipt, seat, sheet, sleet, street, suite, sweet, treat, tweet, wheat

- beneath, teeth, wreath

- breathe, teethe

- achieve, believe, cleave, conceive, deceive, eave, eve, grieve, heave, leave, perceive, receive, relieve, reprieve, retrieve, sleeve, weave, we've

- breeze, cheese, disease, ease, freeze, peas, pleas, please, seize, sneeze, squeeze, tease, these, trees, wheeze

Long Vowels
Long E Words

Homophones and Compound Words

Homophones

be/bee	heal/heel
beach/beech	hear/here
beat/beet	he'd/heed
breach/breech	knead/need
cede/seed	leach/leech
ceiling/sealing	leak/leek
cereal/serial	lean/lien
cheap/cheep	leased/least
chic/sheik	mean/mien
creak/creek	meat/meet/mete
dear/deer	overseas/oversees
discreet/discrete	pea/pee
eave/eve	peace/piece
feat/feet	peak/peek/pique
flea/flee	peal/peel
genes/jeans	peer/pier
grease/Greece	pleas/please

Compound Words

beanpole	peanut
beanstalk	piecemeal
beechnut	policeman
beehive	seafood
beekeeper	seagull
cheeseburger	seashore
earache	seasick
eardrum	seaweed
feedback	southeast
fieldhouse	speedway
freeway	steamboat
greenhouse	steamship
hearsay	sweetheart
keyboard	teacup
keychain	teammate
keyhole	teapot
kneecap	teaspoon
meatloaf	treehouse
nearby	weekday
northeast	weekend
overseas	wheelchair
oversee	yearbook

© Shell Education

151921—The Everything Guide to Phonics

99

Long Vowels
Long I Words

Long I Patterns

VCe Syllables with I

High-Frequency Words

life	mile	while
like	side	white
line	time	write

Rule Breakers

give	live

Words with Two Sounds

ice	isle

Words with Three Sounds

bide	guise	nine	tile
bike	hide	pike	time
bile	hike	pile	tine
bite	hive	pine	vice
chide	jive	pipe	vile
chime	kite	rice	vine
chive	knife	ride	while
cite	lice	rife	whine
dice	life	rile	white
dike	like	rime	wide
dime	lime	ripe	wife
dine	line	rise	wine
dive	live	rite	wipe
fife	mice	shine	wise
file	mile	side	write
fine	mime	sire	
five	mine	site	
guide	mite	size	
guile	nice	tide	

Words with Four Sounds

bribe	lives	slime	swipe
bride	price	smile	thrice
brine	pride	smite	thrive
crime	prime	snide	tribe
drive	prize	spice	trike
glide	quite	spike	trite
grime	shrine	spine	twice
gripe	slice	spite	twine
knives	slide	swine	wives

Words with Five Sounds

scribe	sprite	strife	stripe
splice	stride	strike	strive

Words with a Stressed First Syllable

lifeless	nineteen	wisely
nicely	ninety	

Words with a Stressed Second Syllable

advice	confide	divide	provide
advise	confine	divine	recite
alive	decide	excite	recline
arrive	decline	ignite	refine
awhile	despite	invite	revise
beside	device	oblige	revive
collide	devise	polite	surprise
combine	disguise	precise	unite

Words with Three or More Syllables

advisor	recital	revival
excitement	refinery	survival

100   151921— The Everything Guide to Phonics   © Shell Education

Long I Patterns

VCe Syllables with Y

Words with Three Sounds

hype	rhyme	tyke
pyre	thyme	type

Words with Four Sounds

style

Words with a Stressed First Syllable

rhyming	stylist
stylish	typist

IE Words

Words with Two Sounds

die	pie	vie
lie	tie	

IGH Words

High-Frequency Words

high	might	right
light	night	

Words with Two Sounds

high	sigh
nigh	thigh

Words with Three Sounds

fight	light	right
height	might	sight
knight	night	tight

Words with Four Sounds

blight	fright	tights
bright	plight	
flight	slight	

Words with a Stressed First Syllable

brighten	highest	mighty
brightness	highly	nightmare
fighter	lighten	slightly
frighten	lightly	tighten
higher	lightning	

Words with a Stressed Second Syllable

alright	delight	tonight

Words with Three or More Syllables

enlighten	frightening

Long Vowels
Long I Words

Long I Patterns

ILD and IND

High-Frequency Words

find	kind

Words with Four Sounds

bind	kind	wild
child	mild	wind
find	mind	
hind	rind	

Words with Five Sounds

blind	grind

Words with a Stressed First Syllable

binder	childish	mildly
blindness	kindly	mindful
childhood	kindness	wildly

Words with a Stressed Second Syllable

behind	rewind
remind	unkind

Words with Three or More Syllables

reminder

Open Syllables with Y or YE

High-Frequency Words

by	try
my	why

Words with One Sound

eye

Words with Two Sounds

buy	guy	shy
by	lye	thy
bye	my	why
dye	rye	wry

Words with Three Sounds

cry	ply	spy
dry	pry	sty
fly	sky	try
fry	sly	

Words with Four Sounds

spry

Words with a Stressed First Syllable

dryer	hybrid	nylon
cycle	hydrant	python
cyclone	hygiene	tyrant
flyer	hyphen	

Words with a Stressed Second Syllable

apply	defy	rely
awry	deny	reply
bely	imply	supply
comply	July	

Long I Patterns

Long Vowels
Long I Words

Open Syllables with I

High-Frequency Words

I

Words with Two Sounds

hi

Words with a Stressed First Syllable

bias	iron	spider
biker	item	spiny
bison	ivy	spiral
briar	liar	tidal
bridal	lilac	tidy
bridle	lion	tiger
China	migrate	timer
cider	mileage	tiny
client	minor	title
climate	minus	trial
climax	miser	triumph
crisis	pilot	vial
dial	pirate	vinyl
diamond	pliers	violence
diaper	private	violent
diet	quiet	violet
diner	rhino	visor
diver	rifle	virus
driver	riot	visor
final	ripen	vital
finance	rival	whiny
friar	shiny	widen
Friday	silence	writer
giant	silent	
glider	sinus	
grimy	siren	
icy	slimy	
iris	spicy	

Words with Three or More Syllables

appliance	Ohio
bicycle	privacy
compliance	reliance
Idaho	rivalry
Iowa	South Carolina
itemize	tidiness
miserly	tricycle
North Carolina	

© Shell Education

Long Vowels
Long I Words

Rhyming Sets

- apply, awry, buy, by, bye, comply, cry, deny, die, dry, dye, eye, fly, fry, guy, hi, high, imply, July, lie, lye, my, nigh, pie, ply, pry, rely, reply, rye, shy, sigh, sky, sly, spry, spy, sty, supply, thigh, thy, tie, try, vie, why, wry

- bribe, scribe, tribe

- dice, ice, lice, mice, nice, price, rice, slice, spice, splice, thrice, twice, vice

- beside, bide, bride, chide, cried, died, dried, dyed, fried, glide, guide, hide, lied, pride, pried, provide, ride, side, sighed, slide, snide, spied, stride, tide, tied, tried, vied, wide

- fife, knife, life, rife, strife, wife

- bike, dike, hike, like, mic, pike, spike, strike, trike, tyke

- aisle, bile, dial, file, guile, I'll, isle, mile, Nile, pile, rile, smile, style, tile, trial, vial, vile, while

- child, dialed, filed, mild, piled, smiled, styled, tiled, wild

- chime, climb, crime, dime, grime, lime, mime, prime, rhyme, rime, slime, thyme, time

- assign, brine, design, dine, fine, line, mine, nine, pine, resign, shine, shrine, sign, spine, swine, tine, twine, vine, whine, wine

- assigned, bind, blind, designed, find, grind, hind, kind, lined, mind, mined, pined, remind, resigned, rewind, rind, unkind, whined, wind

- gripe, hype, pipe, ripe, stripe, swipe, type, wipe

- acquire, admire, briar, choir, crier, desire, dire, dryer, fire, friar, fryer, higher, hire, inspire, liar, mire, plier, pyre, require, retire, shire, sire, spire, squire, tire, wire

- guise, guys, prize, revise, rise, size, wise

- bite, blight, bright, byte, cite, excite, fight, flight, fright, height, ignite, invite, kite, knight, light, might, mite, night, plight, polite, quite, recite, right, rite, sight, site, slight, smite, spite, sprite, tight, white, write

- arrive, chive, dive, drive, five, hive, jive, live, strive

- fives, knives, lives, wives

- applies, buys, complies, cries, denies, dies, dries, dyes, eyes, flies, fries, guise, guys, pries, relies, sighs, size, supplies, ties, tries, wise

Long Vowels
Long I Words

Homophones and Compound Words

Homophones

aisle/I'll/isle
bite/byte
bridal/bridle
buy/by/bye
cite/sight/site
die/dye
died/dyed
drier/dryer
eye/I
friar/fryer
guise/guys
hi/high
higher/hire
idle/idol
knight/night
lie/lye
might/mite

mind/mined
miner/minor
pried/pride
rhyme/rime
right/rite/write
rye/wry
side/sighed
sighs/size
stile/style
thyme/time
tidal/title
tide/tied
vial/vile
vice/vise
whine/wine
whined/wind

Compound Words

blindfold
bypass
childcare
driveway
eyeball
eyebrows
eyelid
eyesight
eyesore
firefighter
fireproof
firetruck
goodbye
highchair
highlight
highway
hindsight
iceberg
lifeguard
lifelong
lifesaver
lifetime
lighthouse
lightweight
livestock
nightfall

nightgown
nightlight
nightshirt
nightstand
nighttime
outside
pineapple
sidekick
sidestep
sidetrack
sidewalk
sideways
sightsee
skylight
skyscraper
slideshow
timekeeper
timeline
typewriter
upright
uptight
whiteboard
widespread
wildfire
wildlife
worthwhile

© Shell Education

Long Vowels
Long O Words

Long O Patterns

VCe Syllables

High-Frequency Words

close	home	those

Rule Breakers

above	glove	move	shove
come	gone	none	some
done	lose	one	whose
dove	love	prove	

Words with One Sound

owe

Words with Two Sounds

ode

Words with Three Sounds

bode	hole	nope	sole
bone	home	nose	those
choke	hone	note	tome
chose	hope	phone	tone
code	hose	poke	tote
cone	joke	pole	vole
cope	lobe	pone	vote
cove	lode	pope	whole
dole	loge	pose	woke
dome	lone	robe	wove
dope	lope	rode	wrote
dose	mode	role	yoke
dote	mole	rope	zone
dove	mope	rose	
doze	mote	rote	
gnome	node	shone	

VCe Syllables *(cont.)*

Words with Four Sounds

broke	drone	prone	spoke
chrome	drove	prose	stoke
clone	froze	quote	stole
close	globe	scone	stone
clothes	grope	scope	stove
clove	grove	slope	throne
crone	probe	smoke	trove

Words with Five Sounds

strobe	strode	stroke	strove

Words with a Stressed First Syllable

homeless	hopeless
hopeful	wholesome

Words with a Stressed Second Syllable

alone	explode	invoke	provoke
compose	expose	promote	revoke
console	implode	propose	suppose

OA Words

Rule Breakers

broad

Words with Two Sounds

oaf	oath
oak	whoa
oat	

Long Vowels
Long O Words

Long O Patterns

OA Words *(cont.)*

Words with Three Sounds

boat	goal	loathe	roan
coach	goat	moan	shoal
coal	hoax	moat	soak
coat	load	poach	soap
foal	loaf	roach	toad
foam	loam	road	
goad	loan	roam	

Words with Four Sounds

bloat	coast	gloat	throat
boast	coax	groan	toast
broach	croak	loaves	
cloak	float	roast	

Words with a Stressed First Syllable

boastful	coaster	hoagie	toaster
coastal	goalie	roaster	

Words with a Stressed Second Syllable

afloat	encroach	reproach
approach	reload	unload

OE Words

Rule Breakers

does	doesn't	shoe

Words with Two Sounds

doe	hoe	roe	woe
foe	joe	toe	

Words with Three Sounds

<u>floe</u>	goes

OW Words

High-Frequency Words

below	grow	own
follow	know	show

Words with Two Sounds

bow	mow	show
know	own	sow
low	row	tow

Words with Three Sounds

blow	glow	slow
bowl	grow	snow
crow	known	stow
flow	shown	throw

Words with Four Sounds

blown	grown	thrown
flown	growth	

Words with a Stressed First Syllable

lower	owner	slowly
lowly	slower	

Words with a Stressed Second Syllable

below	bestow

Words with Three or More Syllables

lawnmower	tomorrow	widower
marshmallow	wheelbarrow	

Long O Patterns

OLD, OLK, OLL, OLT, OST, and OTH Words

High-Frequency Words

almost	most
both	old

Rule Breakers

cost	doll	lost

Words with Three Sounds

both	old	toll
folk	poll	yolk
knoll	roll	

Words with Four Sounds

bold	gold	post
bolt	hold	sold
cold	host	told
dolt	jolt	troll
droll	mold	volt
fold	molt	
ghost	most	

Words with Five Sounds

scold	scroll	stroll

Words with a Stressed First Syllable

colder	hostess	postal
coldest	moldy	poster
coldly	molten	roller
coldness	mostly	smolder
folder	older	soldier
golden	oldest	stroller
holder	polka	voltage
holster	postage	

Words with a Stressed Second Syllable

control	extol	revolt
enroll	patrol	withhold

Words with Three or More Syllables

controller	enrollment

Long Vowels
Long O Words

Long O Patterns

OUGH and OUL Words

Words with Two Sounds

dough   though

Words with Three Sounds

soul

Words with a Stressed First Syllable

borough   furlough   shoulder
boulder   poultry   thorough

Words with a Stressed Second Syllable

although

ON Words

High-Frequency Words

don't   only

Words with a Stressed First Syllable

only

Open Syllables with O

High-Frequency Words

also   no   over
go   open   so

Rule Breakers

do   who   women
to   woman

Words with Two Sounds

go   no   so

Words with Three Sounds

fro   pro

Open Syllables with O *(cont.)*

Words with a Stressed First Syllable

bonus	grocer	over	rotor
bony	local	phony	slogan
broken	locate	photo	smoky
chosen	lotion	poem	social
closure	lotus	poet	soda
clover	mobile	polar	sofa
cobra	molar	pony	solar
cocoa	moment	potent	solo
cozy	motion	potion	spoken
donate	motor	profile	stolen
donor	noble	program	token
dosage	notice	pronoun	total
focal	notion	protein	totem
focus	ocean	robot	trophy
frozen	odor	rodent	vocal
global	open	rosy	voter
gopher	oval	rotate	

Words with a Stressed Second Syllable

ago

Words with Three or More Syllables

Arizona	explosion	opponent
commotion	exposure	promotion
composure	inconsolable	proposal
condolences	macaroni	socialize
devotion	Minnesota	South Dakota
disposal	North Dakota	Wyoming
erosion	Oklahoma	

© Shell Education

151921—The Everything Guide to Phonics

109

Long Vowels
Long O Words

Rhyming Sets

- ago, although, beau, below, bestow, blow, bow, bro, crow, doe, dough, floe, flow, foe, fro, glow, go, grow, hoe, joe, know, low, mow, no, owe, pro, roe, row, sew, show, slow, snow, so, sow, stow, though, throw, toe, tow, whoa, woe

- globe, lobe, probe, robe, strobe

- approach, broach, coach, encroach, poach, reproach, roach

- bode, code, explode, goad, implode, load, lode, mode, mowed, node, ode, owed, road, rode, rowed, sewed, sowed, showed, slowed, snowed, stowed, strode, toad, towed

- loaf, oaf

- broke, choke, cloak, croak, folk, invoke, joke, oak, poke, provoke, revoke, soak, smoke, spoke, stoke, stroke, woke, yoke, yolk

- bowl, coal, control, dole, droll, enroll, extol, foal, goal, hole, knoll, mole, patrol, pole, poll, role, roll, scroll, shoal, sole, soul, stole, stroll, toll, troll, vole, whole

- bold, cold, doled, fold, gold, hold, mold, old, rolled, scold, sold, told, withhold

- bolt, colt, dolt, jolt, molt, volt

- chrome, comb, dome, foam, gnome, home, loam, roam, tome

- alone, blown, bone, clone, cone, crone, disown, drone, flown, groan, grown, hone, known, loan, lone, moan, own, phone, pone, prone, roan, scone, sewn, shone, shown, stone, throne, thrown, tone, unknown, zone

- cope, dope, grope, hope, lope, mope, nope, pope, rope, scope, slope, soap, taupe

- close, dose, gross

- boast, coast, ghost, host, most, post, roast, toast

- bloat, boat, coat, dote, float, gloat, goat, moat, note, oat, promote, quote, rote, throat, tote, vote, wrote

- both, growth, oath

- clove, cove, dove, drove, grove, stove, trove, wove

- chokes, cloaks, coax, croaks, folks, hoax, invokes, jokes, pokes, provokes, revokes, smokes, soaks, spokes, strokes, yokes, yolks

- blows, bows, chose, close, clothes, compose, crows, doze, flows, foes, froze, glows, goes, grows, hoes, hose, knows, lows, mows, nose, owes, pose, propose, prose, rose, rows, sews, shows, slows, snows, sows, stows, suppose, those, throws, toes, tows, woes

Long Vowels
Long O Words

Homophones and Compound Words

Homophones

beau/bow	pros/prose
bode/bowed	road/rode
bolder/boulder	roe/row
close/clothes	role/roll
doe/dough	rose/rows
floe/flow	rote/wrote
groan/grown	sew/so/sow
hoes/hose	sewed/sowed
hole/whole	sews/sows
holy/wholly	shone/shown
know/no	sole/soul
knows/nose	throne/thrown
load/lode	toad/towed
loan/lone	toe/tow
moan/mown	toes/tows
mode/mowed	whoa/woe
ode/owed	yoke/yolk
oh/owe	yokes/yolks
pole/poll	

Compound Words

blowhole	overstock
boathouse	postcard
bowtie	postmark
clothesline	roadblock
coastline	roadside
crowbar	roadwork
folklore	rosebush
folktale	rowboat
globetrotter	showcase
goldfish	slowpoke
goldmine	smokehouse
homemade	smokestack
homeroom	snowball
homesick	snowflake
hometown	snowman
homework	snowplow
notebook	snowshoe
nowhere	snowstorm
oatmeal	stovetop
overalls	toadstool
overcoat	toenail
overflow	tollbooth
overload	towpath

© Shell Education

151921—The Everything Guide to Phonics

111

Long Vowels
Long U Words

Long U Patterns

VCe Syllables with U

Words with Three Sounds

chute	June	nude	tube
dude	jute	nuke	tune
duke	lube	rude	
dupe	luge	rule	
juke	lute	ruse	

Words with Four Sounds

brute	fluke	flute	prune
crude	flume	plume	truce

Words with Five Sounds

spruce

Words with a Stressed First Syllable

rudely	rudeness	tuneful

Words with a Stressed Second Syllable

astute	dilute	pollute	reduce
conclude	exclude	preclude	resume
consume	include	produce	salute

VCe Syllables with O or OO

Words with Three Sounds

choose	lose	noose
goose	moose	soothe
loose	move	whose

Words with Four Sounds

groove	prove	snooze	stooge

VCe Syllables with O or OO (cont.)

Words with a Stressed First Syllable

loser	movement	proven

Words with a Stressed Second Syllable

approve	improve
disprove	remove

Words with Three or More Syllables

approval	improvement
disapproval	removal

EU or EW Words

High-Frequency Words

new

Rule Breakers

sew

Words with Two Sounds

chew	Jew	new
dew	knew	yew

Words with Three Sounds

blew	drew	news	slew
brew	flew	newt	stew
crew	grew	shrew	threw

Words with Four Sounds

screw	shrewd	strew

Long U Patterns

EU or EW Words *(cont.)*

Words with Five Sounds

strewn

Words with a Stressed First Syllable

jewel   neutral   sewer
Jewish   sewage

Words with a Stressed Second Syllable

eschew   renew   withdrew

Words with Three or More Syllables

jeweler   jewelry   pseudonym

O Words

High-Frequency Words

do   two
to   who

Words with Two Sounds

do   two
to   who

Words with a Stressed Second Syllable

redo   undo

Words with Three or More Syllables

overdo

OO Words

High-Frequency Words

food   school   soon   too

Rule Breakers

blood   flood

Words with Two Sounds

boo	goo	ooze	too
coo	loo	poo	woo
doo	moo	shoo	zoo

Words with Three Sounds

boom	goon	mood	root
boon	goop	moon	shoot
boot	hoop	moot	soon
booth	hoot	noon	tool
cool	kook	pooch	toot
coop	loom	poof	tooth
doom	loon	pool	whoop
food	loop	poop	zoom
fool	loot	roof	
goof	mooch	room	

Words with Four Sounds

bloom	gloom	sloop	spoon
boost	groom	smooch	stool
brood	proof	snood	stoop
broom	roost	snoop	swoon
croon	school	spoof	swoop
drool	scoop	spook	troop
droop	scoot	spool	

Long Vowels
Long U Words

Long U Patterns

OO Words *(cont.)*

Words with a Stressed First Syllable

cooler	goofy	oodles	scooter
doodle	google	poodle	smoothly
doozy	moody	roomy	spooky
gloomy	noodle	rooster	woozy

Words with a Stressed Second Syllable

aloof	cartoon	monsoon	tattoo
baboon	cocoon	raccoon	
balloon	lagoon	redo	
bamboo	maroon	shampoo	

Words with Three or More Syllables

afternoon   kangaroo

UE Words

Rule Breakers

guess   guest

Words with Two Sounds

due   rue   sue

Words with Three Sounds

blue	dues	glue
clue	<u>flue</u>	true

Words with Four Sounds

cruel   gruel

Words with a Stressed First Syllable

duel   Tuesday

Words with a Stressed Second Syllable

ensue   pursue   subdue

U and UI Words

Words with Three Sounds

juice   suit

Words with Four Sounds

bruise   cruise   fruit   truth

Words with a Stressed First Syllable

Buddhist   fruity   juicy   nuisance

Words with a Stressed Second Syllable

pursuit   recruit

Words with Three or More Syllables

suitable

Long U Patterns

OU and OUGH Words

High-Frequency Words

group through you

Words with Two Sounds

you

Words with Three Sounds

| ghoul | route | through |
| rouge | soup | youth |

Words with Four Sounds

croup group troupe wound

Words with a Stressed First Syllable

| cougar | crouton | wounded |
| coupon | ghoulish | youthful |

Words with a Stressed Second Syllable

routine uncouth

Open Syllables with U

Words with a Stressed First Syllable

brutal	plumage	truly
crucial	prudent	tuba
duty	ruby	tulip
fluent	ruin	tumor
fluid	ruler	tuna
frugal	rumor	tutor
junior	student	
lunar	super	

Words with Three or More Syllables

constitution	illusion	numeral
consumer	juvenile	solution
contusion	Massachusetts	

Long Vowels
Long U Words

Rhyming Sets

- accrue, bamboo, blew, blue, boo, brew, chew, crew, clue, coo, cue, dew, do, doo, drew, due, ensue, ewe, few, flew, flu, flue, glue, goo, grew, hew, hue, Jew, knew, loo, moo, new, outgrew, overdo, pew, phew, poo, pursue, queue, redo, renew, rue, screw, shampoo, shoe, shoo, shrew, skew, slew, spew, stew, strew, subdue, sue, tattoo, threw, through, to, too, true, two, undo, view, who, withdrew, woo, yew, you, zoo

- cube, lube, tube

- brewed, brood, chewed, conclude, crude, dude, exclude, feud, glued, include, mood, nude, preclude, rude, rued, screwed, shrewd, snood, stewed, viewed

- aloof, goof, poof, proof, roof, spoof

- huge, luge, stooge

- duke, fluke, juke, nuke, puke, spook

- cool, cruel, drool, dual, duel, fool, fuel, ghoul, gruel, jewel, mule, pool, rule, school, spool, stool, tool, who'll

- bloom, boom, broom, consume, doom, flume, fume, gloom, groom, loom, perfume, plume, resume, room, tomb, womb, zoom

- baboon, balloon, boon, cartoon, cocoon, croon, dune, goon, hewn, June, loon, maroon, monsoon, moon, noon, prune, raccoon, soon, spoon, strewn, swoon, tune

- coop, croup, droop, dupe, goop, group, hoop, loop, poop, scoop, sloop, snoop, soup, stoop, swoop, troop, troupe

- deuce, excuse, goose, juice, loose, moose, noose, produce, puce, spruce, truce

- boost, roost

- astute, boot, brute, chute, cute, flute, fruit, hoot, jute, lute, moot, mute, newt, pollute, pursuit, recruit, root, route, scoot, shoot, suit, toot

- booth, tooth, truth, youth

- approve, disprove, groove, move, prove, remove

- amuse, bruise, chews, choose, confuse, crews, cruise, fuse, lose, muse, news, refuse, ruse, screws, shoes, snooze, use, who's, whose

116   151921— The Everything Guide to Phonics   © Shell Education

Long Vowels
Long U Words

Homophones and Compound Words

Homophones	Compound Words
blew/blue	afternoon
brewed/brood	blueberry
brews/bruise	bluebird
chews/choose	broomstick
chute/shoot	jukebox
crews/cruise	lukewarm
dew/do/doo/due	moonbeam
dual/duel	moonlight
flew/flu/flue	newborn
gnu/knew/new	newlywed
loot/lute	newspaper
overdo/overdue	newsroom
root/route	overdo
roots/routes	overdue
rude/rued	proofread
shoe/shoo	screwdriver
through/threw	shoemaker
to/too/two	suitcase
troop/troupe	throughout
who's/whose	toolbox
yew/you	toothache
	toothbrush
	toothpaste
	toothpick
	yuletide

© Shell Education

151921—The Everything Guide to Phonics

117

Long Vowels
Glided Long U Words

Glided Long U Patterns

VCe Syllables with Glided U

High-Frequency Words

use

Words with Two Sounds

use

Words with Three Sounds

cube	huge	puce
cute	mule	puke
fume	muse	
fuse	mute	

Words with a Stressed First Syllable

cuteness   hugely

Words with a Stressed Second Syllable

abuse	compute	excuse
acute	confuse	perfume
amuse	dispute	refuse

Glided EU and Glided EW Words

Words with One Sound

ewe

Words with Two Sounds

few	mew	phew
hew	pew	view

Words with Three Sounds

feud   skew   spew

Words with a Stressed First Syllable

feudal   pewter   skewer

Glided EU and Glided EW Words *(cont.)*

Words with a Stressed Second Syllable

review

Words with Three or More Syllables

eulogy   euphemism   interview

Glided UE Words

Words with Two Sounds

cue   hue

Words with Three Sounds

fuel

Words with a Stressed Second Syllable

imbue

Open Syllables with Glided U

Words with a Stressed First Syllable

bugle	cutest	humid	union
Cuba	futile	humor	unit
Cuban	future	music	usage
cuter	human	pupil	Utah

Words with Three or More Syllables

confusion	musical	reunion	usually
humorous	peculiar	usual	

Long Vowels
Glided Long U Words

Rhyming Sets and Homophones

Rhyming Sets

- cue, few, hew, pew, queue, skew, spew
- fuel, mule
- fume, perfume
- cute, mute
- amuse, confuse, fuse, muse, refuse, use

Homophones

cue/queue
ewe/yew/you
hew/hue/Hugh
review/revue

The Everything Guide to Phonics

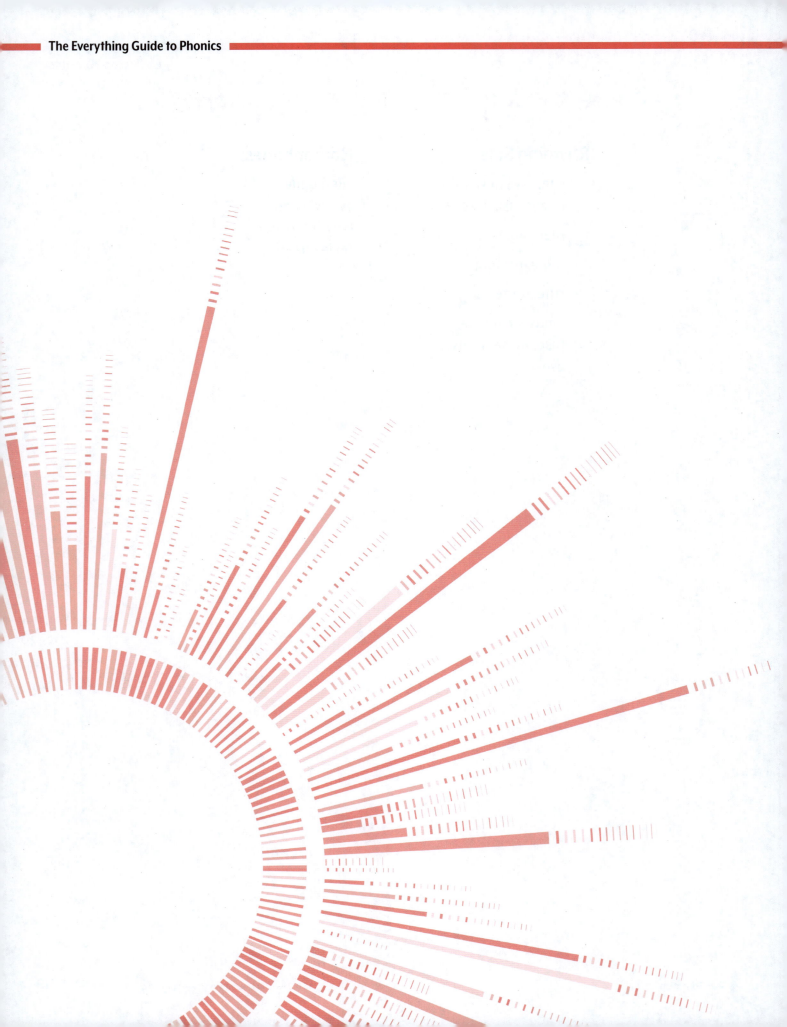

Advanced Vowel Teams Table of Contents

/aw/ Words 122

/aw/ (as in saw) Words 122
AW Words 122
A Words 122
AL and ALL Words 122
AU and AUGH Words 123
O and OA Words 124
OUGH Words 125
QUA and WA Words 125

Rhyming Sets 126
Homophones and Compound Words 127

/o͝o/ Words 128

/o͝o/ (as in book) Words 128
OO Words 128
OU Words 128
U and ULL Words 128

Rhyming Sets 129
Homophones and Compound Words 130

/ow/ Words 131

/ow/ (as in cow) Words 131
OW Words 131
OU and OUGH Words 132

Rhyming Sets 133
Homophones and Compound Words 134

/oy/ Words 135

/oy/ (as in boy) Words 135
OY Words 135
OI Words 135

Rhyming Sets 136
Homophones and Compound Words 137

Notes: High-frequency words only include Fry's first 300 words. Rule breakers are only one-syllable words. For most patterns, words are listed only if their stressed syllable follows the focus pattern.

© Shell Education   151921—The Everything Guide to Phonics   **121**

Advanced Vowel Teams
/aw/ Words

/aw/ (as in saw) Words

AW Words

High-Frequency Words

saw

Rule Breakers

drawer   lawyer

Words with One Sound

awe

Words with Two Sounds

awl	jaw	raw
caw	law	saw
gnaw	paw	thaw

Words with Three Sounds

bawl	draw	hawk	slaw
claw	fawn	lawn	yawn
craw	flaw	pawn	
dawn	gawk	shawl	

Words with Four Sounds

brawl	drawl	spawn
brawn	drawn	straw
crawl	prawn	trawl

Words with Five Sounds

scrawl	sprawl	squawk

Words with a Stressed First Syllable

awesome	brawny	gawky	trawler
awful	dawdle	lawless	
awkward	drawing	scrawny	
awning	flawless	tawny	

Words with Three or More Syllables

strawberry

A Words

High-Frequency Words

father

Words with Two Sounds

ma	pa

Words with a Stressed First Syllable

mama	papa	saga

Words with a Stressed Second Syllable

collage

Words with Three or More Syllables

Colorado	sabotage
lasagna	Washington

AL and ALL Words

High-Frequency Words

all	always	small	walk
also	called	talk	

Rule Breakers

shall

Words with Two Sounds

all

Advanced Vowel Teams
/aw/ Words

/aw/ (as in saw) Words

AL and ALL Words *(cont.)*

Words with Three Sounds

balk	fall	psalm
ball	gall	talk
balm	hall	tall
call	mall	walk
calm	pall	wall
chalk	palm	

Words with Four Sounds

bald	malt	squall
false	salt	stalk
halt	small	stall

Words with Five Sounds

scald	waltz

Words with a Stressed First Syllable

almond	falter	wallet
almost	halter	wallop
also	salty	wallow
altar	scallop	walnut
alter	swallow	walrus

Words with a Stressed Second Syllable

appalled	exalt	install

Words with Three or More Syllables

Halloween	talkative
installment	unsalted

AU and AUGH Words

High-Frequency Words

because

Rule Breakers

laugh

Words with Three Sounds

aunt	gauze	sauce
caught	haul	taught
caulk	maul	taut
cause	pause	

Words with Four Sounds

clause	gaunt	launch
daunt	haunch	paunch
fault	haunt	taunt
fraud	jaunt	vault

Words with Five Sounds

flaunt	staunch

Words with a Stressed First Syllable

auction	faucet	saucer
audit	faulty	sauna
August	gaudy	saunter
author	haughty	sausage
auto	haunches	slaughter
autumn	jaundice	trauma
cauldron	laundry	
caustic	naughty	
caution	nausea	
cautious	nauseous	
daughter	pauper	

© Shell Education

151921—The Everything Guide to Phonics

123

Advanced Vowel Teams
/aw/ Words

/aw/ (as in saw) Words

AU and AUGH Words (cont.)

Words with a Stressed Second Syllable

applaud	assault	default
applause	because	exhaust

Words with Three or More Syllables

audible	automobile	inauguration
audience	cauliflower	
autograph	exhaustion	

O and OA Words

High-Frequency Words

along	off	song
long	often	

Rule Breakers

gross

Words with Two Sounds

off

Words with Three Sounds

boss	gong	moss	toss
doff	long	moth	wrong
gone	loss	song	

Words with Four Sounds

broad	floss	honk	sloth
broth	font	loft	soft
cloth	froth	lost	solve
cost	gloss	prong	
cross	golf	scoff	

O and OA Words (cont.)

Words with Five Sounds

frost	strong

Words with a Stressed First Syllable

bossy	frosty	office
chocolate	glossy	often
coffee	lofty	posse
coffin	lozenge	sophomore
costly	mossy	toffee
frosting	offer	

Words with a Stressed Second Syllable

absolve	dissolve	lacrosse
across	emboss	resolve

Words with Three or More Syllables

glossary	officer

Advanced Vowel Teams
/aw/ Words

/aw/ (as in saw) Words

OUGH Words

High-Frequency Words

thought

Words with Two Sounds

ought

Words with Three Sounds

bought   fought   thought
cough   sought

Words with Four Sounds

brought   trough

Words with a Stressed First Syllable

thoughtful   thoughtless

QUA and WA Words

High-Frequency Words

walk   watch   water

Words with Three Sounds

quad   walk   wash
quash   wall   watch
wad   wan   watt

Words with Four Sounds

swab   swatch   want
swan   swath   wasp
swap   waft
swat   wand

Words with Five Sounds

squad   squash   swamp
squall   squat   waltz

Words with a Stressed First Syllable

squabble   wallet   wander
squalid   wallow   water
squander   walnut   wattage
waffle   walrus

Words with Three or More Syllables

equality   quality
inequality   quantify
qualify   quantity

Advanced Vowel Teams
/aw/ Words

Rhyming Sets

- awe, caw, claw, draw, flaw, gnaw, jaw, law, paw, raw, saw, slaw, straw, thaw

- applaud, broad, laud, quad, squad, wad

- bald, called, crawled, hauled, scald, scrawled, sprawled

- cough, doff, off, scoff, trough

- coughed, loft, soft

- balk, caulk, chalk, gawk, hawk, squawk, stalk, talk, walk

- all, awl, ball, bawl, brawl, call, crawl, drawl, fall, gall, hall, haul, mall, maul, pall, scrawl, shawl, small, sprawl, squall, stall, tall, trawl, wall

- bald, called, hauled, scrawled, sprawled, stalled

- balm, calm, palm, psalm

- assault, default, exalt, fault, halt, malt, salt, vault

- brawn, dawn, drawn, fawn, gone, lawn, pawn, prawn, spawn, swan, wan, yawn

- haunch, launch, paunch, staunch

- along, belong, gong, long, prong, song, strong, throng, tong, wrong

- daunt, flaunt, font, gaunt, haunt, jaunt, taunt, want

- across, boss, cross, emboss, floss, gloss, lacrosse, loss, moss, sauce, toss

- cost, frost, lost

- bought, brought, caught, fought, fraught, ought, sought, squat, swat, taught, taut, thought, watt

- broth, cloth, froth, moth, sloth, swath

- absolve, dissolve, resolve, solve

- applause, because, cause, clause, draws, jaws, laws, pause, paws, straws

Advanced Vowel Teams
/aw/ Words

Homophones and Compound Words

Homophones

all/awl
altar/alter
bald/balled
ball/bawl
balm/bomb
cause/caws
clause/claws
hall/haul
mall/maul
pause/paws
taught/taut

Compound Words

chalkboard
crosswalk
crossword
drawstring
frostbite
hallway
lawmaker
lawnmower
lawsuit
longshot
pawnshop
rawhide
saucepan
sawmill
smallpox
strawberry
wallpaper
watercolor
waterfall
watermelon
waterproof
withdraw

Advanced Vowel Teams
/o͝o/ **Words**

/o͝o/ (as in *book*) Words

OO Words

High-Frequency Words

book	look
good	took

Words with Three Sounds

book	hook	took
cook	look	wood
foot	nook	woof
good	rook	wool
hood	shook	
hoof	soot	

Words with Four Sounds

brook	hooves	wolf
crook	stood	woods

Words with a Stressed First Syllable

cookie	goodness	wooden
footage	hoodie	woolen
goodie	rookie	

Words with a Stressed Second Syllable

unhook

OU Words

High-Frequency Words

could	should	would

Words with Three Sounds

could	should	would

Words with a Stressed First Syllable

couldn't	shouldn't	wouldn't
could've	should've	would've

U and ULL Words

High-Frequency Words

put

Words with Three Sounds

bull	pull	shush
bush	push	
full	put	

Words with a Stressed First Syllable

bullet	fulcrum	pudding
butcher	fullness	pushy
cushion	fully	

Words with Three or More Syllables

bulletin

128   151921— The Everything Guide to Phonics   © Shell Education

Advanced Vowel Teams
/o͞o/ **Words**

Rhyming Sets

- could, good, hood, should, stood, wood, would
- hoof, woof
- book, brook, cook, crook, hook, look, nook, rook, shook, took
- bull, full, pull, wool
- bush, mush, push, shush
- foot, put, soot

Advanced Vowel Teams
/o͞o/ **Words**

Homophones and Compound Words

Homophones

pudding/putting
wood/would

Compound Words

bookcase
bookkeeper
bookmark
bookshelf
bookworm
cookbook
football
footprint
footsteps
footstool
lookout
woodchuck

Advanced Vowel Teams
/ow/ Words

/ow/ (as in cow) Words

OW Words

High-Frequency Words

down	how	now

Words with One Sound

ow

Words with Two Sounds

bow	now	vow
cow	owl	wow
chow	pow	
how	sow	

Words with Three Sounds

brow	gown	town
down	howl	plow
fowl	jowl	prow

Words with Four Sounds

brown	crown	prowl
browse	drown	scowl
clown	frown	
crowd	growl	

Words with a Stressed First Syllable

brownie	dowry	shower
chowder	drowsy	towel
coward	flower	tower
cower	glower	trowel
crowded	prowler	vowel
dowdy	powder	
dowel	rowdy	

Words with a Stressed Second Syllable

allow	endow	renown
allowed	meow	

Words with Three or More Syllables

allowance	powerful
endowment	powerless

Advanced Vowel Teams
/ow/ Words

/ow/ (as in cow) Words

OU and OUGH Words

High-Frequency Words

about	house	out
around	mountains	sound
found	our	without

Words with Two Sounds

bough	ouch	out
hour	our	

Words with Three Sounds

bout	loud	pouch
couch	louse	pout
doubt	lout	shout
dour	mouse	sour
douse	mouth	tout
foul	noun	vouch
gouge	ounce	
house	oust	

Words with Four Sounds

blouse	grouch	scout
bounce	grouse	shroud
bound	grout	slouch
cloud	hound	snout
clout	lounge	sound
count	mound	spouse
crouch	mount	spout
drought	pounce	stout
found	pound	trout
fount	proud	wound
flour	round	
flout	scour	

Words with Five Sounds

ground	sprout

Words with Six Sounds

scrounge

Words with a Stressed First Syllable

bouncy	founder	outage
boundary	foundry	outer
bounty	fountain	outlet
cloudy	grouchy	outrage
council	hourly	proudly
counsel	louder	scoundrel
counter	loudly	thousand
county	lousy	trousers
doubtful	mountain	voucher
flouncy	mouthful	
flounder	ouster	

Words with a Stressed Second Syllable

abound	around	profound
about	astound	pronounce
account	denounce	renounce
aloud	devour	surmount
amount	expound	surround
announce	impound	

Words with Three or More Syllables

accountant	bountiful	mountainous
announcement	counterfeit	surrounded

Advanced Vowel Teams
/ow/ Words

Rhyming Sets

- allow, bough, bow, brow, chow, cow, endow, how, meow, now, ow, plow, pow, prow, sow, vow, wow

- couch, crouch, grouch, ouch, pouch, slouch, vouch

- allowed, bowed, chowed, cloud, crowd, loud, plowed, proud, shroud, vowed, wowed

- bowel, dowel, foul, fowl, growl, howl, jowl, owl, prowl, scowl, towel, trowel, vowel

- brown, clown, crown, down, drown, frown, gown, noun, renown, town

- announce, bounce, denounce, flounce, ounce, pounce, pronounce, renounce

- abound, around, astound, bound, crowned, found, ground, hound, mound, pound, profound, round, sound, surround, wound

- lounge, scrounge

- account, amount, count, fount, mount, surmount

- cower, devour, dour, flour, flower, hour, our, power, scour, sour, tower

- blouse, douse, grouse, house, louse, mouse, spouse

- about, bout, clout, doubt, drought, flout, grout, lout, out, pout, scout, shout, snout, spout, sprout, stout, tout, trout

- mouth, south

- bows, browse, cows, plows

© Shell Education

Advanced Vowel Teams

/ow/ Words

Homophones and Compound Words

Homophones

allowed/aloud
bough/bow
brows/browse
council/counsel
councilor/counselor
coward/cowered
flour/flower
foul/fowl
hour/our
hours/ours

Compound Words

countdown
cowboy
cowhand
downfall
downhill
download
downpour
downstairs
downstream
downtown
hourglass
household
housewife
housework
housetop
however
mountainside
mousetrap

mouthwash
outburst
outcast
outcome
outdoors
outfield
outhouse
outline
output
outside
songbird
songbook
songwriter
southeast
southwest
townspeople
without

Advanced Vowel Teams
/oy/ Words

/oy/ (as in boy) Words

OY Words

High-Frequency Words

boy

Words with Two Sounds

boy	joy
choy	soy
coy	toy

Words with Three Sounds

cloy	ploy

Words with a Stressed First Syllable

boycott	joyful
boyish	joyous
buoyant	royal
foyer	voyage
loyal	

Words with a Stressed Second Syllable

annoy	employ
deploy	enjoy
destroy	

Words with Three or More Syllables

clairvoyant	flamboyant
employee	loyalty
employer	royalty
employment	voyager
enjoyment	

OI Words

High-Frequency Words

point

Words with Two Sounds

oil	poi
koi	

Words with Three Sounds

boil	oink
choice	poise
coil	roil
coin	soil
foil	toil
join	voice
loin	void
noise	

Words with Four Sounds

broil	joist
droid	moist
groin	point
hoist	spoil
joint	

Words with a Stressed First Syllable

broiler	oily
doily	ointment
foible	pointless
moisten	pointy
moisture	poison
noisy	toilet

© Shell Education

151921—The Everything Guide to Phonics

135

/oy/ (as in boy) Words

OI Words (cont.)

Words with a Stressed Second Syllable

adjoin
anoint
appoint
avoid
embroil

enjoin
exploit
recoil
rejoice

Words with Three or More Syllables

appointment
avoidance
boisterous
disappoint
disappointment
embroider
Illinois
moisturize
poisonous

Advanced Vowel Teams
/oy/ Words

Rhyming Sets

- annoy, boy, choy, cloy, deploy, destroy, employ, enjoy, joy, koi, ploy, poi, soy, toy

- choice, rejoice, voice

- annoyed, avoid, droid, enjoyed, void

- boil, broil, coil, embroil, foil, loyal, oil, recoil, roil, royal, soil, spoil, toil

- adjoin, coin, groin, join, loin

- anoint, appoint, joint, point

- hoist, joist, moist, voiced

- boys, destroys, employs, enjoys, noise, ploys, poise, toys

Advanced Vowel Teams
/oy/ Words

Homophones and Compound Words

Homophones

coy/koi
roil/royal

Compound Words

boyfriend
noisemaker
soybean
toybox
toymaker
voicemail

R-Controlled Vowels Table of Contents

/ar/ Words 140

/ar/ (as in car) Words 140
AR Words.................................140
EAR Words................................140

Rhyming Sets............................ 141
Homophones and Compound Words 142

/er/ Words 143

/er/ (as in her) Words 143
ER Words.................................143
EAR Words................................143
IR and YR Words 144
UR Words.................................144
EUR and OUR Words.....................145
URE and UR_ Words 145
Glided URE and Glided UR_ Words 145
WOR Words...............................145

Rhyming Sets............................146
Homophones and Compound Words 147

/or/ Words 148

/or/ (as in more) Words..................148
OR Words.................................148
ORE Words...............................149
OAR Words...............................149
OOR Words 149
OUR Words...............................150
QUAR and WAR Words 150

Rhyming Sets............................ 151
Homophones and Compound Words 152

"AIR" Words 153

"AIR" (as in care) Words................153
AIR Words................................153
ARE Words...............................153
AR and ARR Words 154
EAR and EIR Words 154
ER, ERE, and ERR Words 154
UR Words.................................154

Rhyming Sets............................155
Homophones and Compound Words 156

"EER" Words 157

"EER" (as in deer) Words 157
EAR Words................................157
EER Words................................157
ERE Words................................158
IR, IER, and YR Words 158

Rhyming Sets............................159
Homophones and Compound Words 160

"IRE" Words 161

"IRE" (as in fire) Words.................161
IRE and YRE Words 161

Rhyming Sets............................162
Homophones and Compound Words 163

"OOR" Words 164

"OOR" (as in moor) Words..............164
OOR Words...............................164
OUR Words...............................164
URE Words................................164

**Rhyming Sets, Homophones,
and Compound Words** 165

Notes: High-frequency words only include Fry's first 300 words. Rule breakers are only one-syllable words. For most patterns, words are listed only if their stressed syllable follows the focus pattern.

R-Controlled Vowels
/ar/ Words

/ar/ (as in car) Words

AR Words

High-Frequency Words

are	far	hard	part
car	farm	large	started

Rule Breakers

quart	ward	warmth	warp
war	warm	warn	wart

Words with One Sound

are

Words with Two Sounds

arc	arm	car	jar
arch	art	char	par
ark	bar	far	tar

Words with Three Sounds

barb	charm	harsh	scar
bard	chart	hart	shard
barf	dark	heart	shark
barge	darn	lard	sharp
bark	dart	large	spar
barn	farm	lark	star
carb	garb	march	tarp
card	gnarl	mark	tart
carp	guard	marsh	yard
cart	hard	mart	yarn
carve	hark	parch	
chard	harm	park	
charge	harp	part	

Words with Four Sounds

scarf	snarl	starch	start
smart	spark	stark	starve

AR Words *(cont.)*

Word with a Stressed First Syllable

arbor	charcoal	hardy	parsley
Arctic	charter	harmful	partial
argue	darkness	harness	partner
armor	darling	harvest	partridge
army	farmer	jargon	party
artist	farther	larva	scarlet
barber	garbage	marble	sharpen
bargain	garden	margin	sparkle
barley	gargle	market	startle
barter	garland	marshal	tardy
carbon	garlic	martyr	target
carcass	garment	parcel	tarnish
cargo	garnet	parchment	tartar
carpet	garnish	pardon	varnish
carton	harbor	parka	
cartridge	hardly	parlor	

Words with a Stressed Second Syllable

afar	alarm	depart	guitar
ajar	apart	embark	remark

Words with Three or More Syllables

apartment	carnivore	marvelous
Arkansas	compartment	partnership
barbecue	department	sarcasm
cardinal	departure	
carnival	margarine	

EAR Words

Words with Three Sounds

heart	hearth

140   151921— The Everything Guide to Phonics

Rhyming Sets

- bar, car, char, far, jar, par, scar, spar, star, tar
- barb, carb, garb
- arch, march, parch, starch
- bard, barred, card, chard, guard, hard, lard, scarred, shard, starred, yard
- barge, charge, large
- arc, ark, bark, dark, embark, hark, lark, mark, park, remark, shark, spark, stark
- alarm, arm, charm, disarm, farm, harm
- barn, darn, yarn
- carp, harp, sharp, tarp
- apart, art, cart, chart, dart, depart, hart, heart, mart, part, smart, start, tart

R-Controlled Vowels
/ar/ Words

Homophones and Compound Words

Homophones

arc/ark
bard/barred
hart/heart
marshal/martial

Compound Words

artwork
barnyard
cardboard
carsick
cartwheel
farmhouse
farmland
farmyard
guardrail
hardware
heartache
heartbreak
starfish
starlight
yardstick

/er/ (as in her) Words

ER Words

High-Frequency Words

her	were

Words with Two Sounds

her	herb	per

Words with Three Sounds

berg	jerk	perm	verge
berm	merge	pert	verse
berth	nerd	serve	verve
fern	nerve	term	
germ	perch	tern	
herd	perk	verb	

Words with Four Sounds

clerk	stern	swerve	twerp

Words with a Stressed First Syllable

certain	hermit	mermaid	serpent
clergy	jerky	nervous	service
derby	jersey	perfect	thermal
desert	kerchief	perjure	thermos
fertile	kernel	perky	verbal
fervor	merchant	permit	verdict
gerbil	mercy	person	version
herbal	merger	sermon	versus

Words with a Stressed Second Syllable

alert	deserve	observe
concern	dessert	prefer
confer	diverge	preserve
conserve	emerge	refer
converge	exert	reserve
converse	infer	reverse
defer	insert	submerge

ER Words (cont.)

Words with Three or More Syllables

certify	mercury	reversal
emergency	New Jersey	terminate
exertion	permanent	thermostat
herbivore	personal	versatile
merchandise	referral	vertical

EAR Words

High-Frequency Words

earth	learn

Words with Two Sounds

earl	earn	earth

Words with Three Sounds

dearth	learn	search
heard	pearl	yearn

Words with a Stressed First Syllable

early	learner	research
earthen	pearly	yearning

Words with a Stressed Second Syllable

rehearse	research

Words with Three or More Syllables

rehearsal

R-Controlled Vowels
/er/ Words

/er/ (as in her) Words

IR and YR Words

High-Frequency Words

first   girl

Words with Two Sounds

fir   myrrh   sir   whir

Words with Three Sounds

birch	dirt	mirth	third
bird	firm	shirk	whirl
birth	girl	shirt	
chirp	girth	stir	

Words with Four Sounds

first	skirt	swirl	twirl
flirt	smirk	thirst	

Words with Five Sounds

squirm   squirt

Words with a Stressed First Syllable

circle	firmly	skirmish	syrup
circuit	girdle	squirmy	thirsty
circus	myrtle	squirrel	thirty
dirty	sirloin	stirrups	virtue

Words with a Stressed Second Syllable

thirteen

Words with Three or More Syllables

circular   virtual

UR Words

High-Frequency Words

turn

Words with Two Sounds

burr	purr	urn
fur	urge	

Words with Three Sounds

blur	curd	hurl	purse
burn	curl	hurt	slur
burp	curse	lurch	spur
church	curt	lurk	turf
churn	curve	nurse	turn
curb	furl	purge	

Words with Four Sounds

blurb	burst	spurn
blurt	slurp	spurt

Words with Six Sounds

splurge

Words with a Stressed First Syllable

blurry	curtain	jury	surplus
burden	curtsy	murder	Thursday
burger	curvy	murky	turban
burglar	during	murmur	turkey
burlap	furnace	nurture	turmoil
burner	furnish	plural	turnip
burrow	furrow	purchase	turquoise
curdle	furry	purple	turret
curfew	further	purpose	turtle
curly	gurgle	rural	urban
current	hurdle	scurry	
cursive	hurry	sturdy	
cursor	juror	surface	

144   151921— The Everything Guide to Phonics   © Shell Education

R-Controlled Vowels
/er/ Words

/er/ (as in her) Words

UR Words *(cont.)*

Words with a Stressed Second Syllable

disturb   return   unfurl   usurp

Words with Three or More Syllables

burdensome	hurricane	suburban
currency	nursery	surgery
curvature	refurbish	universe
disturbance	Saturday	
furniture	security	

EUR and OUR Words

Words with a Stressed First Syllable

courage	flourish	journey
Europe	journal	nourish

Words with Three or More Syllables

discourage	journalism	Missouri
encourage	journalist	nourishment

URE and UR_ Words

Words with Two Sounds

sure

Words with a Stressed Second Syllable

assure	ensure	unsure
brochure	insure	
endure	mature	

Words with Three or More Syllables

assurance	immature	maturity
endurance	insurance	

Glided URE and Glided UR_ Words

Words with Three Sounds

cure   pure

Words with a Stressed First Syllable

fury

Words with a Stressed Second Syllable

impure	procure
obscure	secure

Words with Three or More Syllables

furious	insecure	security
furiously	insecurity	
impurities	obscurity	

WOR Words

High-Frequency Words

words   work   world

Words with Three Sounds

word	worm	worth
work	worse	

Words with a Stressed First Syllable

worker	worsen	worthless
worry	worship	worthy

R-Controlled Vowels
/er/ Words

Rhyming Sets

- blur, burr, confer, cure, defer, fir, fur, her, infer, per, prefer, pure, purr, refer, sir, slur, spur, stir, sure, were, whir
- blurb, curb, disturb, herb, verb
- birch, church, lurch, perch, research, search
- bird, blurred, curd, cured, heard, herd, nerd, purred, slurred, spurred, stirred, third, whirred, word
- converge, diverge, emerge, merge, purge, splurge, submerge, urge, verge
- clerk, jerk, lurk, perk, shirk, smirk, work
- jerky, murky, perky, smirky, turkey
- curl, earl, furl, girl, hurl, pearl, squirrel, swirl, twirl, whirl
- curled, furled, hurled, swirled, twirled, whirled, world
- burly, curly, early, girly, pearly, swirly, twirly
- berm, firm, germ, perm, squirm, term, worm
- germy, squirmy, wormy
- burn, churn, concern, earn, fern, learn, spurn, stern, tern, turn, yearn
- burp, chirp, slurp, twerp, usurp
- blurry, furry, fury, hurry, jury, scurry, worry
- converse, curse, nurse, purse, rehearse, reverse, verse, worse
- burst, cursed, first, nursed, thirst, worst
- alert, blurt, curt, dessert, dirt, flirt, hurt, insert, pert, shirt, skirt, spurt, squirt
- berth, birth, dearth, earth, girth, mirth, worth
- conserve, curve, deserve, nerve, observe, preserve, reserve, serve, swerve, verve

R-Controlled Vowels
/er/ Words

Homophones and Compound Words

Homophones

berth/birth
borough/burrow
colonel/kernel
currant/current
earn/urn
fir/fur
heard/herd
per/purr
tern/turn
were/whir
whirled/world
whirred/word

Compound Words

birdbath
birdfeeder
birdhouse
birdseed
birthday
birthmark
birthplace
birthstone
curbstone
earthquake
earthworm
furthermore
girlfriend
searchlight
surfboard
whirlpool
whirlwind
workload
workout
workroom
worksheet

R-Controlled Vowels
/or/ Words

/or/ (as in *more*) Words

OR Words

High-Frequency Words

for	or
important	story

Words with One Sound

or

Words with Two Sounds

for	nor	orb

Words with Three Sounds

born	form	pork
chord	fort	port
cord	forth	shorn
cork	gorge	short
corn	horn	sort
corps	horse	sword
dork	lord	thorn
dorm	morph	torch
force	New York	torn
ford	norm	worn
forge	north	
fork	porch	

Words with Four Sounds

corpse	snort	stork
scorch	spork	storm
scorn	sport	sworn

Words with a Stressed First Syllable

border	gorgeous	porpoise
boring	hornet	porridge
choral	horrid	portal
chorus	horror	porter
coral	moral	portion
cordial	morning	portrait
corner	morsel	shortage
dormant	mortal	shorten
floral	mortar	shorter
florist	mortgage	shortest
forage	Nordic	snorkel
forceful	normal	sporty
forest	northern	storage
forfeit	orange	stormy
formal	orbit	story
fortress	orchard	torment
fortune	order	torrent
forty	organ	torso
forward	orphan	tortoise
glory	porous	torture

Words with a Stressed Second Syllable

abhor	distort	reform
absorb	divorce	report
adorn	endorse	retort
afford	enforce	support
conform	inform	transport
deformed	perform	
deport	record	

R-Controlled Vowels
/or/ Words

/or/ (as in *more*) Words

OR Words *(cont.)*

Words with Three or More Syllables

adorable	Georgia	portable
auditorium	horrible	reinforce
California	important	reporter
contortions	majority	supportive
deported	minority	unfortunately
Florida	Oregon	victorious
formula	organize	
fortunate	performance	

ORE Words

High-Frequency Words

before   more

Words with One Sound

ore

Words with Two Sounds

bore	lore	tore
chore	more	wore
core	pore	yore
fore	shore	
gore	sore	

Words with Three Sounds

score	spore	swore
snore	store	

Words with a Stressed First Syllable

boredom	gory
boring	scoreless

ORE Words *(cont.)*

Words with a Stressed Second Syllable

adore	explore	implore
before	galore	restore
deplore	ignore	

OAR Words

Words with One Sound

oar

Words with Two Sounds

boar	roar	soar

Words with Three Sounds

board	hoard
coarse	hoarse

Words with a Stressed First Syllable

coarsely   hoarsely   hoarseness

OOR Words

Words with Two Sounds

door   poor

Words with Three Sounds

floor

Words with a Stressed First Syllable

flooring   poorest   poorly

© Shell Education   151921—The Everything Guide to Phonics   **149**

R-Controlled Vowels
/or/ Words

/or/ (as in *more*) Words

OUR Words

High-Frequency Words

four   your

Words with Two Sounds

four   pour   your

Words with Three Sounds

course   fourth   source
court   mourn   yours

Words with a Stressed First Syllable

mournful

Words with a Stressed Second Syllable

fourteen

Words with Three or More Syllables

resourceful

QUAR and WAR Words

Words with Two Sounds

war

Words with Three Sounds

dwarf   warm   wart
quart   warn
ward   warp

Words with Four Sounds

quartz   swarm   warmth

Words with a Stressed First Syllable

quarrel   wardrobe   warren
quarter   warning
warble   warrant

Words with a Stressed Second Syllable

award   reward

Words with Three or More Syllables

quarantine   warranty   warrior

or

Rhyming Sets

R-Controlled Vowels
/or/ Words

- adore, before, boar, bore, chore, core, corps, door, drawer, explore, floor, for, fore, four, gore, ignore, implore, indoor, lore, more, nor, oar, or, ore, outdoor, poor, pore, pour, restore, roar, score, shore, s'more, snore, soar, sore, store, sword, swore, tore, war, wore, yore, your, you're

- absorb, orb

- porch, scorch, torch

- accord, adored, afford, board, bored, chord, cord, cored, ford, hoard, ignored, implored, lord, pored, poured, record, restored, roared, scored, snored, soared, stored, sword, toward, ward

- engorge, forge, gorge

- cork, dork, fork, pork, spork, stork

- conform, dorm, form, inform, norm, perform, reform, storm, swarm, warm

- adorn, born, borne, corn, horn, morn, mourn, scorn, shorn, sworn, thorn, torn, warn, worn

- coarse, course, divorce, endorse, enforce, force, hoarse, horse, source

- court, distort, export, import, fort, port, quart, report, retort, short, snort, sort, sport, support, torte, transport, wart

- forth, fourth, north

- pours, yours

R-Controlled Vowels
/or/ Words

Homophones and Compound Words

Homophones

aural/oral
boar/bore
board/bored
boarder/border
born/borne
chord/cord/cored
coarse/course
core/corps
for/fore/four
forth/fourth
hoarse/horse
morn/mourn
morning/mourning
oar/or/ore
pore/poor/pour
pored/poured
pours/yours
quarts/quartz
soar/sore
war/wore
warn/worn
yore/you're/your

Compound Words

boardroom
boardwalk
cornfield
cornmeal
cornstalk
cornstarch
courthouse
courtroom
courtyard
doorbell
doorknob
doorstep
floorboards
horseback
horsefly
horseman
horseshoe
indoor
northeast
northwest
outdoor
quarterback
shoreline
shortcake
shortstop
storefront
storekeeper

"AIR" (as in care) Words

AIR Words

High-Frequency Words

air

Words with Two Sounds

air

Words with Three Sounds

chair   hair   pair
fair   lair

Words with Four Sounds

flair

Words with Five Sounds

stairs

Words with a Stressed First Syllable

dairy   fairy   prairie

Words with a Stressed Second Syllable

affair   despair   impair   repair

ARE Words

Rule Breakers

are

Words with Three Sounds

bare   fare   pare
care   hare   rare
dare   mare   share

Words with Four Sounds

blare   scare   stare
flare   snare   wares
glare   spare

Words with Five Sounds

square

Words with Six Sounds

squared

Words with a Stressed First Syllable

barely   careless   scary
careful   rarely

Words with a Stressed Second Syllable

aware   compare   ensnare
beware   declare   prepare

R-Controlled Vowels
"AIR" Words

"AIR" (as in care) Words

AR and ARR Words

High-Frequency Words

carry

Words with a Stressed First Syllable

arrow	carrot	parents
baron	carry	Paris
barracks	harry	parish
barrel	larynx	parrot
barren	marriage	sparrow
carat	marrow	tariff
carol	marry	tarry
carrel	narrate	vary
carriage	narrow	wary

Words with Three or More Syllables

apparel	comparison	mascara
aquarium	disparage	narrator
area	disparity	parachute
arrogant	embarrass	paradise
barricade	garrulous	parallel
barrier	librarian	paralyze
caramel	library	parasol
caravan	marathon	popularity
charity	marinate	scenario
clarify	Maryland	similarity

EAR and EIR Words

High-Frequency Words

their

Words with Two Sounds

heir

EAR and EIR Words (cont.)

Words with Three Sounds

bear	tear	wear
pear	their	

Words with Four Sounds

swear

ER, ERE, and ERR Words

High-Frequency Words

America	very
there	where

Words with Three Sounds

there	where

Words with a Stressed First Syllable

berry	error	merit	sterile
cherish	ferret	merry	terrace
cherry	herald	peril	terror
cherub	heron	perish	very
cleric	herring	sheriff	

Words with Three or More Syllables

America	hysterical	serrated	terrible
clerical	merrily	severity	terrify
hysteria	merriment	sterilize	territory

UR Words

Words with a Stressed First Syllable

bury

Words with Three or More Syllables

burial

R-Controlled Vowels
"AIR" Words

Rhyming Sets

- affair, air, aware, bare, bear, blare, care, chair, compare, dare, declare, despair, fair, fare, flare, flair, glare, hair, hare, heir, impair, lair, mare, pair, pare, pear, rare, repair, scare, share, snare, spare, stair, stare, swear, tear, their, there, they're, ware, wear, where

- barrel, carol, carrel, peril, sterile

- carrot, ferret, merit, parrot

- arrow, marrow, narrow, sparrow

- berry, bury, cherry, dairy, fairy, ferry, marry, merry, scary, vary, very, wary

R-Controlled Vowels
"AIR" Words

Homophones and Compound Words

Homophones

air/heir
bare/bear
baron/barren
berry/bury
carat/carrot
carol/carrel
fair/fare
fairy/ferry
flair/flare
hair/hare
marry/merry
pair/pare/pear
parish/perish
stair/stare
stairs/stares
their/there/they're
vary/very
ware/wear/where

Compound Words

aircraft
airline
airplane
airport
airtight
barefoot
carefree
chairlift
chairman
downstairs
fairground
hairbrush
haircut
hairdo
hairstyle
spareribs
staircase
stairwell
upstairs
warehouse

R-Controlled Vowels
"EER" Words

"EER" (as in *deer*) Words

EAR Words

Words with Two Sounds

ear

Words with Three Sounds

dear	near	tear
fear	rear	year
gear	sear	
hear	shear	

Words with Four Sounds

beard	smear
clear	spear

Words with a Stressed First Syllable

clearing	fearful	tearful
clearly	fearless	weary
dearest	nearest	
dearly	nearly	

Words with a Stressed Second Syllable

appear

Words with Three or More Syllables

appearance	disappear	reappear

EER Words

Words with Three Sounds

beer	jeer	sheer
cheer	leer	steer
deer	peer	veer

Words with Four Sounds

queer	sneer	steer

Words with a Stressed First Syllable

cheerful	leery	steering
cheery	queerly	

Words with a Stressed Second Syllable

career

Words with Three or More Syllables

engineer	pioneer	veneer

R-Controlled Vowels
"EER" Words

"EER" (as in deer) Words

ERE Words

High-Frequency Words

here

Words with Three Sounds

here   mere

Words with Four Sounds

sphere

Words with a Stressed First Syllable

cashmere   merely

Words with a Stressed Second Syllable

adhere   revere   sincere
austere   severe

Words with Three or More Syllables

interfere   severely   spherical
interference   sincerely

IR, IER, and YR Words

Words with Three Sounds

pier   tier

Words with a Stressed First Syllable

cirrus   lyrics   mirror

Words with Three or More Syllables

chandelier   irritate   myriad
irrigate   miracle   pyramid

R-Controlled Vowels
"EER" Words

Rhyming Sets

- adhere, appear, austere, beer, career, cheer, clear, dear, deer, ear, fear, gear, hear, here, interfere, jeer, mere, near, peer, pier, queer, rear, revere, sear, severe, shear, sheer, sincere, smear, sneer, spear, sphere, steer, tear, tier, veer, year

- beard, cheered, feared, geared, jeered, leered, neared, peered, reared, seared, steered, tiered, veered, weird

- cheery, leery, smeary, teary, weary

- clearly, dearly, merely, nearly, queerly, severely, sincerely

R-Controlled Vowels
"EER" Words

Homophones and Compound Words

Homophones

cereal/serial
dear/deer
hear/here
peer/pier
shear/sheer
tear/tier

Compound Words

cheerleader
deerskin
earache
earlobe
earring
gearshift
hearsay
nearby
rearview
spearhead
spearmint
teardrop
yearbook

R-Controlled Vowels
"IRE" Words

"IRE" (as in *fire*) Words

IRE and YRE Words

Words with Two Sounds

ire

Words with Three Sounds

dire	mire	tire
fire	pyre	wire
hire	shire	
lyre	sire	

Words with Four Sounds

spire

Words with Five Sounds

squire

Words with a Stressed First Syllable

bonfire	gyrate	satire
empire	haywire	umpire
esquire	quagmire	vampire

Words with a Stressed Second Syllable

acquire	enquire	rehire
afire	entire	require
aspire	expire	retire
attire	inquire	rewire
barbwire	inspire	transpire
bemire	misfire	
desire	perspire	

© Shell Education

R-Controlled Vowels
"IRE" Words

Rhyming Sets

- acquire, afire, aspire, attire, desire, dire, entire, expire, fire, hire, inquire, inspire, ire, lyre, mire, misfire, perspire, pyre, rehire, require, retire, rewire, shire, sire, spire, squire, tire, transpire, wire

R-Controlled Vowels
"IRE" Words

Homophones and Compound Words

Homophones

hire/higher
shire/shier/shyer
sire/sigher

Compound Words

backfire
bushfire
campfire
ceasefire
crossfire
drumfire
grandsire
gunfire
hardwire
newswire
spitfire
tightwire
wildfire

R-Controlled Vowels
"OOR" Words

"OOR" (as in *moor*) Words

OOR Words

Words with Three Sounds

moor   poor

Words with Four Sounds

spoor

OUR Words

High-Frequency Words

your

Words with Three Sounds

pour   tour   your

Words with Four Sounds

yours

Words with a Stressed First Syllable

touring   tourist

Words with Three or More Syllables

tourism

URE Words

Words with Three Sounds

cure   pure
lure   sure

Words with a Stressed First Syllable

purely
surely

164   151921— The Everything Guide to Phonics   © Shell Education

R-Controlled Vowels
"OOR" Words

Rhyming Sets, Homophones, and Compound Words

Rhyming Sets

- cure, lure, moor, poor, pure, spoor, sure, tour, your

Homophones

poor/pour
you're/your

Compound Words

purebred
surefire
thoroughbred

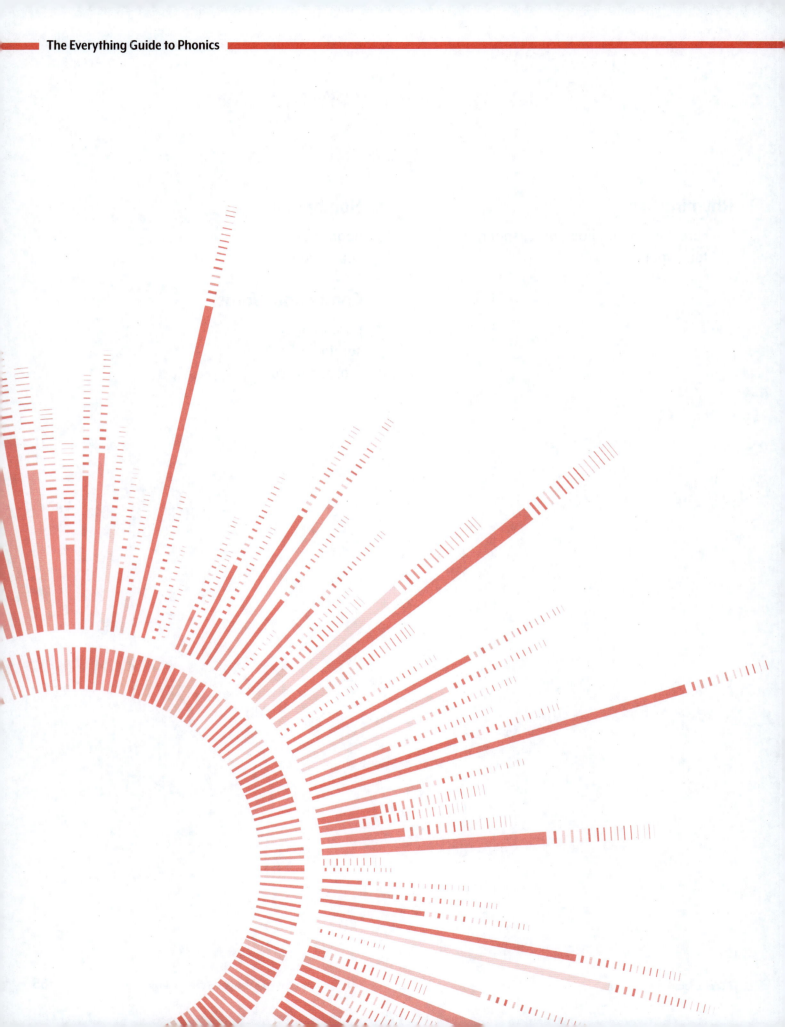
The Everything Guide to Phonics

Consonant Patterns Table of Contents

Initial Blends 168
Initial L Blends. 168
Initial R Blends 170
Initial S Blends. .172
Initial W Blends .175

Final Blends 176
Final C Blends 176
Final F Blends 177
Final L Blends 178
Final M Blends. 179
Final N Blends 180
Final P Blends 182
Final S Blends 183
Final T Blends 184
Final X Blends 185

Final Double-Letter Digraphs 186
DD Words 186
FF Words 186
LL Words 186
SS Words 186
TT Words 186
ZZ Words 186

Consonant-*le* Words 187

© Shell Education

Consonant Patterns
Initial Blends

Initial L Blends

BL Words

blab	bleep	blond
black	blend	blood
blade	bless	bloom
blame	blew	blot
blanch	blight	blouse
bland	blimp	blow
blank	blind	blown
blare	bling	blue
blast	blink	bluff
blaze	blip	blunt
bleach	bliss	blur
bleat	bloat	blurb
bleak	blob	blurt
bled	block	blush
bleed	blog	

CL Words

clad	cleft	cloth
claim	clench	clothes
clam	clerk	cloud
clamp	click	clout
clan	cliff	clove
clang	climb	clown
clap	clinch	cloy
clash	cling	club
clasp	clink	cluck
class	clip	clue
claw	cloak	clump
clay	clock	clung
clean	clod	clunk
clear	clog	clutch
cleat	clone	
cleave	close	
clef	clot	

FL Words

flab	fleet	floss
flag	flesh	flour
flail	flew	flout
flair	flex	flow
flake	flick	flower
flame	flight	flown
flank	flinch	flu
flap	fling	flue
flare	flint	flub
flash	flip	fluff
flat	flirt	flume
flaunt	flit	flung
flaw	float	flunk
flay	flob	flush
flea	flock	flute
fleck	floe	flux
fled	flood	fly
flee	floor	
fleece	flop	

GL Words

glad	glean	globe
glade	glee	gloom
glam	glen	gloss
glance	glib	glove
gland	glide	glue
glare	glimpse	glum
glass	glint	glut
glaze	glitch	
gleam	gloat	

Consonant Patterns
Initial Blends

Initial L Blends

PL Words

place	play	ploy
plaid	plea	pluck
plain	plead	plug
plait	please	plum
plan	pleat	plume
plane	pledge	plump
plank	plight	plus
plant	plod	plush
plague	plop	ply
plaque	plot	
plate	plow	

SL Words

slab	sleigh	slope
slack	slept	slosh
slam	slew	slot
slang	slice	sloth
slant	slick	slow
slap	slid	sludge
slash	slide	slug
slat	slight	slum
slate	slim	slump
slave	slime	slur
slaw	sling	slurp
slay	slink	slush
sled	slip	sly
sleek	slit	
sleep	slob	
sleet	slog	
sleeve	slop	

SPL Words

splash	splendid	splurge
splat	splice	splutter
splatter	splint	
splay	split	
spleen	splotchy	

© Shell Education

151921—The Everything Guide to Phonics

169

Consonant Patterns
Initial Blends

Initial R Blends

BR Words

brace	bray	bride	brood
brad	breach	bridge	brook
brag	bread	brie	broom
braid	breadth	brief	broth
brain	break	bright	brought
brake	breast	brim	brow
bran	breath	brine	brown
branch	breathe	bring	browse
brand	bred	brink	bruise
brash	breech	brisk	brunch
brass	breed	broach	brunt
brat	breeze	broad	brush
brave	brew	brogue	brute
brawl	bribe	broil	
brawn	brick	broke	

CHR Words

christen	chrome	chronology
Christmas	chronicle	chrysalis

CR Words

crab	cray	crimp	crown
crack	crayon	crisp	crud
craft	craze	croak	crude
crag	creak	crock	cruel
cram	cream	crone	cruise
cramp	crease	crook	crumb
crane	creed	croon	crunch
crank	creek	crop	crush
crash	creep	cross	crust
crass	crept	crotch	crutch
crate	crest	crouch	crux
crave	crew	croup	cry
craw	crib	crow	
crawl	crime	crowd	

DR Words

drab	drawer	drew	droop
draft	drawl	drift	drop
drag	drawn	drill	drought
drain	dray	drink	drove
drake	dread	drip	drown
dram	dream	drive	drug
drank	dredge	droid	drum
drape	dreg	droll	drunk
drat	drench	drone	dry
draw	dress	drool	

FR Words

frail	free	friend	frond
frame	freeze	fright	front
France	freight	frill	frost
frank	French	frisk	froth
frat	fresh	frizz	frown
fraud	fret	frock	froze
fray	fridge	frog	fruit
freak	fried	from	fry

GR Words

grab	gray	grind	grove
grace	graze	grip	grow
grade	grease	gripe	growl
graft	great	grist	grown
grail	greed	grit	growth
grain	green	groan	grub
gram	greet	groin	grudge
grand	grew	groom	gruel
grant	grid	groove	gruff
grape	grief	grope	grump
graph	grieve	gross	grunt
grasp	grill	grouch	
grass	grim	ground	
grate	grime	group	
grave	grin	grout	

Consonant Patterns
Initial Blends

Initial R Blends

PHR Words

phrase phrasing

PR Words

praise	press	prince	proof
pram	prey	print	prop
prance	price	prize	prose
prank	prick	pro	proud
prawn	pride	probe	prove
pray	priest	prod	prowl
prayer	pried	prom	prune
preach	prim	prompt	pry
preen	prime	prone	
prep	primp	prong	

SCR Words

scrag	scree	scrip	scruff
scram	screech	script	scrum
scrap	screen	scrod	scrunch
scrape	screw	scroll	scry
scratch	scribe	scrounge	
scrawl	scrim	scrub	
scream	scrimp	scrubs	

SHR Words

shrank	shrill	shrub
shred	shrimp	shrug
shrew	shrine	shrunk
shrewd	shrink	
shriek	shroud	

SPR Words

sprain	spread	sprinkle	spruce
sprang	spree	sprint	sprung
sprawl	sprig	sprite	spry
spray	spring	sprout	

STR Words

straight	stream	stride	stroke
strain	street	strife	stroll
strait	strength	strike	strong
strand	strep	string	strove
strange	stress	strip	struck
strap	stretch	stripe	strum
straw	strew	strive	strung
stray	strewn	strobe	strut
streak	strict	strode	

THR Words

thrash	threw	throat	throw
thread	thrice	throb	thrown
threat	thrift	throne	thrum
three	thrill	throng	thrush
thresh	thrive	through	thrust

TR Words

trace	tray	trill	trowel
track	tread	trim	truce
tract	treat	trip	truck
trade	tree	tripe	trudge
trail	trek	trite	true
train	trench	trod	trump
traipse	trend	troll	trunk
trait	tress	troop	trust
tram	trial	trot	truth
trance	tribe	trough	try
trap	trick	troupe	
trash	tried	trout	
trawl	trike	trove	

© Shell Education

151921—The Everything Guide to Phonics

171

Consonant Patterns
Initial Blends

Initial S Blends

SC Words

scab	scarce	scoop	scout
scald	scare	scoot	scowl
scale	scarf	scope	scuff
scalp	scat	scorch	sculpt
scam	scathe	score	scum
scan	scoff	scorn	scup
scant	scold	Scot	
scar	scone	scour	

SCH Words

schedule	scheme	school

SCR Words

scrag	scree	scrip	scruff
scram	screech	script	scrum
scrap	screen	scrod	scrunch
scrape	screw	scroll	scry
scratch	scribe	scrounge	
scrawl	scrim	scrub	
scream	scrimp	scrubs	

SK Words

skate	skiff	skip
skein	skill	skirt
sketch	skim	skit
skew	skimp	skulk
ski	skin	skunk
skid	skink	sky

SL Words

slab	sled	slim	sloth
slack	sleek	slime	slouch
slain	sleep	sling	slough
slam	sleet	slink	slow
slang	sleeve	slip	sludge
slant	sleigh	slit	slug
slap	slept	slob	slum
slash	slew	slog	slump
slat	slice	sloop	slung
slate	slick	slop	slur
slave	slid	slope	slurp
slaw	slide	slosh	slush
slay	slight	slot	sly

SM Words

smack	smell	smite	smooch
small	smelt	smith	smooth
smart	smidge	smock	smudge
smash	smile	smog	smug
smear	smirk	smoke	

SN Words

snack	sneak	snob	snow
snag	sneer	snood	snub
snail	sneeze	snoop	snuck
snake	snide	snooze	snuff
snap	sniff	snore	snug
snare	snip	snort	
snarl	snit	snot	
snatch	snitch	snout	

172   151921— The Everything Guide to Phonics   © Shell Education

Consonant Patterns
Initial Blends

Initial S Blends

SP Words

spa	spay	spin	spork
space	speak	spine	sport
spade	speck	spire	spot
Spain	sped	spit	spouse
spam	speech	spite	spout
span	speed	spoil	spree
spank	spell	spoke	spud
spar	spend	sponge	spunk
spare	spent	spoof	spur
spark	spew	spook	spurn
spasm	spice	spool	spurt
spat	spike	spoon	spry
spawn	spill	spore	spy

SPH Words

sphere	sphinx

SPL Words

splash	splay	splice	splotchy
splat	spleen	splint	splurge
splatter	splendid	split	splutter

SPR Words

sprain	spread	sprinkle	spruce
sprang	spree	sprint	sprung
sprawl	sprig	sprite	spry
spray	spring	sprout	

SQU Words

squad	squat	squeeze	squire
squall	squawk	squelch	squirm
square	squeak	squid	squish
squash	squeal	squint	

ST Words

stab	start	stern	store
stack	starve	stew	stork
staff	stash	stick	storm
stag	state	stiff	stove
stage	stats	still	stow
staid	staunch	sting	stout
stain	stave	stink	stub
stairs	stay	stint	stuck
stake	stead	stir	stuff
stale	steak	stitch	stump
stalk	steal	stock	stun
stall	stealth	stoke	stung
stamp	steam	stole	stunk
stance	steed	stomp	stunt
stand	steel	stone	sty
stank	steep	stood	style
star	steer	stooge	
starch	stem	stool	
stare	stench	stoop	
stark	step	stop	

© Shell Education

151921—The Everything Guide to Phonics

173

Consonant Patterns
Initial Blends

Initial S Blends

STR Words

straight	stream	stride	stroke
strain	street	strife	stroll
strait	strength	strike	strong
strand	strep	string	strove
strange	stress	strip	struck
strap	stretch	stripe	strum
straw	strew	strive	strung
stray	strewn	strobe	strut
streak	strict	strode	

SW Words

swab	sway	swift	Swiss
swag	swear	swig	switch
swam	sweat	swill	swoon
swamp	Swede	swim	swoop
swan	sweep	swine	swoosh
swap	sweet	swing	swore
swarm	swell	swipe	sworn
swat	swept	swirl	swum
swatch	swerve	swish	swung

Consonant Patterns
Initial Blends

Initial W Blends

DW Words

dwarf   dwell   dwindle
dweeb   dwelling

SW Words

swab   sweep   swish
swag   sweet   Swiss
swam   swell   switch
swamp   swept   swoon
swan   swerve   swoop
swap   swift   swoosh
swarm   swig   swore
swat   swill   sworn
swatch   swim   swum
sway   swine   swung
swear   swing
sweat   swipe
Swede   swirl

TW Words

twang   twelve   twine
tweak   twerp   twinge
tweed   twice   twinkle
tweet   twig   twirl
tweezers twill   twit
twelfth   twin   twitch

© Shell Education

151921—The Everything Guide to Phonics

175

Consonant Patterns
Final Blends

Final C Blends

CT Words

act	distract	pact
affect	district	perfect
aspect	duct	predict
attract	effect	project
collect	eject	protect
concoct	elect	protract
conduct	enact	react
conflict	exact	reflect
connect	expect	reject
constrict	extract	respect
construct	fact	restrict
contact	impact	retract
contract	induct	select
correct	inject	strict
deduct	inspect	subject
destruct	instruct	subtract
detect	neglect	suspect
detract	object	tact
direct	obstruct	tract

Consonant Patterns
Final Blends

Final F Blends

FT Words

aft	graft	shift
cleft	heft	sift
craft	left	soft
daft	lift	swift
deft	loft	theft
draft	raft	thrift
drift	rift	tuft
gift	shaft	

FTH Words

fifth
twelfth

Consonant Patterns
Final Blends

Final L Blends

LB Words

bulb

LCH Words

belch   gulch   squelch
filch   mulch   zilch

LD Words

bald	fold	mold	told
bold	gold	old	weld
build	guild	scald	wield
child	held	scold	wild
cold	hold	shield	yield
field	mild	sold	

LF Words

elf   golf   self   wolf
engulf   gulf   shelf

LGE Words

bulge   divulge   indulge

LK Words

balk	chalk	silk	talk
bilk	elk	skulk	walk
bulk	hulk	stalk	
caulk	milk	sulk	

LM Words

balm   helm   psalm
calm   overwhelm   qualm
film   palm   realm

LN Words

kiln

LP Words

gulp   kelp   scalp   yelp
help   pulp   whelp

LSE Words

else   false   impulse   pulse

LT Words

adult	dolt	kilt	silt
assault	exalt	knelt	smelt
belt	exult	lilt	tilt
bolt	fault	malt	vault
built	felt	melt	volt
colt	guilt	molt	welt
consult	halt	pelt	wilt
cult	hilt	quilt	
dealt	insult	result	
default	jolt	salt	

LTH Words

filth   health   stealth   wealth

LVE Words

absolve	evolve	salve	twelve
delve	involve	selves	valve
dissolve	resolve	shelves	wolves
elves	revolve	solve	

178   151921— The Everything Guide to Phonics   © Shell Education

Consonant Patterns
Final Blends

Final M Blends

MP Words

amp	hemp	shrimp
blimp	hump	skimp
bump	imp	slump
camp	jump	stamp
champ	lamp	stomp
chimp	limp	stump
chomp	lump	swamp
clamp	pomp	tamp
clomp	plump	temp
clump	primp	thump
cramp	pump	trump
crimp	ramp	ump
damp	romp	
dump	rump	
grump	scrimp	

MPSE Words

glimpse

MPT Words

attempt	kempt	tempt
contempt	preempt	unkempt
exempt	prompt	

© Shell Education

151921—The Everything Guide to Phonics

179

Consonant Patterns
Final Blends

Final N Blends

NCE Words

announce	fence	<u>once</u>	renounce
bounce	flounce	ounce	since
chance	France	pence	stance
commence	glance	pounce	trance
dance	hence	prance	wince
denounce	lance	prince	
dunce	mince	pronounce	

NCH Words

bench	crunch	hunch	scrunch
blanch	drench	launch	staunch
branch	finch	lunch	stench
bunch	flinch	munch	trench
cinch	French	paunch	winch
clench	Grinch	pinch	wrench
clinch	haunch	punch	

NCT Words

defunct	instinct
distinct	precinct
extinct	succinct

ND Words

abound	demand	hind	send
amend	depend	hound	sound
and	end	kind	spend
around	expand	land	stand
astound	extend	lend	strand
band	fend	mend	surround
bend	find	mind	suspend
beyond	fond	mound	tend
bind	found	pond	trend
bland	friend	pound	unkind
blend	frond	profound	vend
blind	fund	remind	wand
blond	gland	rend	wind
bond	grand	respond	wound
bound	grind	rewind	
brand	ground	round	
command	hand	sand	

NGE Words

arrange	expunge	lounge	singe
binge	fringe	lunge	sponge
change	grange	plunge	strange
cringe	grunge	range	syringe
exchange	hinge	scrounge	tinge

Consonant Patterns
Final Blends

Final N Blends

NK Words

bank	drunk	mink	slink
blank	dunk	monk	slunk
blink	fink	oink	spank
bonk	flank	pink	spunk
brink	flunk	plank	stank
bunk	frank	prank	stink
chink	funk	punk	stunk
chunk	gunk	rank	sunk
clink	honk	rink	tank
clunk	hunk	sank	thank
conk	ink	shrank	think
crank	junk	shrink	trunk
dank	kink	sink	wink
drank	lank	skink	yank
drink	link	skunk	

NSE Words

condense	dense	rinse	tense
defense	immense	sense	

NT Words

account	dent	joint	sent
acquaint	descent	lint	shunt
amount	dissent	meant	slant
anoint	faint	mint	spent
ant	flaunt	mount	splint
appoint	flint	paint	sprint
ascent	font	pant	squint
assent	fount	pent	stint
bend	front	plant	stunt
blunt	gaunt	point	surmount
brunt	gent	print	taint
bunt	glint	punt	taunt
cement	grant	quaint	tent
chant	grunt	rant	tint
consent	haunt	rent	vent
content	hint	runt	want
count	hunt	scant	went
daunt	jaunt	scent	

NTH Words

eleventh	month	tenth
fifteenth	ninth	thirteenth
fourteenth	seventh	

Consonant Patterns
Final Blends

Final P Blends

PSE Words

collapse	elapse	lapse
corpse	ellipse	relapse
eclipse	glimpse	traipse

PT Words

abrupt	Egypt	rapt
accept	erupt	slept
corrupt	except	swept
crept	interrupt	wept
crypt	opt	
disrupt	kept	

PTH Words

depth

Consonant Patterns
Final Blends

Final S Blends

SK Words

ask	dusk	risk
bask	flask	task
brisk	frisk	tusk
cask	husk	whisk
desk	mask	
disk	musk	

SM Words

chasm	sarcasm
prism	spasm

SP Words

clasp	grasp	wasp
crisp	lisp	wisp

ST Words

adjust	dust	last	roost
arrest	east	least	rust
assist	exist	lest	taste
beast	fast	list	test
best	feast	lost	thirst
blast	fest	mast	thrust
boast	fist	mist	toast
boost	first	moist	trust
breast	frost	most	twist
burst	ghost	must	vast
bust	gist	nest	vest
cast	grist	oust	waist
chest	guest	past	west
coast	gust	persist	worst
consist	heist	pest	wrest
cost	hoist	post	wrist
crest	host	priest	yeast
crust	insist	quest	zest
cyst	jest	resist	
disgust	joist	rest	
distrust	just	roast	

Consonant Patterns
Final Blends

Final T Blends

TCH Words

batch	glitch	Scotch
blotch	hatch	snatch
botch	hitch	snitch
catch	hutch	stitch
clutch	itch	swatch
crotch	latch	switch
crutch	match	thatch
ditch	notch	watch
Dutch	patch	witch
etch	pitch	
fetch	retch	

TZ Words

blitz	quartz	waltz
klutz	spritz	

Consonant Patterns
Final Blends

Final X Blends

XT Words

betwixt	next	text
context	pretext	

© Shell Education

151921—The Everything Guide to Phonics

185

Consonant Patterns
Final Double-Letter Digraphs

Final Double-Letter Words

DD Words

add   odd

FF Words

bailiff	huff	puff	snuff
bluff	jiff	quaff	staff
buff	mastiff	riff	stiff
chaff	midriff	scoff	stuff
cliff	miff	scruff	tariff
cuff	muff	scuff	tiff
doff	off	sheriff	whiff
fluff	plaintiff	skiff	
gruff	pontiff	sniff	

LL Words

all	gall	pill	stroll
ball	gill	poll	swell
bell	grill	pull	swill
bill	gull	quell	tall
bull	hall	quill	tell
call	hill	roll	thrill
cell	hull	scroll	till
chill	ill	sell	toll
cull	install	shall	trill
dell	instill	shell	twill
dill	kill	shrill	wall
doll	knell	sill	well
drill	knoll	skill	will
droll	krill	skull	yell
dull	loll	small	
dwell	lull	smell	
fall	mall	spell	
fell	mill	spill	
fill	mull	squall	
frill	null	stall	
full	pall	still	

SS Words

across	cuss	hiss	progress
address	digress	impress	recess
assess	dismiss	kiss	regress
bass	dress	lass	sass
boss	emboss	less	stress
bless	express	loss	surpass
bliss	floss	mass	Swiss
brass	fuss	mess	toss
caress	glass	miss	tress
chess	gloss	moss	unless
class	grass	muss	
crass	gross	pass	
cross	guess	press	

TT Words

boycott	mitt	putt
butt	mutt	watt

ZZ Words

abuzz	frizz	pizzazz
buzz	fuzz	whizz
fizz	jazz	

Consonant Patterns
Consonant-*le* Words

Consonant-*le* Words

Consonant-*le* words

able	dongle	marble	simple
aisle	eagle	middle	single
ample	fable	mingle	sparkle
angle	feeble	muddle	sprinkle
apple	fickle	mumble	stable
bangle	fiddle	myrtle	staple
battle	gable	needle	supple
beetle	gamble	nimble	table
bible	gentle	paddle	tackle
bottle	giggle	pebble	tangle
bubble	handle	pickle	temple
buckle	hassle	puddle	tickle
bundle	huddle	purple	tingle
bungle	hurdle	puzzle	title
cable	hustle	raffle	topple
candle	jangle	rattle	treble
castle	jingle	riddle	triple
cattle	juggle	ripple	tumble
circle	jumble	rubble	turtle
couple	jungle	ruble	twinkle
cradle	kettle	sable	uncle
crinkle	little	saddle	whittle
cycle	mangle	sample	wrangle
dangle	mantle	settle	wrinkle
dazzle	maple	shingle	

© Shell Education

151921—The Everything Guide to Phonics

187

The Everything Guide to Phonics

Consonant Digraphs Table of Contents

CH Digraph ...190
/ch/ (as in *chip*) Words ...190
/ch/ Rhyming Sets ...191
/ch/ Homophones and
Compound Words ...192
/k/ (as in *echo*) Words ...193
/k/ Homophones and
Compound Words ...195
/sh/ (as in *chef*) Words ...195

CK Digraph ...196
CK Words ...196
CK Rhyming Sets ...197
CK Compound Words ...198

GH Digraph ...199
/f/ (as in *tough*) Words and
Rhyming Sets ...199
/g/ (as in *ghost*) Words ...200
Silent GH (as in *high*) Words ...201
Silent GH Rhyming Sets ...202
Silent GH Homophones and
Compound Words ...203

NG Digraph ...204
NG Words ...204
NG Rhyming Sets and Homophones ...205
NG Compound Words ...206

PH Digraph ...207
PH Words ...207
PH Compound Words ...208

SH Digraph ...209
SH Words ...209
SH Rhyming Sets and
Compound Words ...210

TH Digraph ...211
/th/ (as in *both*) Words ...211
/th/ Rhyming Sets and Homophones ...212
/th/ Compound Words ...213
/th/ (as in *them*) Words ...214
/th/ Rhyming Sets and Homophones ...215
/th/ Compound Words ...216

WH Digraph ...217
/w/ (as in *wheel*) Words ...217
/w/ Homophones and
Compound Words ...218
/h/ (as in *who*) Words ...219
/h/ Homophones and
Compound Words ...220

Notes: High-frequency words only include Fry's first 300 words. Rule breakers are only one-syllable words. For most patterns, words are listed only if their stressed syllable follows the focus pattern.

Consonant Digraphs
CH Digraph

/ch/ (as in chip) Words

High-Frequency Words

change	each	such	which
children	much	watch	

Words with Two Sounds

arch	chew	each	itch
char	chow	etch	ouch

Words with Three Sounds

batch	cheese	churn	poach
beach	chess	coach	porch
beech	chick	couch	pouch
birch	chide	ditch	reach
botch	chief	Dutch	retch
catch	chill	fetch	rich
chafe	chime	hatch	roach
chain	chin	hitch	search
chair	chip	hutch	such
chalk	chirp	inch	teach
chap	chive	latch	thatch
chard	chock	leach	torch
charge	choice	leech	touch
charm	choke	lurch	vouch
chart	choose	march	watch
chase	chop	match	which
chat	chore	much	witch
cheap	chose	notch	wretch
cheat	chuck	parch	
check	chug	patch	
cheek	chum	peach	
cheer	church	pitch	

Words with Four Sounds

belch	chimp	gulch	scorch
bench	chink	haunch	Scotch
bleach	chunk	hunch	sketch
blotch	chomp	launch	slouch
breach	cinch	lunch	snatch
breech	clutch	lynch	snitch
broach	conch	mulch	speech
bunch	crotch	munch	stitch
champ	crouch	paunch	swatch
change	crutch	pinch	switch
chant	finch	preach	twitch
chest	glitch	punch	winch
child	grouch	ranch	wrench

Words with Five Sounds

blanch	crunch	quench	stench
branch	drench	scratch	stretch
brunch	flinch	screech	trench
clench	French	splotch	
clinch	grinch	staunch	

Words with Six Sounds

scrunch

Words with a Stressed First Syllable

butcher	cherish	merchant	teacher
chapter	hatchet	ostrich	
cheddar	kitchen	sandwich	

Words with a Stressed Second Syllable

approach	beseech	reproach
attach	encroach	

Consonant Digraphs
CH Digraph

/ch/ Rhyming Sets

- blanch, branch, ranch
- arch, march, parch, starch
- batch, catch, hatch, latch, match, patch, scratch, snatch, thatch
- haunch, launch, paunch, staunch
- beach, beech, beseech, bleach, breach, breech, each, leach, leech, peach, preach, reach, screech, speech, teach
- bench, clench, drench, French, stench, trench, wrench
- etch, fetch, retch, sketch, wretch
- cinch, clinch, finch, flinch, grinch, inch, lynch, pinch, winch
- ditch, glitch, hitch, itch, pitch, rich, snitch, stitch, switch, twitch, which, witch
- approach, broach, coach, encroach, poach, reproach, roach
- blotch, botch, crotch, notch, Scotch, splotch
- couch, crouch, grouch, ouch, pouch, slouch, vouch
- brunch, bunch, crunch, hunch, lunch, munch, punch, scrunch
- clutch, crutch, Dutch, hutch, much, such, touch

© Shell Education

151921—The Everything Guide to Phonics

191

Consonant Digraphs
CH Digraph

/ch/ Homophones and Compound Words

Homophones

beach/beech
breach/breech
leach/leech
which/witch

Compound Words

chairlift
chalkboard
cheerleader
cheeseburger
hatchback
lunchroom
matchstick
patchwork
pitchfork
touchscreen
witchcraft

Consonant Digraphs
CH Digraph

/k/ (as in echo) Words

High-Frequency Words

school

Words with Two Sounds

ache

Words with Three Sounds

chord

Words with Four Sounds

chasm	chrome	school
choir	scheme	

Words with a Stressed First Syllable

anchor	chorus	monarch
archives	Christian	orchid
chaos	Christmas	schedule
chemist	chronic	scholar
chlorine	echo	stomach

Words with a Stressed Second Syllable

technique

Words with Three or More Syllables

arachnid	charisma	mechanic
archaic	chemical	monarchy
architect	chemistry	orchestra
bronchitis	choreograph	patriarch
chameleon	chronology	scholarship
chaotic	chrysalis	technical
character	Hanukkah	
characteristics	matriarch	

© Shell Education

151921—The Everything Guide to Phonics

193

Consonant Digraphs
CH Digraph

/k/ Homophones and Compound Words

Homophones

chord/cord

Compound Words

earache
headache
schoolhouse
schoolyard
toothache

Consonant Digraphs
CH Digraph

/sh/ (as in chef) Words

High-Frequency Words

machine

Words with Three Sounds

chef   chute   quiche

Words with a Stressed First Syllable

chevron   fuchsia   mustache

Words with a Stressed Second Syllable

brochure   charade   crochet
chagrin   chauffeur   machine
chalet   chiffon
champagne   cliché

Words with Three or More Syllables

chandelier   chivalry   parachute
chaparral   machinery   pistachio
chaperone   Michigan
Chicago   nonchalant

© Shell Education   151921—The Everything Guide to Phonics   **195**

Consonant Digraphs
CK Digraph

CK Words

High-Frequency Words

back

Rule Breakers

flak	soccer	wok
picnic	trek	yak

Words with Three Sounds

back	huck	nick	sock
beck	jack	pack	suck
buck	jock	peck	tack
check	kick	pick	thick
chick	knack	pock	tick
chock	knock	puck	tuck
chuck	lack	rack	whack
deck	lick	rock	wick
dock	lock	sack	wreck
duck	luck	shack	yuck
hack	mock	shock	
heck	muck	shuck	
hock	neck	sick	

Words with Four Sounds

black	crock	quick	stack
block	fleck	slack	stick
brick	flick	slick	stock
click	flock	smack	stuck
clock	frock	smock	track
cluck	pluck	snack	trick
crack	prick	snuck	truck
crick	quack	speck	

Words with Five Sounds

struck

Words with a Stressed First Syllable

bicker	hacker	package	sticker
bucket	heckle	packet	stocking
buckle	hockey	picket	suckle
cackle	jackal	pickle	tackle
chicken	jacket	pocket	thicket
chuckle	jockey	pricker	ticket
cockroach	knickers	prickle	tickle
cracker	knuckle	pucker	trickle
crackle	locker	racket	wicked
cricket	locket	rocker	wicker
docket	lucky	snicker	wicket
fickle	necklace	socket	wreckage
flicker	nickel	spackle	
freckle	nickname	speckle	

Words with a Stressed Second Syllable

attack	unlock	unpack

Words with Three or More Syllables

hickory	mockery	sickening

Consonant Digraphs
CK Digraph

CK Rhyming Sets

- back, black, crack, hack, jack, knack, lack, pack, plaque, quack, rack, sack, shack, slack, smack, snack, stack, tack, track, whack, yak
- beck, check, deck, fleck, heck, neck, peck, speck, trek, wreck
- brick, chick, click, crick, flick, kick, lick, nick, pick, prick, quick, sick, slick, stick, thick, tick, trick, wick
- block, chock, clock, crock, dock, flock, frock, hock, jock, knock, lock, mock, pock, rock, shock, smock, sock, stock, wok
- buck, chuck, cluck, duck, huck, luck, muck, pluck, puck, shuck, snuck, struck, stuck, suck, truck, tuck, yuck
- backer, cracker, hacker, packer, slacker, stacker, tracker
- bicker, flicker, pricker, quicker, sicker, snicker, sticker, wicker
- docker, locker, rocker, shocker
- pucker, shucker, sucker, trucker
- bracket, jacket, packet, racket
- cricket, picket, ticket, wicket
- docket, locket, pocket, rocket, socket
- bucket, tucket
- cackle, crackle, jackal, spackle, tackle
- freckle, heckle, speckle
- fickle, nickel, pickle, prickle, tickle, trickle
- buckle, chuckle, knuckle, suckle
- haddock, paddock

© Shell Education

Consonant Digraphs
CK Digraph

CK Compound Words

aftershock	horseback
backbone	kickball
background	kickstand
backpack	leatherback
backstop	livestock
backtrack	lumberjack
backyard	matchstick
bedrock	overstock
blackbird	paperback
blackboard	piggyback
blacksmith	potluck
blacktop	quarterback
bottleneck	racetrack
broomstick	roadblock
candlestick	seasick
carsick	shipwreck
drumstick	sidekick
feedback	sidetrack
flashback	smokestack
hatchback	sunblock
haystack	thumbtack
homesick	toothpick

Consonant Digraphs
GH Digraph

/f/ (as in tough) Words and Rhyming Sets

Words

High-Frequency Words

enough

Words with Three Sounds

cough   rough
laugh   tough

Words with Four Sounds

slough   trough

Words with a Stressed First Syllable

laughter   roughly   tougher
roughage   toughen   toughest

Words with a Stressed Second Syllable

enough

Rhyming Sets

- bluff, buff, cuff, enough, fluff, gruff, huff, puff, rough, scruff, scuff, slough, snuff, stuff, tough

- cough, doff, off, scoff, trough

© Shell Education   151921—The Everything Guide to Phonics   **199**

Consonant Digraphs

GH Digraph

/g/ (as in ghost) Words

Words with Two Sounds

ugh

Words with Three Sounds

ghoul

Words with Four Sounds

ghost

Words with a Stressed First Syllable

ghastly   ghetto

Words with a Stressed Second Syllable

aghast

Consonant Digraphs
GH Digraph

Silent GH (as in high) Words

High-Frequency Words

| high | might | thought |
| light | night | through |

Words with Two Sounds

bough	neigh	thigh
dough	nigh	though
eight	ought	weigh
high	sigh	

Words with Three Sounds

bought	light	sought
caught	might	taught
fight	night	thought
fought	right	through
height	sight	tight
knight	sleigh	

Words with Four Sounds

blight	fraught	sleight
bright	freight	slight
brought	fright	tights
flight	plight	

Words with a Stressed First Syllable

brighten	highly	neighbor
daughter	lighten	nightmare
eighty	lightly	slaughter
frighten	lightning	slightly
higher	mighty	tighten
highest	naughty	

Words with a Stressed Second Syllable

| alright | delight | tonight |
| although | eighteen | |

Words with Three or More Syllables

| enlighten | frightening | neighborhood |

© Shell Education

151921—The Everything Guide to Phonics

201

Consonant Digraphs
GH Digraph

Silent GH Rhyming Sets

- bought, brought, caught, fought, fraught, ought, sought, squat, swat, taught, taut, thought, watt

- apply, awry, buy, by, bye, comply, cry, deny, die, dry, dye, eye, fly, fry, guy, hi, high, imply, July, lie, lye, my, nigh, pie, ply, pry, rely, reply, rye, shy, sigh, sky, sly, spry, spy, sty, supply, thigh, thy, tie, try, vie, why, wry

- bite, blight, bright, byte, cite, excite, fight, flight, fright, height, ignite, invite, kite, knight, light, might, mite, night, plight, polite, quite, recite, right, rite, sight, site, slight, smite, spite, sprite, tight, white, write

- ago, although, beau, below, bestow, blow, bow, bro, crow, doe, dough, floe, flow, foe, fro, glow, go, grow, hoe, joe, know, low, mow, no, owe, pro, roe, row, sew, show, slow, snow, so, sow, stow, though, throw, toe, tow, whoa, woe

- allow, bough, bow, brow, chow, cow, endow, how, meow, now, ow, plow, pow, prow, sow, vow, wow

Consonant Digraphs
GH Digraph

Silent GH Homophones and Compound Words

Homophones

ate/eight
bough/bow
doe/dough
hi/high
knight/night
might/mite
nay/neigh
right/rite
sight/site
slay/sleigh
slight/sleight
taught/taut
threw/through
wait/weight
way/weigh

Compound Words

copyright
daylight
eyesight
flashlight
headlights
heavyweight
highchair
highlight
highway
lighthouse
lightweight
moonlight
nightgown
nightlight
nightshirt
nightstand
nighttime
sightsee
spotlight
sunlight
tonight

Consonant Digraphs
NG Digraph

NG Words

High-Frequency Words

along	long	thing
being	something	young
following	song	

Words with Three Sounds

bang	lung	tang
ding	pang	thing
dung	ping	tongue
fang	rang	wing
gang	ring	wring
gong	rung	wrong
hang	sang	young
hung	sing	zing
king	song	
long	sung	

Words with Four Sounds

bling	length	swing
bring	prong	swung
clang	slang	throng
cling	sling	tongs
clung	slung	twang
fling	sting	
flung	stung	

Words with Five Sounds

sprang	string	strung
spring	strong	

Words with a Stressed First Syllable

hangar	lengthy	tangy
hanger	singer	

Words with a Stressed Second Syllable

along	among	belong

Consonant Digraphs
NG Digraph

NG Rhyming Sets and Homophones

Rhyming Sets

- bang, clang, fang, gang, hang, pang, rang, sang, slang, sprang, tang, twang

- bling, bring, cling, ding, fling, king, ping, ring, sing, sling, spring, sting, string, swing, thing, wing, wring, zing

- along, belong, gong, long, prong, song, strong, throng, tong, wrong

- among, clung, dung, flung, hung, lung, rung, slung, strung, stung, sung, swung, tongue, wrung, young

Homophones

hangar/hanger
ring/wring
rung/wrung

Consonant Digraphs
NG Digraph

NG Compound Words

anything
bedsprings
drawstring
everything
gangplank
hamstring
handspring
lifelong
longshot
nothing
ringmaster
something
songbird
songbook
songwriter
springboard
springtime
stingray

Consonant Digraphs
PH Digraph

PH Words

Words with Three Sounds

phase   phone

Words with Four Sounds

glyph   phrase
graph   sphere

Words with a Stressed First Syllable

dolphin   phonics
gopher   phony
graphics   photo
hyphen   physics
nephew   triumph
orphan   trophy
pamphlet

Words with Three or More Syllables

alphabet   paraphrase
amphibian   peripheral
apostrophe   pharmacist
atmosphere   pharmacy
atrophy   phenomenon
autograph   philosophy
biography   phobia
catastrophe   photocopy
decipher   photogenic
elephant   photograph
emphasis   photographer
emphasize   photosynthesis
esophagus   physical
geography   physician
hemisphere   saxophone
homophone   sophisticated
metamorphosis   sophomore
metaphor   symphony
microphone   telephone
orphanage   triumphant
paragraph   xylophone

© Shell Education   151921—The Everything Guide to Phonics   **207**

Consonant Digraphs
PH Digraph

PH Compound Words

phonebook
phonebooth
photocopy

Consonant Digraphs
SH Digraph

SH Words

High-Frequency Words

she	should	show

Rule Breakers

sugar	sure

Words with Two Sounds

ash	shoe	show
she	shore	shy

Words with Three Sounds

bash	shack	ship
bush	shade	shire
cash	shag	shirk
dash	shake	shirt
dish	shale	shoal
fish	sham	shock
gash	shame	shod
gnash	shape	shone
gush	shard	shook
harsh	share	shop
hash	shark	shorn
hush	sharp	short
lash	shave	shot
leash	shawl	should
lush	sheaf	shout
marsh	shear	shove
mash	shed	shown
mesh	sheen	shrew
mush	sheep	shuck
nosh	sheer	shun
posh	sheet	shush
push	sheik	shut
rash	shell	wash
rush	shin	whoosh
sash	shine	wish

Words with Four Sounds

blush	shelf	smash
brash	shield	smoosh
brush	shift	squish
clash	shred	stash
crash	shriek	swish
crush	shrill	thrash
flash	shrine	thresh
flesh	shrub	thrush
flush	shrug	trash
fresh	shunt	Welsh
plush	slash	
shaft	slush	

Words with Five Sounds

shrimp	shrunk
shrink	splash

Words with a Stressed First Syllable

bushy	mushy	shuffle
cushion	pushy	slushy
freshman	shepherd	
mushroom	shingle	

Words with Three or More Syllables

marshmallow

Consonant Digraphs
SH Digraph

SH Rhyming Sets and Compound Words

Rhyming Sets

- harsh, marsh

- ash, bash, brash, cash, clash, crash, dash, flash, gash, gnash, hash, lash, mash, rash, sash, slash, smash, splash, stash, trash

- dish, fish, squish, swish, wish

- bush, mush, push, shush

- blush, brush, crush, flush, gush, hush, lush, plush, rush, shush, slush

Compound Words

ashtray	shipyard
cashflow	shoemaker
dashboard	shopkeeper
dishwater	shoreline
flashback	shortcake
flashlight	shortstop
fishbowl	showcase
hashtag	showdown
pushcart	showerhead
sheetrock	wishbone
shipwreck	

/th/ (as in *both*) Words

High-Frequency Words

both	thing	three
earth	think	through
something	thought	

Rule Breaker

thyme

Words with Two Sounds

earth	thaw	thigh
oath	the	

Words with Three Sounds

bath	mouth	thorn
berth	myth	thought
birth	north	three
booth	path	threw
both	pith	through
dearth	south	throw
death	teeth	thud
fifth	thatch	thug
forth	theft	thumb
girth	theme	tooth
hearth	thick	worth
lithe	thief	wrath
math	thin	wreath
mirth	thing	
moth	third	

Words with Four Sounds

breath	tenth	throat
broth	thank	throb
cloth	think	throne
froth	thirst	thrown
growth	thrash	thrum
month	thread	thrush
sloth	threat	thump
smith	thrill	
swath	thrive	

Words with Five Sounds

thrift	thrust

Words with a Stressed First Syllable

theory	thirsty	threaten
thermal	thirty	thrifty
thermos	thorough	thunder
thimble	thousand	Thursday

Words with a Stressed Second Syllable

beneath

Words with Three or More Syllables

thermostat

Consonant Digraphs
TH Digraph

/th/ Rhyming Sets and Homophones

Rhyming Sets

- bath, math, path, wrath
- health, stealth, wealth
- breath, death
- beneath, teeth, wreath
- berth, birth, dearth, earth, girth, mirth, worth
- fifth, myth, pith, smith
- both, growth, oath
- broth, cloth, froth, moth, sloth, swath
- forth, north
- mouth, south

Homophones

berth/birth

Consonant Digraphs
TH Digraph

/th/ Compound Words

bathroom
bathtub
birthday
birthmark
birthstone
earthquake
northeast
northwest
southeast
southwest
Thanksgiving
throughout
thumbnail
toothache
toothbrush
toothpaste
toothpick

Consonant Digraphs
TH Digraph

/th/ (as in them) Words

High-Frequency Words

father	them	those
other	then	together
than	there	with
that	these	without
the	they	
their	this	

Rule Breaker

thyme

Words with Two Sounds

though

Words with Three Sounds

bathe	their	this
lithe	them	those
teethe	then	tithe
than	there	with
that	these	

Words with Four Sounds

breathe

Words with a Stressed First Syllable

father	northern	whether
heather	southern	
leather	weather	

Words with a Stressed Second Syllable

although

Words with Three or More Syllables

together

Consonant Digraphs
TH Digraph

/th/ Rhyming Sets and Homophones

Rhyming Sets

- feather, heather, leather, weather, whether

- breathe, teethe

Homophones

weather/whether

Consonant Digraphs
TH Digraph

/th/ Compound Words

withdraw
within
without

Consonant Digraphs
WH Digraph

/w/ (as in wheel) Words

High-Frequency Words

what	which	why
when	while	
where	white	

Words with Two Sounds

whey	whir	why

Words with Three Sounds

whack	when	whine
whale	where	whip
wharf	whet	whirl
what	which	white
wheat	whiff	whiz
wheel	while	
wheeze	whim	

Words with Four Sounds

whisk

Words with a Stressed First Syllable

wheedle	whisker	whitish
whether	whisper	whittle
whimper	whistle	whopper
whinny	whiten	

© Shell Education   151921—The Everything Guide to Phonics   **217**

Consonant Digraphs
WH Digraph

/w/ Homophones and Compound Words

Homophones

wail/whale
ware/wear/where
way/whey
weal/wheel
weather/whether
were/whir
wet/whet
which/witch
whine/wine

Compound Words

whalebone
wheelchair
whirlpool
whistleblower
whiteboard
whitecap
whitetail
whitewash

Consonant Digraphs
WH Digraph

/h/ (as in who) Words

High-Frequency Words

who

Words with Two Sounds

who

Words with Three Sounds

whole
whom
whose

© Shell Education

151921—The Everything Guide to Phonics

219

Consonant Digraphs
WH Digraph

/h/ Homophones and Compound Words

Homophones

hole/whole
who's/whose

Compound Words

whoever
wholehearted
whosoever

Soft Consonants Table of Contents

Soft C Patterns 222
Soft C Words 222
Soft C Preceded by Hard C: CC 223
Soft C Preceded by S: SC 224
Soft C Preceded by X: XC 225
Rhyming Sets 226
Homophones and Compound Words 227

Soft G Patterns 228
Soft G Words 228
Soft G Preceded by D: DG 230
Soft G Preceded by Hard G: GG 231
Soft G Preceded by N: NG 232
Rhyming Sets 233
Homophones and Compound Words 234

Notes: High-frequency words only include Fry's first 300 words. Rule breakers are only one-syllable words. For most patterns, words are listed only if their stressed syllable follows the focus pattern.

© Shell Education

Soft Consonants

Soft C Patterns

Soft C Words

High-Frequency Words

city   once   sentence

face   place

Rule Breakers

cello

Words with Two Sounds

ace   ice

Words with Three Sounds

cease	face	nice	race
cede	farce	niece	rice
cell	force	ounce	sauce
choice	juice	pace	source
cite	lace	peace	vice
deuce	lice	piece	voice
dice	mice	puce	

Words with Four Sounds

bounce	fence	once	space
brace	fierce	pierce	spice
cent	fleece	place	trace
chance	grace	pounce	truce
cinch	Greece	price	twice
cyst	hence	scent	wince
dance	lance	since	
dunce	mince	slice	

Words with Five Sounds

cents	glance	scarce	stance
flounce	prance	splice	trance
France	prince	spruce	

Words with a Stressed First Syllable

balance	citrus	grimace	practice
bracelet	city	juicy	princess
cancel	civic	justice	rancid
cedar	civil	lettuce	recent
ceiling	concept	malice	recess
cellar	council	menace	resource
census	crevice	mercy	sentence
center	cycle	necklace	service
central	cyclone	notice	species
certain	cymbol	novice	stencil
cider	decent	office	surface
circle	entrance	palace	terrace
circuit	fancy	parcel	
circus	furnace	pencil	

Words with a Stressed Second Syllable

announce	deceive	percent	receive
apiece	decide	police	recite
cement	denounce	precede	reduce
commence	device	precise	rejoice
conceal	divorce	proceed	renounce
concede	enforce	produce	sincere
conceit	fancy	pronounce	
conceive	incite	recede	
convince	perceive	receipt	

Words with Three or More Syllables

celebrate	circulate	decision
celery	circumstances	necessary
cemetery	citizen	percentage
century	concessions	publicity
cereal	cylinder	reception
cinnamon	deceptive	recipe

Soft Consonants
Soft C Patterns

Soft C Preceded by Hard C: CC

Words with a Stressed First Syllable

accent   access

Words with a Stressed Second Syllable

accept   success   vaccine
succeed   succinct

Words with Three or More Syllables

accelerate   accessible   successful
accelerator   accessory   successor
accentuate   accident   vaccinate
acceptable   accidental   vaccination
acceptance   eccentric

© Shell Education   151921—The Everything Guide to Phonics   **223**

Soft Consonants

Soft C Patterns

Soft C Preceded by S: SC

Words with a Stressed First Syllable

abscess   muscle

Words with a Stressed Second Syllable

ascend   descend   discern
ascent   descent   rescind

Words with Three or More Syllables

adolescent   fascinate   susceptible
condescend   fascination
descendant   fluorescent

Soft Consonants
Soft C Patterns

Soft C Preceded by X: XC

Words with a Stressed First Syllable

excerpt   excess   excise

Words with a Stressed Second Syllable

exceed   except
excel   excite

Words with Three or More Syllables

excellent   exceptional   excitement
exception   excessive   exciting

Soft Consonants

Soft C Patterns

Rhyming Sets

- ace, base, brace, case, chase, erase, face, grace, lace, pace, place, race, replace, space, trace, vase
- chance, dance, France, glance, lance, prance, stance, trance
- commence, condense, defense, dense, fence, hence, immense, sense, tense
- fierce, pierce
- apiece, cease, crease, decrease, fleece, grease, Greece, increase, lease, niece, peace, piece
- dice, ice, lice, mice, nice, price, rice, slice, spice, splice, thrice, twice, vice
- convince, mince, prince, rinse, since, wince
- choice, rejoice, voice
- coarse, course, divorce, endorse, enforce, force, hoarse, horse, source
- announce, bounce, denounce, flounce, ounce, pounce, pronounce, renounce
- deuce, excuse, goose, juice, loose, moose, noose, produce, puce, spruce, truce
- dunce, once

Soft Consonants
Soft C Patterns

Homophones and Compound Words

Homophones

accept/except
ascent/assent
cede/seed
ceiling/sealing
cell/sell
cellar/seller
censor/sensor
cent/scent/sent
cents/sense
cereal/serial
chance/chants
cite/sight/site
council/counsel
descent/dissent
grease/Greece
mince/mints
muscle/mussel
peace/piece
presence/presents
prince/prints
principal/principle
residence/residents
vice/vise

Compound Words

facelift
icebox
icepick
piecemeal
placemat
policeman
racehorse
racetrack
spaceship
voicemail

Soft Consonants

Soft G Patterns

Soft G Words

High-Frequency Words

large   page

Rule Breakers

camouflage	get	girl
collage	gift	give
gear	gig	massage
geek	gild	
geese	gill	

Words with Two Sounds

age   gee   urge

Words with Three Sounds

barge	gist	rage
cage	gorge	sage
charge	gouge	siege
forge	gym	stage
gauge	huge	surge
gel	large	verge
gem	merge	wage
gene	page	
germ	purge	

Words with Four Sounds

| bulge | stage |
| gist | stooge |

Words with Five Sound

splurge

Words with a Stressed First Syllable

agent	image	refuge
baggage	larger	region
bandage	largest	rigid
cabbage	legend	roughage
carriage	legion	rummage
college	logic	salvage
cottage	luggage	sausage
courage	magic	savage
damage	manage	scrimmage
digit	margin	sewage
dosage	marriage	shortage
drainage	message	spillage
footage	mileage	storage
forage	mortgage	surgeon
fragile	outage	tragic
garbage	outrage	urgent
genius	package	usage
gentle	pageant	village
gerbil	passage	vintage
German	pigeon	voltage
gesture	pillage	voyage
giant	plumage	wattage
gorgeous	postage	wreckage
gymnast	rampage	

Words with a Stressed Second Syllable

| digest | enlarge | garage |
| engage | enrage | |

228   151921— The Everything Guide to Phonics   © Shell Education

Soft Consonants
Soft G Patterns

Soft G Words

Words with Three or More Syllables

advantage	encourage	original
agency	energy	orphanage
agenda	foliage	oxygen
apologize	general	percentage
apology	generation	religion
average	geologist	sabotage
beverage	geology	strategy
digestion	imagine	surgeon
diligent	intelligent	tragedy
disadvantage	logical	vegetable
discourage	magical	
emergency	margarine	

© Shell Education

Soft Consonants

Soft G Patterns

Soft G Preceded by D: DG

Words with Two Sounds

edge

Words with Three Sounds

badge	hedge	nudge
budge	judge	ridge
dodge	ledge	sedge
fudge	lodge	wedge

Words with Four Sounds

bridge	pledge	smudge
dredge	sledge	trudge
fridge	sludge	
grudge	smidge	

Words with a Stressed First Syllable

badger	fudgy	pudgy
budget	gadget	smidgen
cartridge	knowledge	stodgy
dodgy	partridge	
fidget	porridge	

Words with a Stressed Second Syllable

abridge   misjudge

Words with Three or More Syllables

acknowledge   drudgery   knowledgeable

Soft Consonants
Soft G Patterns

Soft G Preceded by Hard G: GG

Words with a Stressed Second Syllable

suggest

Words with Three or More Syllables

suggestion
suggestive

© Shell Education

Soft Consonants

Soft G Patterns

Soft G Preceded by N: NG

High-Frequency Words

change

Words with Four Sounds

binge	lounge	singe
change	lunge	tinge
hinge	range	

Words with Five Sounds

cringe	grunge	twinge
fringe	plunge	
grange	sponge	

Words with Six Sounds

scrounge	strange

Words with a Stressed First Syllable

angel	engine	plunger
challenge	ginger	stingy
danger	grungy	stranger
dingy	mangy	vengeance
dungeon	orange	

Words with a Stressed Second Syllable

arrange	expunge	syringe
avenge	ingest	
exchange	revenge	

Words with Three or More Syllables

angelic	congestion	engineer
arrangement	dangerous	rearrange
congested	endanger	

Soft Consonants

Soft G Patterns

Rhyming Sets

- cage, gauge, page, rage, sage, stage, wage
- arrange, change, exchange, grange, range, strange
- barge, charge, large
- dredge, edge, hedge, ledge, pledge, sedge, wedge
- converge, diverge, emerge, merge, purge, submerge, urge, verge
- bridge, fridge, ridge, smidge
- binge, cringe, fringe, hinge, singe, syringe, tinge, twinge
- dodge, garage, lodge
- engorge, forge, gorge
- lounge, scrounge
- budge, fudge, grudge, judge, nudge, sludge, smudge, trudge
- expunge, grunge, lunge, plunge, sponge

Soft Consonants
Soft G Patterns

Homophones and Compound Words

Homophones

genes/jeans
gym/Jim
page/Paige

Compound Words

birdcage
dodgeball
drawbridge
stagecoach
stagehand

Silent Letters Table of Contents

Silent Letter: B 236
BT Words 236
MB Words 236

Silent Letter: C 237
SC Words 237

Silent Letter: D 238
DG Words 238
ND Words 238
Another Example 238

Silent Letter: G 239
GN Words 239

Silent Letters: GH 240
GH Words 240

Silent Letter: H 241
GH Words 241
H Words 241
RH Words 241
WH Words 241
More Examples 241

Silent Letter K 242
KN Words 242

Silent Letter: L 243
LD Words 243
LF Words 243
LK Words 243
LM Words 243
LV Words 243

Silent Letter: M 244
MN Words 244

Silent Letter: N 245
MN Words 245

Silent Letter: P 246
PS Words 246
More Examples 246

Silent Letter: S 247
S Words 247

Silent Letter: T 248
ST Words 248
Another Example 248

Silent Letter: U 249
GU_ Words 249
GUE Words 249

Silent Letter: W 250
SW Words 250
TW Words 250
WH Words 250
WR Words 250

Silent Letters

Silent Letter: B

BT Words

debt	indebted
doubt	subtle
doubtful	

MB Words

bomb	numb
bombshell	plumb
climb	plumber
comb	succumb
crumb	thumb
dumb	tomb
lamb	womb
limb	

Silent Letters

Silent Letter: C

SC Words

abscess	muscle
adolescent	obscene
ascend	resuscitate
coalesce	scene
condescend	scenery
convalescent	scenario
crescent	scent
descend	science
descendant	scientist
disciple	scissors
fascinate	scintillating
fluorescent	susceptible

Silent Letters

Silent Letter: D

DG Words

abridge	knowledge
acknowledge	knowledgeable
badge	ledge
badger	lodge
bridge	misjudge
budge	nudge
budget	partridge
cartridge	pledge
dodge	porridge
dodgy	pudgy
dredge	ridge
drudgery	sedge
edge	sledge
fidget	sludge
fridge	smidge
fudge	smidgen
fudgy	smudge
gadget	stodgy
grudge	trudge
hedge	wedge
judge	

ND Words

handkerchief   sandwich

Another Example

Wednesday

238   151921— The Everything Guide to Phonics   © Shell Education

Silent Letters

Silent Letter: G

GN Words

align	gnash
alignment	gnat
assign	gnaw
assignment	gnome
benign	gnu
campaign	malign
champagne	paradigm
cologne	phlegm
consignment	reign
design	resign
designer	sign
feign	sovereign
foreign	
gnarled	

Silent Letters: GH

GH Words

alright	freight	slaughter
although	fright	sleigh
blight	height	sleight
borough	high	slight
bough	knight	sought
bought	light	taught
bright	might	thigh
brought	<u>naught</u>	thorough
caught	naughty	though
daughter	neigh	thought
delight	neighbor	through
dough	neighborhood	tight
eight	nigh	tights
eighteen	night	tonight
eighty	ought	weigh
fight	plight	weight
flight	right	
fought	sigh	
fraught	sight	

Silent Letter: H

GH Words

ghastly   ghost
ghetto   ghoul

H Words

heir   honest
herb   honor
herbal   honorable
herbivore   hour

RH Words

rhinoceros   rhyme
rhombus   rhythm

WH Words

whack   whey   whisk
whale   which   whisker
wharf   whiff   whisper
what   while   whistle
wheat   whim   white
wheedle whimper   whittle
wheel   whine   whiz
wheeze   whinny   whopper
when   whip   why
where   whir
whet   whirl

More Examples

exhaust   shepherd   vehicle
khaki   Thailand

Silent Letters

Silent Letter: K

KN Words

knack	knickers	knot
knave	knife	know
knead	knight	known
knee	knit	knowledge
kneel	knob	knuckle
knelt	knock	
knew	knoll	

Silent Letter: L

LD Words

could	should	would

LF Words

behalf	calf	half

LK Words

balk	stalk	yolk
chalk	talk	
folk	walk	

LM Words

balm	palm	salmon
calm	psalm	

LV Words

halves
salve

© Shell Education

Silent Letters

Silent Letter: M

MN Words

mnemonic

Silent Letters

Silent Letter: N

MN Words

autumn   condemn   solemn
column   hymn

© Shell Education

Silent Letters

Silent Letter: P

PS Words

psalm	psychiatric	psychologist
pseudonym	psychiatrist	psychology
psyche	psychic	

More Examples

cupboard	raspberry
pneumonia	receipt

Silent Letter: S

S Words

aisle island
debris isle

Silent Letters

Silent Letter: T

ST Words

apostle	hasten	rustle
bristle	hustle	soften
bustle	listen	thistle
castle	mistletoe	whistle
fasten	moisten	wrestle
glisten	nestle	

Another Example

often

Silent Letters

Silent Letter: U

GU_ Words

disguise	guest	guilty
guard	guidance	guitar
guardian	guide	guy
guess	guidelines	vanguard

GUE Words

colleague	league	vague
dialogue	monologue	vogue
epilogue	plague	
fatigue	prologue	
intrigue	synagogue	

© Shell Education

151921—The Everything Guide to Phonics

Silent Letter: W

SW Words

answer   sword

TW Words

two

WH Words

who   whom
whole   whose
wholesome

WR Words

wrangle   wriggle
wrap   wring
wrapper   wrinkle
wrath   wrist
wreath   write
wreck   writer
wreckage   wrong
wren   wrote
wrench   wrung
wrestle   wry
wretched

Contractions Table of Contents

Contractions 252
  High-Frequency Words 252
  Are Words 252
  Has Words 252
  Have Words 252
  He Words 252
  I Words 252
  Is Words 252
  Not Words 252
  She Words 252
  They Words 252
  Us Words 252
  Will Words 252
  Would Words 252
  You Words 252
  Homophones 253

Contractions

High-Frequency Words

don't	it's

Are Words

they're	we're	you're

Has Words

anyone's	it's	someone's
he's	one's	she's

Have Words

could've	they've	you've
I've	we've	
should've	would've	

He Words

he'd	he'll	he's

I Words

I'd	I'm
I'll	I've

Is Words

anyone's	one's	what's
he's	someone's	when's
here's	she's	where's
how's	that's	who's
it's	there's	why's

Not Words

aren't	don't	shouldn't
can't	hadn't	wasn't
couldn't	hasn't	weren't
didn't	haven't	won't
doesn't	isn't	wouldn't

She Words

she'd	she'll	she's

They Words

they'd	they're
they'll	they've

Us Word

let's

Will Words

he'll	she'll	we'll
I'll	that'll	you'll
it'll	they'll	

Would Words

he'd	she'd	we'd
I'd	they'd	you'd

You Words

you'd	you're
you'll	you've

Contractions

Homophones

aisle/I'll
all/I'll
he'd/heed
heel/he'll
he'll/hill
it's/its
their/there/they're
we'd/weed
we're/were
we've/weave
who's/whose
yore/you're
you're/your

The Everything Guide to Phonics

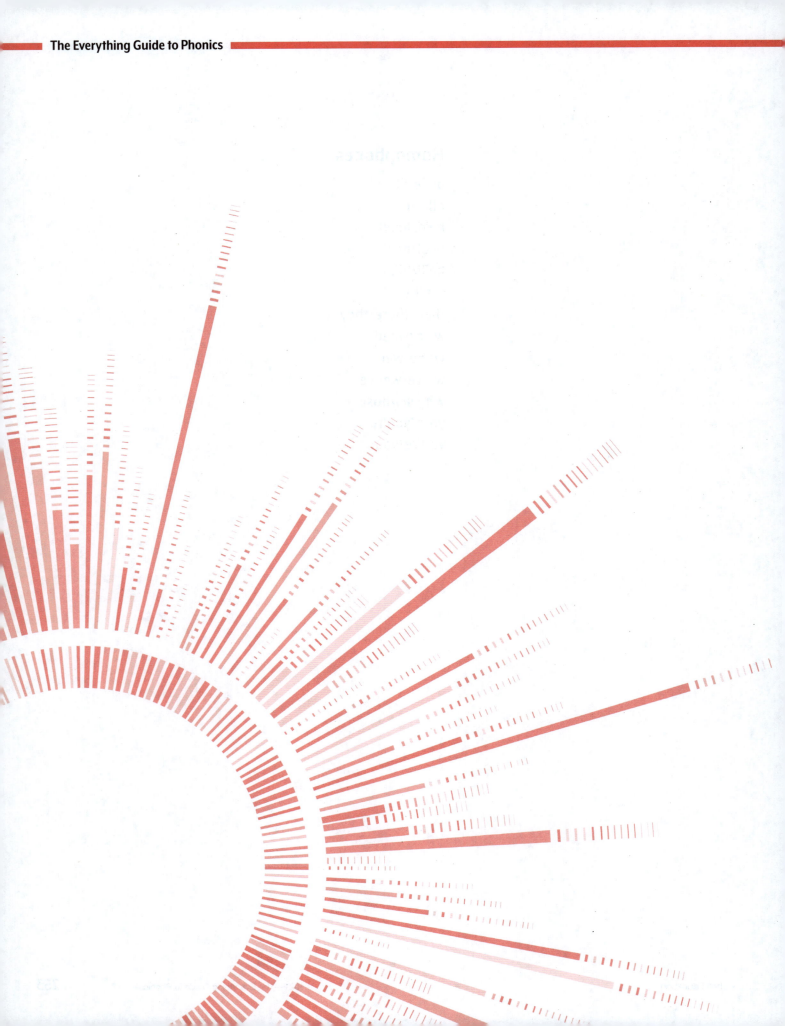

Prefixes Table of Contents

Common Prefixes 257

Anti (against) 257
Bi (two) 257
Inter (between, among) 257
Mis (wrong) 257
Multi (many) 257
Non (not) 257
Over (above) 258
Over (too much) 258
Post (after) 258
Pre (before) 258
Re (again) 258
Re (back) 259
Super (over, beyond) 259
Tele (far away) 259
Trans (across) 259
Tri (three) 259
Un (do the opposite) 260
Un (not) 260
Under (below) 260
Under (not enough) 260
Uni (one) 260

Common Assimilated Prefixes 261

Ad Words (to, toward) 261
A Words 261
Ac Words 261
Ad Words 261
Af Words 261
Ag Words 261
Al Words 261
An Words 261
Ap Words 261
Ar Words 261
As Words 261
At Words 261

Common Assimilated Prefixes *(cont.)*

Com Words (with, together) 262
Co Words 262
Col Words 262
Com Words 262
Con Words 262
Cor Words 262

Dis Words (not, do opposite) 263
Dif Words 263
Dis Words 263

Dis Words (away, apart) 264
Di Words 264
Dif Words 264
Dis words 264

Ex Words (out) 265
E Words 265
Ec Words 265
Ef Words 265
Es Words 265
Ex Words 265

In Words (in) 266
Il Words 266
Im Words 266
In Words 266
Intro Words 266
Ir Words 266

In Words (not) 267
Il Words 267
Im Words 267
In Words 267
Ir Words 267

Prefixes Table of Contents (cont.)

Common Assimilated Prefixes (cont.)

Sub Words (under, below, near) 268
Sub Words 268
Suc Words 268
Suf Words 268
Sug Words 268
Sum Words 268
Sup Words 268
Sur Words 268
Sus Words 268

Advanced Prefixes .269

A Words (not) 269
Auto Words (self) .269
Bene, Beni Words (good) 269
Circum Words (around) 269
De Words (away from, down, off) 269
De Words (completely) 269
De Words (reverse, undo) 269
Epi Words (upon, above) 269
Extra Words (outside, beyond) 269
Fore Words (before) 269
Hypo Words (not enough) 269
Hypo Words (under) 270
Intra Words (within) 270
Mal Words (bad) 270
Mon, Mono Words (one) 270
Oct Words (eight) .270
Para Words (beside, near) 270
Pent Words (five) .270
Per Words
    (through, thoroughly, completely) 270
Peri Words (around, near) 270
Poly Words (many) 270
Pro Words (forward) 271

Advanced Prefixes (cont.)

Pro Words (in advance, in front) 271
Quad Words (four) 271
Semi Words (half) 271
Sur Words (above, beyond) 271

Advanced Assimilated Prefixes 272

Ab Words (off, away from) 272
A Words 272
Ab Words 272

En Words (in, into, cause to be) 273
Em Words 273
En Words 273

Ob Words (against, in the way, toward) 274
Ob Words 274
Oc Words 274
Of Words 274
Op Words 274

Syn Words (with, together) 275
Syl Words 275
Sym Words 275
Syn Words 275
Sys Words 275

Common Prefixes

Anti (against)

antibiotic	antipathy
antibodies	antiseptic
anticlimactic	antithesis
antidepressant	antitoxin
antidote	antitrust
antifreeze	antiwar
antihistamine	

Bi (two)

biannual	binary
bicentennial	binoculars
biceps	bipartisan
bicycle	biped
biennial	biplane
bifocals	bipolar
bilateral	bisect
bilingual	bivalve
bimonthly	biweekly

Inter (between, among)

interact	intermediate
interaction	intermission
intercede	intermittent
intercept	international
intercession	internet
interchange	interpret
interchangeable	interrupt
intercollegiate	intersect
intercom	intersection
interface	interstate
interfere	intervene
interference	interview
interject	introduce
interjection	introvert
interlude	
intermediary	

Mis (wrong)

misbehave	mislead
misconduct	mismanage
miscount	mismatched
misdeal	misplace
misdeed	misprint
misfire	misread
misfit	misspell
misgivings	mistake
misguided	mistreat
mishandle	mistrust
misinform	misunderstand
misjudge	misuse
mislabel	

Multi (many)

multicolored	multinational
multicultural	multiple
multidimensional	multiplex
multifaceted	multiplication
multifamily	multiply
multigrain	multipurpose
multilateral	multitask
multilayered	multitude
multimedia	multivitamin
multimillionaire	

Non (not)

nondairy	nonsense
nonfat	nonslip
nonfiction	nonstick
nonperishable	nonstop
nonprofit	nonviolent
nonrefundable	

Prefixes

Common Prefixes

Common Prefixes

Over (above)

overarching	overlap
overbite	overpass
overcoat	overrule
overhand	oversee
overhang	overtone
overhead	overview
overjoyed	

Over (too much)

overachiever	overkill
overblown	overlook
overcharge	overpaid
overcook	overprotective
overdo	overreact
overdose	overrule
overdraft	oversleep
overdressed	overstate
overdrive	overstep
overdue	overstock
overeat	overtime
overestimate	overtired
overfill	overuse
overflow	overweight
overgrown	overwhelm
overheat	overwork
overindulge	

Post (after)

posterior	postpartum
posterity	postpone
postgame	postscript
posthumous	postseason
postoperative	posttest

Pre (before)

precaution	pregame	prescribe
precede	preheat	preseason
precedent	prehistoric	preserve
precise	prejudge	preset
precook	prelude	preshrunk
precut	premature	presoak
predate	premolars	preteach
predawn	prenatal	preteen
predict	prepackaged	pretest
preexisting	prepare	prevent
prefer	prepay	preview
prefix	preschool	prewashed

Re (again)

readjust	refinish	rerun
reassure	refocus	resend
rebuild	reform	reshape
recharge	refresh	reside
reconcile	refuel	residence
reconsider	regain	retake
reconstruct	reheat	retell
recopy	relearn	retrain
recount	relocate	reuse
recur	remodel	review
recycle	renew	rewrite
reelect	reorder	
reenact	repeat	
reenter	rephrase	
reexamine	replay	
refill	reprint	

Common Prefixes

Re (back)

react
rebound
recall
recapture
recede
receive
recent
recite
reclaim
record
redirect
reduce
refuse
regress
reject
rejoice
relax
release
relieve
rely
remind
remit
repair
repay
repel
repellent
reply
report
require
research
reserve
resolve
resource
respond
restore
result
retrace
return
reverse
revoke
rewind

Super (over, beyond)

superficial
superimpose
superintendent
superior
Superman
supermarket
supermodel
supernatural
superpower
supersede
supersensitive
supersonic
superstition
supervise
supervision
supervisor

Tele (far away)

telecast
telecommunications
telecommute
teleconference
telegram
telegraph
telemarketer
telepathic
telepathy
telephone
telephoto
teleport
telescope
telethon
televise
television

Trans (across)

transaction
transatlantic
transcend
transcontinental
transcribe
transcript
transfer
transform
transfusion
transgender
transgress
transgression
transit
transition
translate
translator
translucent
transmit
transparent
transpire
transplant
transport
transportation
transpose

Tri (three)

triad
triangle
triathlon
triceps
triceratops
tricolor
tricycle
trident
triennial
trillion
trilogy
trimester
trinity
trio
triple
triplets
triplicate
tripod
trivet

Prefixes

Common Prefixes

Common Prefixes

Un (do the opposite)

unbuckle	unpack
unbutton	unplug
uncover	unscramble
undo	untangle
undress	untie
unhook	unwrap
unleash	unzip
unlock	

Un (not)

unable	unheated
unafraid	unhelpful
unappreciative	unkind
unarmed	unlike
unattached	unlucky
unaware	unopened
unbroken	unpaid
uncertain	unplanned
unclean	unreal
unclear	unripe
uncommon	unselfish
uncooked	unstable
unequal	unsteady
uneven	unusual
unfair	
unfortunate	
unhappy	

Under (below)

undercover	undershirt
undercurrent	understand
underfoot	understated
undergo	undertone
underground	undertow
underneath	underwater
underpants	underwear
underpass	

Under (not enough)

undercook	underpaid
underestimate	understate
underfed	underweight
underfunded	underwhelm

Uni (one)

reunion	unique
reunite	unison
unanimous	unit
unicorn	unite
unicycle	unity
uniform	universal
unify	universe
unilateral	university
union	

Prefixes
Common Assimilated Prefixes

Ad Words (to, toward)

A Words
abate   achieve

Ac Words
accelerate   acclaim   accumulate
accent   accommodate   accurate
accept   accomplish   accuse
access   accord   acquiesce
accessory   account   acquire
accident   accrue   acquisition

Ad Words
addend   adjacent   advance
addict   adjective   adventure
address   adjoining   adverse
adhere   admire   advertise
adhesive   admit   advice

Af Words
affable   affiliation   affliction
affair   affinity   affluent
affect   affirm
affection   affix

Ag Words
aggravate   aggressive   agree

Al Words
allege   allow   allusion
alleviate   allude   ally
alliance   allure

An Words
annex   annotate   annul
annihilate   announce

Ap Words
apparatus   applause   apprehend
appeal   application   apprentice
appear   apply   approach
appetite   appoint   appropriate
applaud   appreciate   approve

Ar Words
arraign   arrest   arrogant
arrange   arrive

As Words
aspire   assess   assist
assault   asset   associate
assemble   assiduous   assorted
assent   assign   assume
assert   assimilate   assure

At Words
attach   attempt   attract
attain   attend

© Shell Education   151921—The Everything Guide to Phonics

Prefixes

Common Assimilated Prefixes

Com Words (with, together)

Co Words

coed	coincide	coordinate
coeducational	coincidence	
coexist	cooperate	

Col Words

collaborate	colleague	collision
collapse	collect	collude
collate	collection	
collateral	collide	

Com Words

combine	compass	compound
command	compensate	comprehend
commit	compete	compress
communicate	complete	compulsive
community	complicate	compute
compact	complication	computer
companion	comply	
compare	compose	

Con Words

concentrate	connotation	contact
concern	conquer	contain
conclude	consent	container
conclusion	conserve	context
conduct	consider	contract
confer	consolidate	contrast
conform	conspire	control
confuse	constant	convert
confusion	constrain	convince
congress	construct	
connect	consult	

Cor Words

correct	correspond
correlate	corrupt

Prefixes

Common Assimilated Prefixes

Dis Words (not, do opposite)

Dif Words

difficult

Dis Words

disability	discomfort	dismantle
disable	discontent	disobey
disadvantage	disdain	disorder
disagree	disease	displaced
disappear	disfigure	disprove
disappoint	disgrace	disregard
disapprove	disguise	disrespect
disarm	disgust	dissatisfied
disbelief	dishonest	dissident
discharge	disinfect	dissolve
disclose	dislike	distaste
discolor	disloyal	distrust

Prefixes

Common Assimilated Prefixes

Dis Words (away, apart)

Di Words

digest	diverge	divide
digress	diverse	divorce
direct	divert	

Dif Words

differ	different
difference	diffuse

Dis Words

discard	dispute	distant
disclaim	disrupt	distract
disclaimer	dissect	
dispel	dissection	

Prefixes

Common Assimilated Prefixes

Ex Words (out)

E Words

egress	emancipate	evade
eject	emerge	evict
elope	emigrate	
elude	eminent	

Ec Words

eccentric	eclectic

Ef Words

efface	effervesce	effort
effect	efficient	effusive

Es Words

escape	essay

Ex Words

excavate	exempt	export
exceed	exhale	expose
excerpt	exhaust	express
exchange	exile	exquisite
excite	exit	extend
exclaim	expand	exterior
exclamation	expel	external
exclude	expire	extinct
excrete	explain	extract
excursion	explode	extradite
excuse	explore	extreme

© Shell Education

151921—The Everything Guide to Phonics

265

Prefixes

Common Assimilated Prefixes

In Words (in)

Il Words

illuminate	illustrate
illusion	illustrious

Im Words

immerse	impede	import
immigrate	impel	important
impact	impetus	impostor
impair	implode	

In Words

inboard	influx	inset
incite	infuse	inside
include	ingrown	insidious
income	inhabit	insight
increase	inhale	inspect
incubate	inject	inspire
incumbent	inlaid	instant
incur	inland	instinct
indent	inmate	insult
indoor	innate	intake
induce	inner	internal
industry	input	interior
infield	inquire	intimate
inflammation	inseam	invite
inflate	insert	

Intro Words

introduce	introspective
introduction	introvert

Ir Words

irrigate

266   151921— The Everything Guide to Phonics   © Shell Education

Prefixes

Common Assimilated Prefixes

In Words (not)

Il Words

illegal	illegitimate	illiterate
illegible	illicit	illogical

Im Words

immaculate	imminent	immortal
immaterial	immobile	immune
immature	immobilize	immunize
immeasurable	immoderate	impolite
immediate	immodest	impose
immense	immoral	impossible

In Words

inaccurate	indirect	injustice
inactive	inedible	innumerable
inappropriate	ineffective	inoperable
inaudible	inefficient	insane
incomplete	inept	insecure
inconsiderate	inexpensive	insincere
incorrect	infallible	intact
indecent	inflexible	invisible
indelible	informal	invalid
independent	inhumane	

Ir Words

irrational	irrelevant	irresponsible
irreconcilable	irreparable	irreversible
irrefutable	irreplaceable	
irregular	irresistible	

© Shell Education

Prefixes

Common Assimilated Prefixes

Sub Words (under, below)

Sub Words

subcommittee	submerge	subsoil
subdivision	submission	substitute
subgroup	submit	subtitle
subheading	subsequent	subtotal
subject	subset	subtract
sublet	subside	subway
submarine	subsist	

Suc Words

succeed	succinct
success	succumb

Suf Words

suffer	suffix
suffice	suffocate
sufficient	suffuse

Sug Words

suggest

Sum Words

summon

Sup Words

supplant	supply	suppose
supplement	support	suppress

Sur Words

surreptitious	surrogate

Sus Words

suspend

Advanced Prefixes

Prefixes
Advanced Prefixes

A Words (not)

asexual   asymmetrical   atypical

Auto Words (self)

autobiographical	automobile
autobiography	automotive
autocrat	autonomous
autograph	autonomy
autoimmune	autopilot
automated	autopsy
automatic	

Bene, Beni Words (good)

benediction	beneficiary
benefactor	benefit
benefactress	benevolence
beneficence	benevolent
beneficial	benign

Circum Words (around)

circumambulate	circumpolar
circumference	circumspect
circumlocution	circumstances
circumnavigate	circumvent

De Words (away from, down, off)

debit	degrading	derail
decadent	delay	descend
decay	delete	descent
deceive	delude	destitute
decline	denounce	destroy
decrease	depart	detain
defend	deploy	detract
defer	deport	deviate
deficient	deprecate	devolve
deficit	depreciate	

De Words (completely)

debate	define	deprive
debunk	demonstrate	devoid

De Words (reverse, undo)

debilitate	deflate	deplete
decaffeinated	deforestation	deregulate
declutter	defrost	desegregate
decode	defuse	destabilize
decompose	dehydrated	detach
decongestant	demerits	dethrone
deconstruct	deodorant	detoxify
deescalate	deodorize	

Epi Words (upon, above)

epicenter	epidermis	epithet
epidemic	epigraph	

Extra Words (outside, beyond)

extracurricular	extraordinary	extravagant
extramarital	extrapolate	
extraneous	extraterrestrial	

Fore Words (before)

forearm	forehead	foresight
forecast	foreleg	foretell
foreclose	foreman	forethought
forefather	foremost	forewarn
forefront	forerunner	foreword
foreground	foresee	
forehand	foreshadow	

Hypo Words (not enough)

hypochondriac	hypoglycemic
hypocrisy	hypothermia
hypocrite	

© Shell Education   151921—The Everything Guide to Phonics   **269**

Prefixes
Advanced Prefixes

Advanced Prefixes

Hypo Words (under)

hypodermic	hypothesis
hypotenuse	hypothetical
hypothalamus	

Intra Words (within)

intramural	intrastate
intramuscular	intravenous

Mal Words (bad)

maladapted	malformation
maladjusted	malformed
maladjustment	malfunction
malady	malice
malaria	malign
malcontent	malignant
malediction	malinger
malefactor	malnourished
malevolence	malnutrition
malevolent	malodorous
malfeasance	malpractice

Mon, Mono Words (one)

monarchy	monopoly
monastery	monorail
monochromatic	monotone
monogamy	monotonous
monolith	monotony
monologue	

Oct Words (eight)

octagon	octogenarian
octave	octopus
octet	
October	

Para Words (beside, near)

parachute	paramedic
paraeducator	paraphrase
paragraph	paraprofessional
paralegal	parasite
parallel	

Pent Words (five)

pentagon	pentathlon
pentameter	pentatonic

Per Words (through, thoroughly, completely)

impermeable	permit
impervious	perpetual
percussion	persecute
perennial	persevere
perfect	perspective
perfection	perspiration
perforate	perspire
perform	persuade
perfume	pertain
perish	pervade
perjury	pervasive
permeate	

Peri Words (around, near)

pericardium	peripatetic
perimeter	peripheral
period	periphery
periodontal	periscope

Poly Words (many)

polychromatic	polygraph
polydactyl	polynomial
polygamy	polyp
polygon	polysyllabic

Advanced Prefixes

Pro Words (forward)

proceed
proclaim
procrastinate
produce
product
profess
proficient
profuse
program
progress
project
projector
promise
promote
pronounce
propel
propeller
propose
prosecute
prospect
protract
proverb
provoke

Pro Words (in advance, in front)

prodigy
prohibit
prophesy
prophet
proponent
protect
provide

Quad Words (four)

quadrangle
quadrant
quadriceps
quadrilateral
quadriplegic
quadruped
quadruple
quadruplets

Semi Words (half)

semiannual
semiaquatic
semiautomatic
semicircle
semicolon
semiconscious
semifinal
semiformal
semiprecious
semiprivate
semisolid
semitropical

Sur Words (above, beyond)

surcharge
surface
surpass
surplus
surprise
surreal
surrender
surround
survive

© Shell Education

151921—The Everything Guide to Phonics

271

Prefixes

Advanced Assimilated Prefixes

Ab Words (off, away from)

A Words

averse   avert

Ab Words

absent   absorb

absolute   abstain

absolve   abstract

Prefixes

Advanced Assimilated Prefixes

En Words (in, into, cause to be)

Em Words

embarrass   employ
embroil   empower

En Words

enable   enlarge
enact   enlist
encamp   enrage
encase   enrich
encircle   enroll
enclose   enslave
encode   ensnare
encourage   enter
encrusted   entice
endangered   entomb
endearing   entrails
enforce   entrust
engine   envoy
engulf   envy
enjoy

© Shell Education

151921—The Everything Guide to Phonics

273

Prefixes

Advanced Assimilated Prefixes

Ob Words (against, in the way, toward)

Ob Words

obey	obsess	obstruct
obligation	obsolete	obvious
oblivious	obstacle	

Oc Words

occasion	occupy
occlude	occur
occupation	

Of Words

offend	offensive	offer

Op Words

opponent	oppose	oppress
opportune	opposite	oppressive
opportunity	opposition	

Prefixes

Advanced Assimilated Prefixes

Syn Words (with, together)

Syl Words

multisyllabic   syllable

Sym Words

symbol   sympathy   symptom
symmetry   symphony

Syn Words

sync   synopsis   synthetic
synchronize   syntax
syndrome   synthesize

Sys Words

system   systematic   systemic

© Shell Education

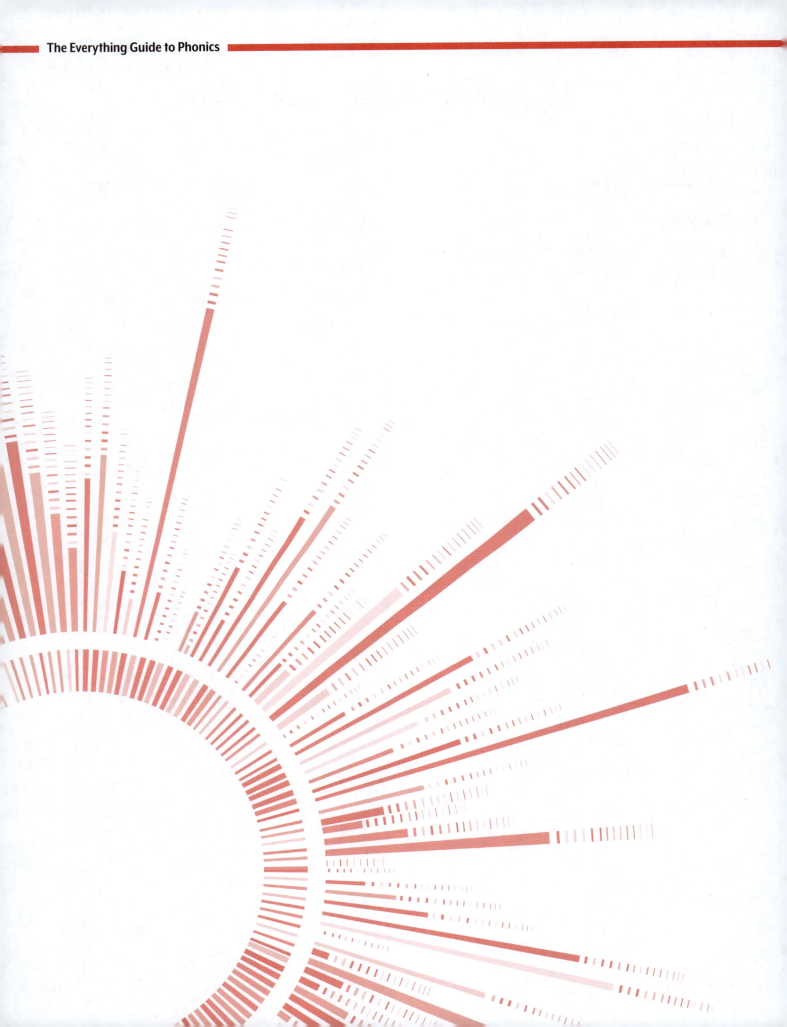

The Everything Guide to Phonics

Roots Table of Contents

Am Words (love, friendship) 281
Ann Words (year) 281
Aqu Words (water) 281
Arch Words (chief, most important) 281
Ast Words (star) 281
Astro Words (star) 281
Aud Words (hear) 281
Bi, Bio Words (life) 281
Cand Words (shine) 281
Cap Words (head) 281
Cap Words (take in, grasp) 281
Card Words (heart) 281
Cease Words (go, yield) 282
Cede Words (go, yield) 282
Ceed Words (go, yield) 282
Ceive Words (take in, grasp) 282
Cent Words (hundred) 282
Cept Words (take in, grasp) 282
Cess Words (go, yield) 282
Chron Words (time) 282
Cide Words (cut off, kill) 282
Cide Words (happen, fall) 282
Cip Words (head) 283
Cip Words (take in, grasp) 283
Circ Words (ring) 283
Cis Words (cut off, kill) 283
Claim Words (cry out, shout) 283
Clam Words (cry out, shout) 283
Clos Words (shut, close) 283
Clud Words (shut, close) 283
Clus Words (shut, close) 283
Cogn Words (know) 283
Cor, Cord Words (heart) 283
Corp Words (body) 283
Cors Words (body) 283
Cosm Words (world) 283
Cour Words (heart) 284

Cour Words (run) 284
Cracy Words (power, strength) 284
Crat Words (power, strength) 284
Cred Words (believe) 284
Crim Words (separate, set apart, choose) 284
Cris Words (separate, set apart, choose) 284
Crit Words (separate, set apart, choose) 284
Cur Words (run) 284
Cuss Words (strike, shake) 284
Cycl Words (circle) 284
Dec Words (ten) 284
Deci Words (a tenth) 284
Dem Words (people) 284
Derm Words (skin) 284
Dent, Dont Words (tooth) 285
Dict Words (say, proclaim) 285
Doc Words (teach) 285
Duc Words (lead, bring) 285
Duce Words (lead, bring) 285
Duct Words (lead, bring) 285
Enn Words (year) 285
Equa Words (equal) 285
Equi Words (equal) 285
Esce Words (become) 285
Fac Words (make, do) 285
Fect Words (make, do) 286
Fen Words (strike, hit, push) 286
Fer Words (bring, carry) 286
Fic Words (make, do) 286
Fid Words (belief, faith, trust) 286
Fin Words (end) 286
Firm Words (strong, steady) 286
Flect Words (bend, curve) 286
Flex Words (bend, curve) 286
Flict Words (strike) 286
Flu Words (flow) 287
Forc Words (strong) 287

© Shell Education

151921—The Everything Guide to Phonics

277

Roots Table of Contents (cont.)

Form Words (having a form/shape) 287
Fort Words (strong) .287
Frac Words (break) .287
Frag Words (break) .287
Fus Words (pour) 287
Gen Words (birth, creation) 287
Geo Words (ground, land, earth) 287
Gest Words (bear, carry) 287
Gin Words (birth, creation) 287
Gno Words (know) .288
Grac Words (pleasing, thankful) 288
Grad Words (step, walk) 288
Gram Words (write) .288
Graph Words (write) 288
Grat Words (pleasing, thankful) 288
Gress Words (step, walk) 289
Hab Words (hold, possess, live in) 289
Hal Words (breathe) 289
Hib Words (hold, possess, live in) 289
Homo Words (same) 289
Hos Words (host, guest) 289
Hydr Words (water) .289
Ject Words (throw) .289
Jud Words (lawful, right) 289
Junct Words (join) .289
Just Words (lawful, right) 289
Lang, Ling Words (language) 289
Lect Words (gather, select) 290
Leg Words (gather, select) 290
Leg Words (law) 290
Li Words (tie, bind) .290
Lig Words (gather, select) 290
Lig Words (tie, bind) 290
Lit Words (letter) 290
Loc Words (place) .290
Loc Words (speak) .290
Log Words (word) 290

Logue Words (word) 290
Logy Words (science/study of something) 290
Logy Words (word) .290
Loqu Words (speak) 291
Luc Words (light, bright, of the moon) 291
Lud Words (play, fool) 291
Lum Words (light, bright, of the moon) 291
Lun Words (light, bright, of the moon) 291
Lus Words (light, bright, of the moon) 291
Lus Words (play, fool) 291
Ly Words (tie, bind) 291
Magn Words (great) 291
Man Words (hand) 291
Mar Words (sea) 291
Mater Words (mother) 291
Matri Words (mother) 291
Med Words (take appropriate measures) 291
Medi Words (middle) 291
Mega Words (great) 291
Mem Words (remember) 292
Men Words (think about) 292
Meter Words (measure) 292
Metric Words (measure) 292
Micro Words (small) 292
Min Words (make smaller) 292
Miss Words (send) .292
Mit Words (send) 292
Mne Words (think about, forget, remember) 292
Mob Words (move) .292
Mod Words (take appropriate measures) 293
Mom Words (move) .293
Mon Words (advise, remind, reveal, warn) 293
Mor Words (harm, death) 293
Morph Words (having a form/shape) 293
Mot Words (move) .293
Mov Words (move) .293
Mur Words (harm, death) 293

Roots Table of Contents (cont.)

Nat Words (birth, creation) 293

Ne Words (not, nothing) .293

Nil Words (not, nothing) .293

Nom Words (name) 294

Nov Words (new) 294

Nul Words (not, nothing) 294

Ny Words (not, nothing) .294

Onym Words (name) 294

Ortho Words (straight, correct) 294

Pan Words (all) 294

Par Words (equal) 294

Par, Pair Words (produce, make ready) 294

Pare Words (produce, make ready) 294

Part Words (separate, divide, allot) 294

Pass Words (feeling, suffering) 294

Pater Words (father) 294

Path Words (feeling, suffering) 295

Patr Words (father) 295

Ped Words (child) 295

Ped Words (foot) 295

Pel Words (push, drive, strike) 295

Pend Words (hang, stretch) 295

Pens Words (hang, stretch) 295

Phon Words (sound) 295

Photo Words (light) 295

Phys Words (nature) 295

Ple Words (fill up, make complete) 295

Plic Words (fold, lay, bend) 296

Ply Words (fill up, make complete) 296

Ply Words (fold, lay, bend) 296

Pod Words (foot) 296

Pol Words (city) 296

Pon Words (put, place) 296

Pop Words (people) 296

Port Words (carry) 296

Port Words (separate, divide, allot) 296

Pos Words (put, place) 296

Press Words (press, hold fast, cover) 297

Prim Words (earliest form, first) 297

Prin Words (earliest form, first) 297

Priv Words (separate, not shared) 297

Prop Words (one's own) .297

Proto Words (earliest form, first) 297

Psych Words (soul, spirit) 297

Pub Words (people) 297

Puls Words (push, drive, strike) 297

Punc, Punct Words (prick, have a point) 297

Quer, Ques Words (ask, seek) 297

Qui Words (rest, be quiet) 297

Quir Words (ask, seek) 297

Quis Words (ask, seek) 298

Rad Words (ray, spoke of a wheel) 298

Rect Words (guide, keep straight) 298

Reg Words (guide, keep straight) 298

Rod Words (gnaw) 298

Ros Words (gnaw) 298

Rupt Words (break) 298

Sacr Words (blessed, sacred) 298

Sad Words (sit) 298

Sanct Words (blessed, sacred) 298

Scen Words (climb) 298

Sci Words (having knowledge) 298

Scope Words (observe) 298

Scrib Words (write) 298

Script Words (write) 299

Sec Words (follow) 299

Sect Words (cut) 299

Sed Words (sit) 299

Seg Words (cut) 299

Sen Words (old) 299

Sens Words (feel) 299

Sent Words (feel) 299

Sequ Words (follow) 299

Ser Words (attach, join, line up) 299

© Shell Education   151921—The Everything Guide to Phonics   **279**

Roots Table of Contents *(cont.)*

Serv Words (keep safe, protect) 299
Serv Words (serve, be a slave) 299
Sess Words (sit) 300
Sid Words (sit) 300
Sign Words (sign, mark, indication) 300
Sist Words (stand, make firm) 300
Soc Words (follow) 300
Sol Words (alone) 300
Solu Words (loosen, untie) 300
Solv Words (loosen, untie) 300
Son Words (sound) 300
Soph Words (clever, wise) 300
Spec Words (observe) 301
Sphere Words (ball) 301
Spic Words (observe) 301
Spir Words (breathe) 301
Spite Words (observe) 301
Spon Words (pledge, promise) 301
Sta Words (stand, make firm) 301
Stell Words (star) 301
Sti Words (stand, make firm) 302
Strain Words (tie, bind, draw tight) 302
Strict Words (tie, bind, draw tight) 302
String Words (tie, bind, draw tight) 302
Stru Words (build) 302
Tact Words (touch, handle) 302
Tag Words (touch, handle) 302
Tain Words (hold) 302
Tain Words (touch, handle) 302
Tang Words (touch, handle) 302
Tech Words (skill, art) 303
Tect Words (cover, shield) 303
Teg Words (touch, handle) 303
Temp Words (time) .303
Ten Words (hold) 303
Ten Words (stretch) .303
Term Words (an end, boundary) 303

Terr Words (ground, land, earth) 303
Therm Words (heat) .304
Tig, Ting Words (near, touch) 304
Tin Words (hold) 304
Tort Words (twist) 304
Tract Words (pull) 304
Trib Words (allot, pay) 304
Vac Words (empty) 304
Vail Words (strong, worthy) 304
Val Words (strong, worthy) 304
Ven Words (come) 304
Ver Words (true) 305
Vers Words (turn) 305
Vert Words (turn) 305
Vi Words (road, way) 305
Via Words (road, way) 305
Vict Words (conquer) 305
Vid Words (see) 305
Vinc Words (conquer) 305
Vis Words (see) 305
Vit Words (life) 305
Viv Words (life) 305
Voc Words (call) 306
Void Words (empty) .306
Vok Words (call) 306
Vol Words (wish or be willing) 306
Volu Words (roll, turn around) 306
Volv Words (roll, turn around) 306
Vor Words (devour) .306
Voy Words (road, way) 306

Roots

Am Words (love, friendship)

amateur	amicable	amorous
amiable	amity	enamored

Ann Words (year)

annals	annual	annuity
anniversary	annually	semiannual

Aqu Words (water)

aquamarine	aquatic
aquarium	aqueduct

Arch Words (chief, most important)

anarchy	architect	monarch
archangel	architectural	monarchy
archbishop	architecture	oligarchy
archduke	archive	patriarch
archetype	hierarchy	
archipelago	matriarch	

Ast Words (star)

aster	asteroid
asterisk	disaster

Astro Words (star)

astrology	astronomer	astronomy
astronaut	astronomical	astrophysics

Aud Words (hear)

audible	audit	inaudible
audience	audition	
audio	auditorium	
audiologist	auditory	
audiology	audiovisual	

Bi, Bio Words (life)

aerobic	biography
amphibian	biology
amphibious	biome
antibiotic	bionic
autobiographical	biopsy
autobiography	symbiosis
biochemistry	symbiotic
biodegradable	

Cand Words (shine)

candelabra	candle
candescent	candor
candid	incandescent
candidate	

Cap Words (head)

cape	captain
capital	decapitate
capitalize	per capita
capitol	recapitulate
capitulate	

Cap Words (take in, grasp)

capability	captor
capable	capture
capacity	incapable
caption	incapacitate
captivate	incapacitated
captive	recapture
captivity	

Card Words (heart)

cardiac	cardiology
cardiologist	pericardium

Roots

Cease Words (go, yield)

cease	deceased
ceaseless	surcease

Cede Words (go, yield)

accede	precede
antecedent	precedent
cede	recede
concede	secede
intercede	unprecedented

Ceed Words (go, yield)

exceed	succeed
proceed	

Ceive Words (take in, grasp)

conceive	perceive
deceive	preconceived
misconceive	receive
misperceive	

Cent Words (hundred)

bicentennial	centipede
cent	century
centenarian	percent
centennial	percentage
centigrade	percentile
centimeter	

Cept Words (take in, grasp)

accept	exception	perceptive
acceptable	exceptional	receptacle
acceptance	imperceptible	reception
concept	intercept	receptionist
conception	interception	receptive
deception	misconception	susceptibility
deceptive	misperception	susceptible
except	perception	unacceptable

Cess Words (go, yield)

abscess	excessive	recess
access	incessant	recession
accessible	intercession	secession
accessory	necessary	success
ancestor	predecessor	successful
concession	process	successor
excess	procession	

Chron Words (time)

anachronism	chronicle	chronology
chronic	chronological	synchronize

Cide Words (cut off, kill)

decide	homicidal	suicidal
fungicide	homicide	suicide
genocide	insecticide	
herbicide	pesticide	

Cide Words (happen, fall)

accident	coincidence	incident
accidental	coincidental	
coincide	incidence	

Roots

Cip Words (head)

precipice precipitation

Cip Words (take in, grasp)

anticipate   participate   principle
emancipate   participation recipe
participant   principal

Circ Words (ring)

circle   circulated
circuit   circus

Cis Words (cut off, kill)

circumcise   excise   indecisive
circumcision imprecise   precise
concise   incise   precision
decision   incision   scissors
decisive   incisor

Claim Words (cry out, shout)

acclaim   disclaimer   proclaim
claim   exclaim   reclaim

Clam Words (cry out, shout)

acclamation   exclamation   proclamation
declamation   exclamatory   reclamation

Clos Words (shut, close)

close   disclose   reclose
closet   enclose
closure   foreclose

Clud Words (shut, close)

conclude   occlude   secluded
exclude   preclude
include   seclude

Clus Words (shut, close)

conclusion   inclusion   recluse
conclusive   inclusive   reclusive
exclusion   inconclusive   seclusion
exclusive   occlusion

Cogn Words (know)

cognition   metacognition   recognizance
cognizance   metacognitive   recognize
cognizant   precognition
incognito   recognizable

Cor, Cord Words (heart)

accord   cordial   discordant
accordance   core   record
concord   discord

Corp Words (body)

corporal   corps   incorporate
corporate   corpse
corporation   corpulent

Cors Words (body)

corsage   corselet   corset

Cosm Words (world)

cosmic   cosmopolitan   microcosm
cosmography   cosmos
cosmonaut   macrocosm

Roots

Cour Words (heart)

courage	discourage	encourage
courageous	discouraging	encouraging

Cour Words (run)

courier	discourse
course	recourse

Cracy Words (power, strength)

aristocracy	democracy	plutocracy
bureaucracy	meritocracy	

Crat Words (power, strength)

aristocrat	bureaucrat
autocrat	democrat

Cred Words (believe)

credence	credit	creed
credibility	credo	incredible
credible	credulous	incredulous

Crim Words (separate, set apart, choose)

criminal	discrimination	indiscriminate
discriminate	incriminate	recrimination

Cris Words (separate, set apart, choose)

crisis	hypocrisy

Crit Words (separate, set apart, choose)

criteria	criticize
critic	critique
critical	hypocrite
criticism	

Cur Words (run)

currency	excursion	recur
current	incur	recurrent
currently	incursion	recursive
cursive	occur	undercurrent
cursory	occurrence	

Cuss Words (strike, shake)

concussed	discuss	percussion
concussion	discussion	repercussions

Cycl Words (circle)

bicycle	cyclone	tricycle
cycle	encyclopedia	unicycle
cyclical	motorcycle	
cyclist	recycle	

Dec Words (ten)

decade	decameter	December
decagon	decathlon	

Deci Words (a tenth)

decimal	decimate	decimeter

Dem Words (people)

demagogue	demographics	epidemiology
democracy	endemic	pandemic
democrat	epidemic	

Derm Words (skin)

dermatitis	dermatology
dermatologist	epidermis

Roots

Dent, Dont Words (tooth)

al dente	dentist	orthodontist
dental	denture	periodontal
dentin	orthodontics	

Dict Words (say, proclaim)

abdicate	dictator	predict
addict	dictatorship	prediction
addiction	diction	valediction
addictive	dictionary	valedictorian
benediction	edict	valedictory
contradict	indict	verdict
dedicate	jurisdiction	vindicate
dedication	malediction	vindication
dictate	predicate	vindictive

Doc Words (teach)

docent	doctorate	documentary
docile	doctrine	indoctrinate
doctor	document	

Duc Words (lead, bring)

conducive	education
educate	educator

Duce Words (lead, bring)

deduce	produce	reproduce
introduce	reduce	

Duct Words (lead, bring)

abduct	deduction	production
abduction	duct	productive
abductor	induct	reduction
aqueduct	induction	reproduction
conduct	introduction	reproductive
conductor	introductory	viaduct
deduct	product	

Enn Words (year)

bicentennial	millennia	perennial
centennial	millennium	

Equa Words (equal)

adequate	equanimity	inadequate
equal	equation	inequality
equality	equator	

Equi Words (equal)

equidistant	equitable	inequitable
equilateral	equity	inequity
equilibrium	equivalent	
equinox	equivocate	

Esce Words (become)

acquiesce	convalescence	senescence
acquiescence	convalescent	senescent
adolescence	fluorescence	
adolescent	fluorescent	

Fac Words (make, do)

artifact	fact	malefactor
benefactor	faction	manufacture
facile	factors	satisfaction
facilitate	factory	
facsimile	faculty	

Roots

Fect Words (make, do)

affect	defective	ineffective
affection	effect	infect
confection	effective	infection
confectionary	imperfect	perfect
defect	imperfection	perfection

Fen Words (strike, hit, push)

defend	defensive	offend
defendant	fence	offense
defender	fencer	offensive
defense	fender	

Fer Words (bring, carry)

aquifer	difference	prefer
circumference	differentiate	preference
confer	ferry	refer
conference	fertile	reference
conifer	indifferent	referral
defer	infer	suffer
deference	inference	transfer
differ	offer	vociferous

Fic Words (make, do)

artifice	fictional	sacrifice
artificial	insufficient	sacrificial
beneficial	magnificence	self-sufficient
certificate	magnificent	sufficiency
deficient	nonfiction	sufficient
difficult	personification	superficial
efficient	proficiency	
fiction	proficient	

Fid Words (belief, faith, trust)

affidavit	confident	Fido
bona fide	confidential	infidelity
confidant	diffidence	perfidious
confide	diffident	perfidy
confidence	fidelity	

Fin Words (end)

confined	final	infinite
confinement	finale	infinity
define	fine	refine
definite	finial	refinement
definition	finish	refinery
definitive	finite	unfinished

Firm Words (strong, steady)

affirm	confirm	infirm
affirmation	confirmation	infirmary
affirmative	firm	reaffirm

Flect Words (bend, curve)

deflect	reflect	reflector
genuflect	reflection	
inflection	reflective	

Flex Words (bend, curve)

circumflex	flexibility	inflexible
flex	flexible	reflex

Flict Words (strike)

afflict	conflict
affliction	infliction

Roots

Flu Words (flow)

affluence	fluent	influence
affluent	fluid	influential
confluence	fluidity	influx
fluctuate	flush	reflux
fluency	flux	superfluous

Forc Words (strong)

enforce	force	reinforce
enforcement	forceful	reinforcement

Form Words (having a form/shape)

conform	formless	platform
deformed	formula	reform
form	formulate	reformation
formal	inform	transform
formality	informal	transformation
format	information	uniform
formation	nonconformist	uniformity

Fort Words (strong)

comfort	effort	fortify
comfortable	effortless	fortitude
discomfort	forte	fortress

Frac Words (break)

diffract	fractious	refract
diffraction	fracture	refraction
fraction	infraction	

Frag Words (break)

fragile	fragility	fragment

Fus Words (pour)

confuse	infuse	refuse
confusion	infusion	suffuse
diffuse	profuse	transfuse
effusive	profusely	transfusion
fuse	profusion	
fusion	refusal	

Gen Words (birth, creation)

congenial	generator	gentle
congeniality	generic	gentleman
congenital	generosity	genuine
degenerate	generous	indigenous
degenerative	genes	ingenious
engender	genesis	ingenuous
gender	genetic	primogenitor
genealogy	genitals	primogeniture
general	genius	progeny
generate	genocide	regenerate
generation	gentile	

Geo Words (ground, land, earth)

geode	geological	geology
geography	geologist	geothermal

Gest Words (bear, carry)

congested	gestation	ingest
congestion	gestational	suggest
decongestant	gesticulate	suggestion
digest	gesture	
digestion	indigestion	

Gin Words (birth, creation)

engine	origin	originality
engineer	original	

© Shell Education

Roots

Gno Words (know)

agnostic	ignoble	ignore
diagnose	ignorance	
diagnosis	ignorant	

Grac Words (pleasing, thankful)

disgrace	grace	gracious
disgraceful	graceful	

Grad Words (step, walk)

biodegradable	grade	graduation
centigrade	gradient	retrograde
degradable	gradual	upgrade
downgrade	graduate	

Gram Words (write)

anagram	histogram
cryptogram	hologram
diagram	monogram
electrocardiogram	parallelogram
epigram	program
grammar	telegram
grammatical	

Graph Words (write)

autobiography	graphite
autograph	homograph
bibliography	lithograph
biography	oceanography
calligraphy	orthography
cartographer	paragraph
cartography	phonograph
choreographer	photograph
choreography	photographer
cinematographer	photography
cinematography	pictograph
demographics	polygraph
digraph	seismograph
geographer	seismographer
geography	telegraph
graffiti	trigraph
graph	topographical
graphic	topography
graphics	

Grat Words (pleasing, thankful)

congratulate	gratuitous
congratulations	gratuity
grateful	ingrate
gratefulness	ingratiate
gratification	ingratitude
gratify	persona non grata
gratifying	ungrateful
gratitude	

Roots

Gress Words (step, walk)

aggression	progression
aggressive	progressive
congress	regress
congressional	regression
digress	transgress
egress	transgression
progress	

Hab Words (hold, possess, live in)

cohabit	inhabit
habit	inhabitant
habitat	rehabilitate
habituate	uninhabitable

Hal Words (breathe)

exhalation	inhale
exhale	inhaler
inhalation	

Hib Words (hold, possess, live in)

exhibit	prohibit
exhibition	prohibition
inhibit	prohibitive
inhibition	

Homo Words (same)

homogeneous	homophone
homogenize	homosexual
homograph	

Hos Words (host, guest)

hospice	host	hotel
hospitable	hostage	inhospitable
hospital	hostel	
hospitality	hostess	

Hydr Words (water)

dehydrate	hydrate	rehydrate
dehydration	hydration	rehydration
hydra	hydroplane	
hydrant	hydroponics	

Ject Words (throw)

abject	interject	reject
adjective	object	rejection
conjecture	objection	subject
dejected	objective	subjective
eject	project	trajectory
inject	projectile	
injection	projector	

Jud Words (lawful, right)

adjudicate	judicial	prejudice
judge	judiciary	prejudicial
judgment	judicious	

Junct Words (join)

adjunct	disjunction	junction
conjunction	injunction	juncture

Just Words (lawful, right)

injustice	justice	justly
just	justify	unjust

Lang, Ling Words (language)

bilingual	linguist	multilingual
language	linguistics	
lingo	monolingual	

Roots

Lect Words (gather, select)

collect
collection
collective
eclectic
elect
election

elective
intellect
lectern
lecture
neglect
recollect

reelect
reelection
select
selection
selective

Leg Words (gather, select)

elegance
elegant

Leg Words (law)

delegate
delegation
illegal
illegitimate
legacy

legal
legality
legislative
legislator
legislature

legitimacy
legitimate
privilege
relegate

Li Words (tie, bind)

alliance
liable
liaison

lien
reliable
reliance

self-reliance
unreliable

Lig Words (gather, select)

diligence
diligent
eligible

eligibility
ineligible
intelligence

intelligent
negligent

Lig Words (tie, bind)

ligament
obligation

obliged
religion

religious

Lit Words (letter)

alliteration
illiterate
literacy

literal
literary
literate

literature
obliterate

Loc Words (place)

allocate
allocation
dislocate
local

locale
locate
location
locomotion

locomotive
locus
relocate

Loc Words (speak)

circumlocution
elocution
interlocutor

Log Words (word)

catalog
illogical

log
logic

logical
logo

Logue Words (word)

dialogue
epilogue

monologue
prologue

Logy Words (science/study of something)

archaeology
audiology
biology
cardiology
chronology
dermatology
ecology
entomology
genealogy
geology

gerontology
hematology
immunology
meteorology
morphology
mythology
ophthalmology
ornithology
pathology
pharmacology

physiology
psychology
pulmonology
radiology
seismology
sociology
technology
theology
zoology

Logy Words (word)

analogy
anthology

apology
eulogy

terminology

Roots

Loqu Words (speak)

colloquial	eloquent	ventriloquist
colloquialism	loquacious	
eloquence	soliloquy	

Luc Words (light, bright, of the moon)

elucidate	lucid	translucent

Lud Words (play, fool)

allude	elude	prelude
collude	interlude	
delude	ludicrous	

Lum Words (light, bright, of the moon)

illuminate	luminary	luminous

Lun Words (light, bright, of the moon)

lunacy	lunar	lunatic

Lus Words (light, bright, of the moon)

illustrate	illustrator	luster
illustrations	illustrious	lustrous

Lus Words (play, fool)

allusion	delusion	illusion
collusion	elusive	

Ly Words (tie, bind)

ally	rally	rely

Magn Words (great)

Magna Carta	magnate	magnify
magnanimity	magnificence	magnitude
magnanimous	magnificent	magnum

Man Words (hand)

emancipate	mandate	manual
emancipation	maneuver	manually
manacles	manicure	manufacture
manage	manipulate	manuscript
management	manipulation	
manager	manner	

Mar Words (sea)

aquamarine	marine	submarine
marina	maritime	

Mater Words (mother)

maternal	maternity

Matri Words (mother)

matriarch	matrimony
matriarchal	matron

Med Words (take appropriate measures)

medic	medicinal	remedial
medical	medicine	remediate
medicate	meditate	remediation
medication	meditation	remedy

Medi Words (middle)

intermediary	median	mediocre
intermediate	mediate	Mediterranean
media	mediator	medium
medial	medieval	

Mega Words (great)

megabucks	megalopolis
megabyte	megaphone
megalomania	megawatt
megalomaniac	

Roots

Mem Words (remember)

commemorate	memorandum
commemoration	memorial
memento	memorialize
memo	memorize
memoir	memory
memorabilia	remember
memorable	remembrance

Men Words (think about)

comment	mental
commentary	mentality
demented	mentor

Meter Words (measure)

barometer	odometer
centimeter	parameter
chronometer	pedometer
diameter	perimeter
hydrometer	speedometer
kilometer	tachometer
millimeter	thermometer

Metric Words (measure)

barometric	metric
biometrics	metrics

Micro Words (small)

microbe	microfilm
microbiology	micromanage
microchip	micrometer
microcomputer	microorganism
microcosm	microscope
microeconomics	microwave
microfiche	

Min Words (make smaller)

administer	minimize	minor
administration	minimum	minus
diminish	minister	minuscule
mince	ministry	minute
minimal	minnow	

Miss Words (send)

admission	emission	permission
commission	intermission	promise
demise	missile	promissory
dismiss	mission	remission
dismissal	missionary	submission
emissary	omission	transmission

Mit Words (send)

admit	intermittent	remit
commit	omit	submit
emit	permit	transmit

Mne Words (think about, forget, remember)

amnesia	amnesty	mnemonic

Mob Words (move)

automobile	mob
bookmobile	mobile
immobile	mobilize
immobilize	

Roots

Mod Words (take appropriate measures)

accommodate	moderate
accommodation	moderation
commode	modest
commodious	modicum
commodity	modification
immoderate	modify
immodest	modulate
mode	module
model	

Mom Words (move)

moment	momentous
momentarily	momentum
momentary	

Mon Words (advise, remind, reveal, warn)

admonish	monstrous
demonstrate	monument
demonstration	premonition
monitor	remonstrate
monster	summon
monstrosity	

Mor Words (harm, death)

immortal	mortician
morbid	mortify
morbidity	mortuary
morbidly	postmortem
moribund	remorse
mortal	rigor mortis
mortality	
mortgage	

Morph Words (having a form/shape)

amorphous	morpheme
anthropomorphism	morphological
metamorphic	morphology
metamorphosis	

Mot Words (move)

automotive	locomotion	motivate
commotion	locomotive	motor
demote	motel	promote
demotion	motif	promotion
emote	motility	remote
emotion	motion	

Mov Words (move)

movable	movement	remove
move	removable	

Mur Words (harm, death)

murder	murderer	murderous

Nat Words (birth, creation)

innate	nativity	perinatal
natal	natural	prenatal
nation	nature	postnatal
native	neonatal	

Ne Words (not, nothing)

abnegate	negate	neither
necessary	neglect	never
nefarious	negotiate	

Nil Words (not, nothing)

annihilate	annihilation	nil

Roots

Nom Words (name)

anonymous	ignominy	nominate
denomination	misnomer	nominee
eponymous	nominal	renominate

Nov Words (new)

innovate	novelty	renovation
innovation	novice	
novel	renovate	

Nul Words (not, nothing)

annul	null
annulment	nullify

Ny Words (not, nothing)

deny

Onym Words (name)

acronym	homonym	synonymous
antonym	pseudonym	
eponym	synonym	

Ortho Words (straight, correct)

orthodontics	orthodox	orthopedics
orthodontist	orthography	orthopedist

Pan Words (all)

panacea	pandemic	Pangaea
Pan-American	pandemonium	panorama
pancreas	Pandora	pantheon

Par Words (equal)

comparable	disparaging	parity
compare	disparity	subpar
comparison	incomparable	
disparage	par	

Par, Pair Words (produce, make ready)

apparatus	inseparable	reparations
comparable	parade	separate
comparison	preparation	separation
disparate	repair	

Pare Words (produce, make ready)

apparel	pare	prepare

Part Words (separate, divide, allot)

apart	impart	participation
apartment	parcel	particle
bipartisan	part	partisan
compartment	partial	partition
depart	partially	partner
department	participate	party

Pass Words (feeling, suffering)

compassion	passion	passive
compassionate	passionate	

Pater Words (father)

paternal	paternity

Roots

Path Words (feeling, suffering)

antipathy	osteopath	sociopath
apathetic	pathetic	sympathetic
apathy	pathogen	sympathize
empathetic	pathological	sympathy
empathize	pathologist	telepathic
empathy	pathos	telepathy
homeopathic	psychopath	

Patr Words (father)

expatriate	patriot	perpetrate
patriarch	patriotic	repatriated
patriarchal	patron	
patrimony	patronize	

Ped Words (child)

encyclopedia	orthopedist	pediatrician
orthopedic	pediatric	

Ped Words (foot)

biped	millipede	pedestrian
centipede	moped	pedicure
expedite	pedal	pedigree
expedition	peddle	pedometer
impede	peddler	quadruped
impediment	pedestal	sesquipedalian

Pel Words (push, drive, strike)

appellate	dispel	propeller
appellation	expel	rappel
compel	impel	repel
compelling	propel	repellent

Pend Words (hang, stretch)

appendage	expend	pending
appendix	expendable	pendulum
depend	impending	stipend
dependability	independence	suspend
dependable	independent	undependable
dependent	pendant	

Pens Words (hang, stretch)

compensate	expense	propensity
compensation	expensive	recompense
dispensary	pension	suspense
dispense	pensive	suspension

Phon Words (sound)

cacophony	microphone	saxophone
earphone	phoneme	symphony
headphones	phonetic	telephone
homophone	phonics	xylophone
megaphone	phonograph	

Photo Words (light)

photocopier	photograph	photojournalist
photocopy	photographer	photosynthesis
photogenic	photography	telephoto

Phys Words (nature)

physical	physics	physique
physician	physiology	

Ple Words (fill up, make complete)

complete	depletion	supplement
completion	expletive	
deplete	replete	

Roots

Plic Words (fold, lay, bend)

accomplice	complicit	replica
applicable	duplicate	replicate
application	explicit	supplicate
complicated	implicit	
complication	multiplication	

Ply Words (fill up, make complete)

comply   supply

Ply Words (fold, lay, bend)

apply	pliable	ply
imply	pliant	reply

Pod Words (foot)

podiatrist   podium   tripod

Pol Words (city)

acropolis	metropolis	policy
Annapolis	metropolitan	political
cosmopolitan	Minneapolis	politician
Indianapolis	police	politics

Pon Words (put, place)

component	opponent	proponent
exponent	postpone	

Pop Words (people)

populace	popularity	population
popular	populate	populous

Port Words (carry)

comport	opportune	purport
comportment	opportunity	rapport
deportation	port	report
deported	portable	reporter
export	portal	support
import	porter	transport
important	portfolio	transportation

Port Words (separate, divide, allot)

disproportionate	proportional
portion	proportionate
proportion	

Pos Words (put, place)

compose	opposite
composite	opposition
composition	pose
compost	position
decompose	positive
depose	postpone
deposit	posture
deposition	preposition
dispose	proposal
disposable	propose
disposal	proposition
expose	repose
exposure	reposition
impose	superimpose
imposition	suppose
impostor	transpose
oppose	

Roots

Press Words (press, hold fast, cover)

antidepressant	express	oppressor
compress	expression	press
compression	impress	pressure
decompress	impression	repress
depress	impressive	repression
depressant	irrepressible	suppress
depressed	oppress	suppression
depression	oppressive	unimpressive

Prim Words (earliest form, first)

prima donna	prime	primogenitor
primal	primer	primogeniture
primary	primeval	primordial
primate	primitive	

Prin Words (earliest form, first)

prince	principal	principle
princess	principality	

Priv Words (separate, not shared)

deprivation	privateer	privilege
deprive	privation	privy
private	privet	

Prop Words (one's own)

appropriate	proper	propriety
appropriation	property	
improper	proprietor	

Proto Words (earliest form, first)

protocol	prototype
proton	protozoan

Psych Words (soul, spirit)

psyche	psychic	psychology
psychedelic	psycho	psychomotor
psychiatrist	psychological	psychosis
psychiatry	psychologist	psychosomatic

Pub Words (people)

pub	publicist	publish
public	publicity	publisher
publication	publicize	republic

Puls Words (push, drive, strike)

compulsion	impulse	pulse
compulsive	propulsion	repulsion
expulsion	pulsate	repulsive

Punc, Punct Words (prick, have a point)

compunction	punctuality	puncture
punch	punctuate	
punctual	punctuation	

Quer, Ques Words (ask, seek)

conquer	query	questionnaire
conquest	quest	request
inquest	question	

Qui Words (rest, be quiet)

acquiesce	quiet	requiem
acquiescence	quit	tranquil
acquit	quite	tranquility

Quir Words (ask, seek)

acquire	inquire	require
acquisition	inquiry	requirement

Roots

Quis Words (ask, seek)

acquisition	inquisition	requisite
conquistador	inquisitive	requisition
corequisite	perquisite	
exquisite	prerequisite	

Rad Words (ray, spoke of a wheel)

radiance	radiation	radius
radiant	radio	
radiate	radiology	

Rect Words (guide, keep straight)

correct	director	rectangular
correction	erect	rector
direct	indirect	rectory
direction	rectangle	

Reg Words (guide, keep straight)

regal	regiment	regulate
regime	region	regulation
regimen	regular	

Rod Words (gnaw)

corrode	erode	rodent

Ros Words (gnaw)

corrosion	erosion
corrosive	erosive

Rupt Words (break)

abrupt	disrupt	interrupt
abruptly	disruption	interruption
bankrupt	erupt	rupture
corrupt	eruption	uninterrupted

Sacr Words (blessed, sacred)

consecrate	sacrifice	sacrosanct
consecration	sacrilege	sacrum
sacrament	sacrilegious	
sacred	sacristy	

Sad Words (sit)

saddle	saddler	saddlery

Sanct Words (blessed, sacred)

sanctify	sanction	sanctuary
sanctimonious	sanctity	sanctum

Scen Words (climb)

ascend	condescending	descent
ascension	condescension	transcend
ascent	descend	transcendence
condescend	descendant	

Sci Words (having knowledge)

conscience	omniscient	scientific
conscientious	prescience	scientist
conscious	prescient	subconscious
omniscience	science	

Scope Words (observe)

gyroscope	microscope	stethoscope
horoscope	periscope	telescope
kaleidoscope	scope	

Scrib Words (write)

ascribe	prescribe	subscribe
circumscribe	proscribe	transcribe
describe	scribble	
inscribe	scribe	

Roots

Script Words (write)

conscript	nondescript	scripture
conscription	postscript	subscription
description	prescription	superscript
inscription	proscription	transcript
manuscript	script	

Sec Words (follow)

consecutive	prosecute	secondary
persecute	second	

Sect Words (cut)

bisect	intersect	section
dissect	intersection	sector
dissection	resect	
insect	sect	

Sed Words (sit)

sedate	sedan	supersede
sedation	sedentary	
sedative	sediment	

Seg Words (cut)

segment	segmentation	segway

Sen Words (old)

senate	senescent	senior
senator	senile	seniority
senescence	senility	

Sens Words (feel)

consensus	sensational	sensitive
dissension	sense	sensitivity
insensitive	senseless	sensory
nonsense	sensibility	sensuality
sensation	sensible	sensuous

Sent Words (feel)

assent	sentient
consent	sentiment
dissent	sentimental
resent	sentimentality
resentful	sentinel
resentment	sentry
sentence	

Sequ Words (follow)

consequence	sequel
consequently	sequence
inconsequential	sequential
non sequitur	sequester
obsequious	subsequent

Ser Words (attach, join, line up)

assert	exertion
assertion	insert
assertive	insertion
desert	serial
desertion	series
dissertation	sermon
exert	

Serv Words (keep safe, protect)

conservancy	observe
conservation	preservative
conservative	preserve
conservator	reservation
conserve	reserve
deserve	reservoir

Serv Words (serve, be a slave)

servant	service
serve	servile

© Shell Education

Roots

Sess Words (sit)

assess	obsession	possession
assessment	obsessive	possessive
obsess	possess	session

Sid Words (sit)

assiduous	preside	residence
dissidence	president	residential
dissident	presidential	subside
insidious	reside	

Sign Words (sign, mark, indication)

assign	designer	signal
assignment	insignia	signature
consign	insignificant	significance
consignment	resign	significant
cosign	resignation	signify
design	sign	undersign
designate	signage	

Sist Words (stand, make firm)

assist	inconsistent	persistent
assistance	insist	resist
assistant	insistence	resistance
consist	insistent	resistant
consistency	irresistible	subsist
consistent	persist	subsistence
desist	persistence	

Soc Words (follow)

associate	social
association	socialize
sociable	society

Sol Words (alone)

desolate	soliloquy	solitude
desolation	solitaire	solo
sole	solitary	

Solu Words (loosen, untie)

absolute	dissolution	soluble
absolutely	insoluble	solution
absolution	resolute	
dissolute	resolution	

Solv Words (loosen, untie)

absolve	resolve	solvent
dissolve	solve	

Son Words (sound)

assonance	sonar	sonorous
consonant	sonata	unison
dissonance	sonic	ultrasonic
dissonant	sonnet	
resonate	sonogram	

Soph Words (clever, wise)

philosopher	sophistication
philosophical	sophomore
philosophy	unsophisticated
sophisticated	

Roots

Spec Words (observe)

aspect	prospect	specimen
circumspect	prospective	spectacle
disrespect	prospectus	spectacles
expect	respect	spectacular
expectation	retrospect	spectator
inspect	special	specter
inspection	specialist	spectrum
inspector	specialty	speculate
introspection	species	speculation
introspective	specific	speculum
perspective	specificity	suspect

Sphere Words (ball)

atmosphere	hemisphere	spherical
bathysphere	lithosphere	stratosphere
biosphere	sphere	troposphere

Spic Words (observe)

auspicious	despicable	suspicion
conspicuous	perspicacious	suspicious

Spir Words (breathe)

antiperspirant	expiration	respiration
aspirate	expire	respiratory
aspiration	inspiration	spirit
aspire	inspirational	spirometer
conspiracy	inspire	transpire
conspire	perspiration	
dispirited	perspire	

Spite Words (observe)

despite	respite

Spon Words (pledge, promise)

correspond	respond
correspondence	response
correspondent	responsibility
despondence	responsible
despondent	responsive
irresponsible	sponsor

Sta Words (stand, make firm)

circumstance	stance
constancy	stand
constant	standard
distance	state
distant	statement
ecstasy	static
ecstatic	station
establish	stationary
estate	statistics
extant	statue
instability	stature
instant	status
interstate	statute
obstacle	substance
reinstate	substantial
stability	understand
stable	unstable
stamina	

Stell Words (star)

constellation	stellar
interstellar	

Roots

Sti Words (stand, make firm)

armistice	institution
constitute	obstinate
constitution	restitution
constitutional	substitute
destination	substitution
destiny	superstition
destitute	superstitious
institute	

Strain Words (tie, bind, draw tight)

constrain	restraints
constraints	strain
restrain	strainer

Strict Words (tie, bind, draw tight)

boa constrictor	restricted
constrict	restrictions
constriction	restrictive
constrictive	strict
district	stricture
restrict	

String Words (tie, bind, draw tight)

astringent	stringent
string	

Stru Words (build)

construct	instructions
construction	instructor
construe	instrument
destruction	instrumental
destructive	misconstrue
indestructible	obstruct
industrial	obstruction
industrious	reconstruct
industry	self-destruct
infrastructure	structure
instruct	unstructured

Tact Words (touch, handle)

contact	tactful
intact	tactics
tact	tactile

Tag Words (touch, handle)

contagion	contagious

Tain Words (hold)

abstain	obtain
contain	obtainable
container	pertain
detain	retain
entertain	retainer
entertainment	sustain
maintain	

Tain Words (touch, handle)

attain	attainable

Tang Words (touch, handle)

intangible	tangible
tangent	

Roots

Tech Words (skill, art)

technical	technological
technician	technology
technique	

Tect Words (cover, shield)

detect	protection
detective	protective
overprotective	undetected
protect	

Teg Words (touch, handle)

disintegrate	integrate
disintegration	integration
integer	integrity

Temp Words (time)

contemporaneous	tempo
contemporary	temporal
extemporaneous	temporary

Ten Words (hold)

abstention	tenacious
detention	tenacity
maintenance	tenant
pertinent	tenement
retention	tenet
sustenance	tenure
tenable	untenable

Ten Words (stretch)

attend	ostensible
attendance	portend
attendant	portentous
attention	pretend
attentive	superintendence
attenuate	superintendent
contend	tend
contention	tendency
contentious	tender
distend	tendon
extend	tendril
extension	tense
extenuate	tensile
hypotenuse	tension
intend	tent
intense	tenuous
intensify	unattended
intensive	unintentional
intention	

Term Words (an end, boundary)

determine	term
exterminate	terminal
indeterminate	terminate
interminable	termination
predetermine	terminology

Terr Words (ground, land, earth)

extraterrestrial	terrain
interment	terrarium
Mediterranean	terrestrial
subterranean	terrier
terra cotta	territorial
terrace	territory

Roots

Therm Words (heat)

geothermal
thermal
thermodynamic
thermometer
thermonuclear
thermos
thermostat

Tig, Ting Words (near, touch)

contiguous
contingency
contingent

Tin Words (hold)

abstinence
abstinent
continual
continue
continuity
continuous
continuum
discontinue

Tort Words (twist)

contort
contortion
distort
distortion
extort
extortion
retort
torment
torture

Tract Words (pull)

abstract
abstraction
attract
attraction
attractive
contract
contraction
contractor
detract
distract
distractible
distraction
extract
extraction
protract
retract
retraction
subtract
subtraction
tract
traction
tractor

Trib Words (allot, pay)

attribute
attribution
contribute
contribution
distribute
distribution
retribution
tributary
tribute

Vac Words (empty)

evacuate
evacuation
vacancy
vacant
vacate
vacation
vacuous
vacuum

Vail Words (strong, worthy)

avail
prevail

Val Words (strong, worthy)

ambivalence
ambivalent
convalesce
convalescent
devaluate
devalue
equivalence
equivalent
evaluate
evaluation
invalid
invalidate
invaluable
prevalence
prevalent
valediction
valedictorian
valiant
valid
validate
validation
valor
valuable
value

Ven Words (come)

advent
adventure
adventurous
avenue
circumvent
convene
convenient
convention
event
eventually
inconvenient
intervene
intervention
invent
invention
inventive
prevent
preventative
prevention
revenant
revenue
souvenir
venture
venue

Roots

Ver Words (true)

aver	verdict	veritable
veracious	verification	verity
veracity	verify	very

Vers Words (turn)

adverse	conversion	transverse
adversity	diverse	traverse
anniversary	diversion	universal
averse	diversity	universe
aversion	inverse	versatile
controversial	inversion	versatility
controversy	reversal	verse
conversation	reverse	version
converse	subversive	versus

Vert Words (turn)

advertise	introvert	vertex
advertisement	introverted	vertical
avert	invert	vertices
convert	revert	vertigo
divert	subvert	
extrovert	vertebrae	

Vi Words (road, way)

devious	obviously	previously
impervious	pervious	
obvious	previous	

Via Words (road, way)

deviant	trivia	viaduct
deviate	trivial	
deviation	trivialize	

Vict Words (conquer)

convict	eviction	victory
conviction	victor	
evict	victorious	

Vid Words (see)

evidence	provide	video
evident	providence	videographer

Vinc Words (conquer)

convince	invincible	provincial
evince	province	

Vis Words (see)

advice	provisions	visage
advise	revise	visible
advisement	revision	vision
advisor	supervise	visionary
audiovisual	supervision	visit
envision	supervisor	visitor
improvisation	televise	visor
improvise	television	vista
invisible	visa	visual

Vit Words (life)

revitalize	vitality
vital	vitamins

Viv Words (life)

convivial	revive	survivor
conviviality	survival	vivacious
revival	survive	vivid

Roots

Voc Words (call)

advocate	evocative	vocal
convocation	irrevocable	vocalize
equivocal	provocative	vocation
equivocate	unequivocal	vociferate
equivocation	vocabulary	vociferous

Void Words (empty)

avoid	avoidance	unavoidable
avoidable	devoid	void

Vok Words (call)

convoke	invoke	revoke
evoke	provoke	unprovoked

Vol Words (wish or be willing)

benevolence	malevolence	voluntary
benevolent	malevolent	volunteer
involuntary	volition	

Volu Words (roll, turn around)

convoluted	revolution	voluminous
evolution	volume	

Volv Words (roll, turn around)

devolve	involve	revolve
evolve	involvement	revolver

Vor Words (devour)

carnivore	herbivore	omnivore
carnivorous	herbivorous	omnivorous
devour	insectivore	voracious

Voy Words (road, way)

convoy	envoy	voyage

Suffixes Table of Contents

Derivational Suffixes 310

Able Words (change a noun
to an adjective) 310

Able Words (change a verb
to an adjective) 310

Age Words (change a verb
to a noun) 310

Al Words (change a noun
to an adjective) 311

Al Words (change a verb to a noun) 311

Ance Words (change a verb or adjective
to an abstract noun) 311

Ancy Words (change a concrete noun
to an abstract noun) 311

Ancy Words (change an adjective
to an abstract noun) 311

Ant Words (change a noun
to an adjective) 312

Ant Words (change a verb to a noun) 312

Ar Words (change a noun
to an adjective) 312

Ar Words (change a verb to a noun) 312

Ary Words (change a noun or verb
to an adjective) 312

Ary Words (change a verb to a noun) 312

Cian Words (change an adjective or noun
to a noun) 312

En Words (change a noun
to an adjective) 312

En Words (change an adjective or noun
to a verb) 312

Ence Words (change a concrete noun
to an abstract noun) 313

Ence Words (change an adjective or verb
to an abstract noun) 313

Ency Words (change a concrete noun
to an abstract noun) 313

Ency Words (change an adjective
to an abstract noun) 313

Ent Words (change a noun
to an adjective) 313

Ent Words (change an abstract noun
to a concrete noun) 313

Er Words (change a verb to a noun) 314

Ery Words (change a concrete noun
to an abstract noun) 314

Ery Words (change a verb to an abstract
or concrete noun) 314

Ful Words (change a noun
to an adjective) 314

Ian Words (change an abstract noun
to a concrete noun) 314

Ible Words (change a noun or verb
to an adjective) 315

Ic Words (change a noun
to an adjective) 315

Ify Words (change an adjective or
noun to a verb) 315

Ist Words (change an abstract noun
to a concrete noun) 315

Ity Words (change an adjective
to an abstract noun) 316

Ive Words (change a verb to
an adjective) 316

Less Words (change a noun to
an adjective) 316

Ly Words (change a noun to
an adjective) 317

Ly Words (change an adjective
to an adverb) 317

Ment Words (change a verb
to a noun) 317

© Shell Education · 151921—The Everything Guide to Phonics · **307**

Suffixes Table of Contents *(cont.)*

Derivational Suffixes *(cont.)*

Ness Words (change an adjective to a noun) 317

Or Words (change a verb to a noun) 318

Ory Words (change a verb to an adjective) 318

Ous Words (change a noun to an adjective) 318

Sion Words (change a verb to a noun) 319

Tion Words (change a verb to a noun) 319

Sure Words (change a verb to a noun) 320

Ture Words (change a verb to a noun) 320

Ure Words (change a verb to a noun) 320

Y Words (change a noun to an adjective) 320

Inflectional Suffixes 321

ED (marks the simple-past tense) 321

Double the Consonant (one-syllable words) 321

Double the Consonant (multisyllabic words) 321

Just Add ED (multisyllabic words) 321

Drop the E (one-syllable words) 321

Drop the E (multisyllabic words) 322

Change the Y to I (words that end with consonant-Y) 322

Just Add ED (words that end with vowel-Y) 322

Irregular Past-Tense Verbs 323

EN (marks the perfect form) 323

Irregular Past Participles 323

More Irregular Past Participles 323

Inflectional Suffixes *(cont.)*

ING (marks the progressive form) 324

Double the Consonant (one-syllable words) 324

Double the Consonant (multisyllabic words) 324

Just Add ING (words that end with vowel-Y) 324

Just Add ING (multisyllabic words) 325

Drop the E (one-syllable words) 325

Drop the E (multisyllabic words) 325

ER (marks the comparative form) 326

Double the Consonant (one-syllable words that end with vowel-consonant) . 326

Drop the E (one-syllable words that end with silent E) 326

Change the Y to I (words that end with consonant-Y) 326

EST (marks the superlative form) 326

Double the Consonant (one-syllable words that end with vowel-consonant) . 326

Drop the E (one-syllable words) 326

Change the Y to I (words that end with consonant-Y) 326

Suffixes Table of Contents *(cont.)*

Inflectional Suffixes *(cont.)*

S (marks the plural form)........................327

   Add ES (words that end with CH or TCH).....327

   Add ES (some words that end with O)......327

   Add ES (words that end with S or SS).......327

   Add ES (words that end with SH).........327

   Add ES (words that end with X)..........327

   Change F to VES (words that
end with F).....................327

   Change IS to ES (words that end with IS)....327

   Change UM to A (words that
end with UM)....................328

   Change US to I (words that
end with US).....................328

   Change Y to I and Add ES (words that
end with consonant-Y)..............328

   Just Add S (words that
end with vowel-Y).................328

   Irregular Plural Nouns...................328

S (marks the third-person singular form)..........329

   Change the Y to I and Add ES
(words that end with consonant-Y)....329

   Just Add S (words that
end with vowel-Y).................329

Suffixes

Derivational Suffixes

Able Words (change a noun to an adjective)

charitable   objectionable
miserable

Able Words (change a verb to an adjective)

abominable   enforceable
acceptable   excitable
accountable   expandable
adaptable   expendable
adjustable   fashionable
admirable   favorable
adorable   impeccable
affordable   inexcusable
agreeable   irritable
allowable   knowledgeable
amicable   laughable
applicable   lovable
approachable   manageable
available   negotiable
avoidable   notable
believable   noticeable
breakable   operable
changeable   payable
chewable   perishable
comfortable   pleasurable
commendable   predictable
comparable   preferable
considerable   profitable
consumable   punishable
debatable   questionable
dependable   reasonable
deplorable   rechargeable
desirable   recyclable
despicable   refillable
disposable   reliable

Able Words (change a verb to an adjective) *(cont.)*

remarkable   unavoidable
removable   unbelievable
replaceable   undependable
respectable   usable
reusable   valuable
serviceable   variable
sociable   washable
tolerable

Age Words (change a verb to a noun)

baggage   passage
carriage   postage
dosage   spillage
drainage   storage
luggage   usage
marriage   wreckage
package

Derivational Suffixes

Al Words (change a noun to an adjective)

accidental	functional	phenomenal
actual	global	philosophical
alphabetical	horizontal	postal
artificial	hysterical	potential
beneficial	incidental	practical
bridal	inferential	preferential
brutal	influential	prejudicial
central	intentional	presidential
choral	judicial	racial
chronological	logical	regional
circumstantial	magical	residential
coincidental	maternal	sacrificial
colonial	monumental	sequential
commercial	mythical	serial
confidential	national	spatial
controversial	natural	substantial
critical	naval	supplemental
cynical	normal	technical
digital	official	tidal
emotional	original	torrential
essential	ornamental	trivial
exponential	parental	typical
facial	partial	universal
factual	paternal	viral
financial	peripheral	
floral	personal	

Al Words (change a verb to a noun)

betrayal	proposal	signal
dismissal	referral	terminal
disposal	rehearsal	
memorial	reversal	

Ance Words (change a verb or adjective to an abstract noun)

abundance	elegance	nonchalance
acceptance	endurance	observance
acquaintance	extravagance	performance
allegiance	exuberance	petulance
allowance	flamboyance	radiance
arrogance	fragrance	relevance
assistance	grievance	reliance
attendance	guidance	reluctance
brilliance	ignorance	resistance
compliance	importance	significance
defiance	instance	tolerance
distance	insurance	valiance
dominance	maintenance	vigilance

Ancy Words (change a concrete noun to an abstract noun)

infancy	truancy
occupancy	vagrancy

Ancy Words (change an adjective to an abstract noun)

buoyancy	dormancy	redundancy
constancy	poignancy	vacancy
discrepancy	pregnancy	

Derivational Suffixes

Ant Words (change a noun to an adjective)

abundant	extravagant	redundant
allegiant	exuberant	relevant
arrogant	flamboyant	reliant
blatant	fragrant	reluctant
brilliant	hesitant	resistant
buoyant	ignorant	significant
compliant	important	tolerant
constant	instant	triumphant
defiant	nonchalant	truant
discrepant	observant	vacant
distant	petulant	vagrant
dominant	poignant	valiant
dormant	pregnant	vigilant
elegant	radiant	

Ant Words (change a verb to a noun)

applicant	combatant	immigrant
assailant	confidant	informant
assistant	defendant	migrant
attendant	dependant	occupant
claimant	emigrant	servant

Ar Words (change a noun to an adjective)

circular	polar	singular
muscular	rectangular	triangular

Ar Words (change a verb to a noun)

beggar	burglar	liar

Ary Words (change a noun or verb to an adjective)

customary	legendary	revolutionary
exemplary	literary	salivary
fragmentary	monetary	solitary
hereditary	necessary	stationary
imaginary	primary	voluntary

Ary Words (change a verb to a noun)

boundary	documentary	rotary
burglary	military	summary
commentary	missionary	

Cian Words (change an adjective or noun to a noun)

clinician	musician	statistician
electrician	optician	tactician
magician	pediatrician	
mathematician	physician	

En Words (change a noun to an adjective)

earthen	rotten	wooden
flaxen	silken	woolen
golden	waxen	

En Words (change an adjective or noun to a verb)

awaken	frighten	sicken
blacken	harden	soften
brighten	lengthen	strengthen
broaden	lessen	sweeten
dampen	lighten	thicken
darken	loosen	tighten
deafen	redden	weaken
fasten	ripen	whiten
flatten	sharpen	widen
freshen	shorten	worsen

Derivational Suffixes

Ence Words (change a concrete noun to an abstract noun)

adherence	correspondence
adolescence	residence
convalescence	superintendence

Ence Words (change an adjective or verb to an abstract noun)

absence	equivalence	negligence
affluence	evidence	obedience
benevolence	excellence	omniscience
coincidence	expedience	patience
competence	fluorescence	permanence
condolence	impatience	persistence
conference	impudence	preference
confidence	incompetence	presence
congruence	independence	prevalence
consequence	indifference	prudence
convenience	indulgence	pungence
decadence	inference	reference
dependence	influence	resilience
difference	innocence	sequence
diligence	insistence	silence
disobedience	intelligence	substance
effervescence	interference	turbulence
eloquence	magnificence	violence
emergence	malevolence	

Ency Words (change a concrete noun to an abstract noun)

agency	presidency	residency

Ency Words (change an adjective to an abstract noun)

consistency	frequency	pungency
decency	inconsistency	stringency
delinquency	insufficiency	sufficiency
efficiency	leniency	transparency
emergency	potency	urgency
fluency	proficiency	

Ent Words (change a noun to an adjective)

absent	equivalent	negligent
absorbent	evident	obedient
affluent	excellent	omniscient
benevolent	expedient	patient
competent	fluent	permanent
complacent	fluorescent	persistent
confident	frequent	potent
congruent	impatient	present
consequent	impudent	prevalent
consistent	incompetent	proficient
convenient	inconsistent	prominent
decadent	independent	prudent
decent	indifferent	pungent
delinquent	indulgent	resilient
dependent	innocent	silent
different	insistent	stringent
diligent	insufficient	sufficient
disobedient	intelligent	transparent
effervescent	lenient	turbulent
efficient	magnificent	urgent
eloquent	malevolent	violent

Ent Words (change an abstract noun to a concrete noun)

adherent	convalescent	president
adolescent	correspondent	superintendent
agent	resident	

Suffixes

Derivational Suffixes

Er Words (change a verb to a noun)

baker	jogger	scooter
beginner	manager	searcher
binder	marcher	seller
blender	peddler	settler
broiler	photographer	shopper
catcher	pitcher	singer
cleaner	planner	skater
composer	poacher	speaker
consumer	preacher	stretcher
crusher	printer	swimmer
dancer	racer	teacher
dreamer	rancher	timer
drummer	ranger	toaster
dryer	reader	tweezers
employer	receiver	voter
farmer	reminder	waiter
founder	rescuer	washer
freezer	robber	worker
heater	runner	

Ery Words (change a concrete noun to an abstract noun)

lottery	scenery	winery
machinery	slavery	

Ery Words (change a verb to an abstract or concrete noun)

bakery	embroidery	pottery
bravery	fishery	refinery
bribery	flattery	robbery
delivery	forgery	trickery
discovery	mystery	
eatery	nursery	

Ful Words (change a noun to an adjective)

beautiful	helpful	skillful
boastful	hopeful	spoonful
bountiful	joyful	stressful
careful	lawful	successful
cheerful	merciful	tasteful
colorful	mindful	tearful
doubtful	mouthful	thankful
dreadful	painful	thoughtful
dutiful	peaceful	truthful
faithful	pitiful	useful
fearful	playful	wasteful
forgetful	plentiful	wishful
graceful	powerful	wonderful
handful	respectful	youthful
harmful	restful	
hateful	rightful	

Ian Words (change an abstract noun to a concrete noun)

clinician	magician	politician
comedian	mathematician	statistician
cosmetician	musician	technician
custodian	optician	
diagnostician	pediatrician	
electrician	physician	

314 151921— The Everything Guide to Phonics © Shell Education

Suffixes

Derivational Suffixes

Ible Words (change a noun or verb to an adjective)

accessible	incompatible
admissible	incredible
audible	indelible
combustible	indestructible
compatible	indivisible
comprehensible	ineligible
contemptible	infallible
convertible	inflexible
corruptible	intangible
credible	invincible
deductible	invisible
digestible	irresistible
distractible	irreversible
divisible	legible
edible	plausible
eligible	possible
fallible	responsible
feasible	reversible
flexible	sensible
gullible	tangible
horrible	terrible
illegible	visible
impossible	
impressible	

Ic Words (change a noun to an adjective)

academic	dynamic	patriotic
allergic	economic	poetic
angelic	energetic	romantic
Antarctic	fantastic	sarcastic
apathetic	generic	scenic
aquatic	genetic	scientific
artistic	heroic	strategic
athletic	historic	stoic
atomic	majestic	symbolic
chaotic	melodic	sympathetic
cosmic	microscopic	tragic
cubic	nomadic	traumatic
democratic	nostalgic	volcanic
dramatic	organic	

Ify Words (change an adjective or noun to a verb)

beautify	gentrify	objectify
calcify	horrify	ossify
citify	humidify	personify
classify	magnify	signify
detoxify	mystify	solidify
electrify	nullify	verify

Ist Words (change an abstract noun to a concrete noun)

archaeologist	geologist	zoologist
biologist	meteorologist	
cardiologist	psychologist	
dermatologist	radiologist	

Suffixes

Derivational Suffixes

Ity Words (change an adjective to an abstract noun)

ability	enormity	opportunity
abnormality	equality	originality
absurdity	eternity	personality
accessibility	ethnicity	plasticity
accountability	facility	popularity
acidity	familiarity	possibility
activity	fatality	prosperity
actuality	ferocity	publicity
adversity	festivity	purity
affordability	formality	reality
agility	fragility	regularity
anonymity	frivolity	responsibility
antiquity	frugality	sanity
anxiety	futility	scarcity
atrocity	generosity	security
authenticity	gravity	seniority
availability	hilarity	serenity
capability	hospitality	severity
captivity	hostility	similarity
civility	humidity	simplicity
clarity	immaturity	sincerity
community	inferiority	specificity
complexity	insanity	spontaneity
continuity	insecurity	stability
creativity	intensity	stupidity
credibility	legality	superiority
curiosity	liability	technicality
density	majority	toxicity
disability	maturity	uniformity
disparity	minority	validity
diversity	morality	vanity
divinity	nationality	versatility
eccentricity	necessity	visibility
elasticity	neutrality	vitality
electricity	nobility	
eligibility	objectivity	

Ive Words (change a verb to an adjective)

abrasive	decorative	informative
active	destructive	interactive
adhesive	digestive	inventive
adoptive	disruptive	narrative
aggressive	effective	negative
assertive	excessive	passive
attractive	exclusive	possessive
cohesive	expensive	productive
competitive	expressive	progressive
constructive	extensive	protective
cooperative	imaginative	relative
creative	impressive	selective

Less Words (change a noun to an adjective)

ageless	harmless	priceless
bottomless	helpless	reckless
breathless	homeless	regardless
careless	jobless	restless
ceaseless	lawless	scoreless
cheerless	lifeless	seamless
cloudless	limitless	sleepless
defenseless	meaningless	sleeveless
effortless	merciless	speechless
endless	mindless	spotless
faultless	odorless	tasteless
fearless	painless	thankless
formless	penniless	timeless
friendless	pitiless	useless
fruitless	pointless	wordless
graceless	powerless	worthless

Derivational Suffixes

Ly Words (change a noun to an adjective)

beastly	gentlemanly	scholarly
costly	leisurely	timely
cowardly	monthly	worldly
elderly	motherly	yearly
friendly	nightly	

Ly Words (change an adjective to an adverb)

abruptly	deeply	nicely
angrily	directly	precisely
avidly	distinctly	proudly
badly	drily	quickly
barely	eagerly	quietly
beautifully	easily	rudely
blindly	equally	sadly
bravely	falsely	safely
busily	frequently	selfishly
calmly	gladly	sensibly
carefully	greedily	shyly
carelessly	happily	slowly
certainly	hastily	smoothly
clearly	heavily	softly
closely	horribly	steadily
clumsily	hourly	strangely
commonly	hungrily	suddenly
constantly	instantly	surely
correctly	kindly	sweetly
crudely	legally	swiftly
cruelly	loudly	weakly
daintily	nearly	

Ment Words (change a verb to a noun)

achievement	encouragement
adjustment	endorsement
advertisement	enjoyment
agreement	equipment
ailment	establishment
amazement	excitement
amendment	government
announcement	improvement
appointment	investment
argument	involvement
arrangement	management
assignment	measurement
attachment	punishment
commitment	refreshment
development	replacement
disagreement	requirement
disappointment	retirement
employment	settlement

Ness Words (change an adjective to a noun)

awareness	fondness	sadness
blindness	freshness	sharpness
business	fussiness	shyness
closeness	goodness	sickness
cloudiness	happiness	silliness
clumsiness	hardness	sleepiness
coolness	illness	sloppiness
dampness	kindness	stiffness
darkness	laziness	stillness
dizziness	liveliness	tenderness
dryness	loneliness	thickness
dullness	madness	thinness
eagerness	openness	tightness
emptiness	puffiness	ugliness
fairness	readiness	vastness
firmness	ripeness	weakness

© Shell Education

151921—The Everything Guide to Phonics

Suffixes

Derivational Suffixes

Or Words (change a verb to a noun)

actor	educator	protector
advisor	elevator	refrigerator
calculator	escalator	sailor
competitor	governor	sculptor
contractor	illustrator	surveyor
counselor	investor	survivor
director	narrator	translator
donor	operator	vendor
editor	professor	visitor

Ory Words (change a verb to an adjective)

accusatory	mandatory
circulatory	migratory
contradictory	obligatory
discriminatory	respiratory
explanatory	satisfactory
inflammatory	self-explanatory
introductory	

Ous Words (change a noun to an adjective)

adventurous	hazardous	pompous
ambitious	herbivorous	prestigious
anonymous	hilarious	prosperous
anxious	humorous	rebellious
atrocious	indigenous	religious
autonomous	industrious	ridiculous
cancerous	infamous	rigorous
carnivorous	infectious	scrupulous
cautious	luxurious	spacious
contagious	malicious	spontaneous
courageous	marvelous	studious
curious	miraculous	superstitious
dangerous	miscellaneous	suspicious
disastrous	mischievous	synonymous
enormous	mountainous	tedious
envious	mysterious	torturous
famous	nervous	treacherous
ferocious	numerous	unanimous
frivolous	nutritious	various
furious	ominous	venomous
generous	omnivorous	victorious
glamorous	outrageous	vigorous
glorious	perilous	villainous
gracious	poisonous	zealous

Derivational Suffixes

Sion Words (change a verb to a noun)

admission	discussion	permission
aggression	diversion	persuasion
apprehension	division	possession
collision	emission	procession
collusion	erosion	profession
commission	explosion	progression
comprehension	expression	provisions
compression	expulsion	recession
concession	extension	regression
conclusion	impression	remission
concussion	incision	repulsion
condescension	inclusion	revision
confession	indecision	submission
confusion	intrusion	succession
convulsion	invasion	supervision
decision	obsession	suspension
delusion	omission	transgression
depression	oppression	transmission

Tion Words (change a verb to a noun)

abbreviation	description	intuition
action	devotion	investigation
addition	direction	invitation
admiration	donation	irrigation
affection	education	legislation
application	election	location
appreciation	equation	migration
association	eruption	multiplication
attention	evaporation	navigation
cancellation	evolution	notification
celebration	exaggeration	observation
circulation	exclamation	occupation
collection	expectation	operation
combination	expiration	organization
communication	explanation	participation
compensation	exploration	perspiration
competition	fascination	pollution
computation	frustration	population
concentration	infection	prediction
concoction	graduation	preparation
congratulation	hesitation	prescription
connection	hibernation	presentation
conservation	ignition	preservation
construction	illustration	production
consultation	imagination	promotion
contamination	imitation	protection
contraction	immigration	qualification
contradiction	inauguration	ratification
convention	indication	reaction
conversation	infection	reception
correction	information	recognition
deception	injection	reduction
declaration	inspection	reflection
decoration	inspiration	relaxation
definition	instructions	renovation
demonstration	introduction	reservation

Suffixes

Derivational Suffixes

Tion Words (change a verb to a noun) (cont.)

resolution	solution	transformation
respiration	subscription	transportation
restriction	subtraction	unification
revolution	suggestion	vacation
selection	temptation	vibration
separation	transaction	

Sure Words (change a verb to a noun)

closure	enclosure	exposure
composure	erasure	

Ture Words (change a verb to a noun)

creature	fixture	sculpture
curvature	furniture	signature
departure	legislature	
expenditure	mixture	

Ure Words (change a verb to a noun)

failure	seizure

Y Words (change a noun to an adjective)

bony	foggy	rusty
bossy	frosty	salty
breezy	funny	sandy
bubbly	furry	slimy
bumpy	fuzzy	sloppy
buttery	gloomy	snowy
catchy	greasy	soapy
chatty	greedy	speedy
chilly	gritty	starry
choppy	grouchy	stormy
cloudy	grumpy	sugary
creamy	guilty	sunny
creepy	handy	sweaty
crispy	healthy	thirsty
curly	icy	toasty
daily	juicy	tricky
dirty	lucky	wealthy
dressy	messy	windy
dusty	needy	wordy
easy	noisy	worthy
filthy	oily	
floppy	rainy	

Inflectional Suffixes

ED (marks the simple-past tense)

Double the Consonant (one-syllable words that end with a single vowel followed by a single consonant other than W or X)

batted	hummed	skipped
begged	jammed	slammed
blotted	jogged	slapped
blurred	knitted	slipped
bragged	knotted	snagged
canned	logged	snapped
capped	mapped	snipped
chapped	mobbed	sobbed
chatted	mopped	spotted
chipped	napped	stabbed
chopped	netted	starred
chugged	nodded	stepped
clapped	padded	stirred
clipped	patted	stopped
cropped	petted	stripped
dimmed	pinned	swabbed
dipped	planned	swapped
dotted	plodded	swatted
dragged	plotted	tagged
dripped	plugged	tapped
dropped	popped	throbbed
drummed	potted	tipped
fanned	propped	topped
fitted	robbed	trapped
flapped	rubbed	trimmed
flipped	scanned	tripped
flopped	scarred	trotted
grabbed	shipped	tugged
grinned	shopped	wagged
gripped	shrugged	whizzed
hemmed	sipped	wrapped
hopped	skimmed	zipped
hugged	skinned	

Double the Consonant (multisyllabic words with a stressed final syllable that ends with a single vowel followed by a single consonant other than W or X)

acquitted	emitted	preferred
admitted	equipped	propelled
allotted	excelled	rebelled
committed	incurred	referred
compelled	inferred	regretted
concurred	occurred	repelled
controlled	omitted	submitted
deferred	patrolled	transferred
embedded	permitted	transmitted

Just Add ED (multisyllabic words with an unstressed final syllable that ends with a single vowel followed by a single consonant)

benefited	edited	inhabited
considered	entered	limited
credited	exhibited	severed
developed	exited	suffered

Drop the E (one-syllable words that end with silent E)

baked	iced	placed	stared
blamed	liked	raced	stored
cared	lined	raised	tamed
chased	lived	saved	tasted
chimed	loved	scored	traded
dared	mined	shaded	tuned
filed	moved	shaped	used
flamed	named	shared	voted
fumed	noted	shoved	wasted
graded	owed	skated	waved
hiked	pasted	sloped	whined
hoped	piled	smiled	

Suffixes

Inflectional Suffixes

ED (marks the simple-past tense) *(cont.)*

Drop the E (multisyllabic words that end with silent E)

acquired	desired	polluted
adhered	devised	preceded
admired	diluted	prepared
adored	disgraced	produced
advised	disguised	promoted
amazed	divided	proposed
amused	embraced	provided
arranged	engaged	provoked
arrived	engraved	puzzled
aspired	escaped	rattled
battled	exchanged	receded
behaved	excited	recited
cascaded	excluded	reclined
collided	excused	reduced
combined	expired	refined
competed	exploded	refused
completed	exposed	replaced
composed	ignited	required
computed	ignored	restored
conceded	impaled	resumed
concluded	impeded	retired
confided	imploded	revered
confined	implored	revised
confused	included	revived
consoled	inquired	revoked
conspired	inspired	saluted
consumed	invited	seceded
created	invoked	secreted
debated	meddled	settled
decided	nibbled	stampeded
declared	obliged	supposed
declined	paraded	surprised
deleted	perspired	survived
depleted	persuaded	united

Change the Y to I (one-syllable and multisyllabic words that end with consonant-Y)

applied	dried	pried
beautified	electrified	relied
belied	emptied	replied
buried	fortified	scurried
carried	fried	shied
certified	horrified	spied
classified	hurried	supplied
complied	implied	tidied
copied	magnified	tried
cried	married	varied
defied	mystified	verified
denied	pitied	worried

Just Add ED (one-syllable and multisyllabic words that end with vowel-Y)

annoyed	frayed	slayed
betrayed	grayed	spayed
curtseyed	jockeyed	splayed
decayed	monkeyed	sprayed
delayed	obeyed	stayed
deployed	okayed	strayed
destroyed	played	swayed
dismayed	portrayed	toyed
displayed	prayed	volleyed
employed	preyed	
enjoyed	relayed	

322   151921— The Everything Guide to Phonics

Inflectional Suffixes

ED (marks the simple-past tense) *(cont.)*

Irregular Past-Tense Verbs

ate	had	shone
beat	heard	shook
became	held	shot
began	hid	showed
bent	hit	shut
bet	hung	slept
bit	hurt	slid
bled	kept	sold
blew	knew	sped
bought	laid	spent
broke	lay	spoke
brought	led	spread
built	left	spun
came	lent	stole
caught	let	stood
chose	lit	struck
cost	lost	stuck
cut	made	stung
did	meant	swam
dove	met	swept
drank	paid	swore
drew	put	swung
drove	quit	taught
dug	ran	thought
fed	rang	threw
fell	read	told
felt	rode	took
flew	rose	tore
forgot	said	was
fought	sang	went
found	sank	were
froze	sat	woke
gave	saw	won
got	sent	wore
grew	set	wrote

EN (marks the perfect form)

Irregular Past Participles

beaten	forgotten	shaken
bitten	frozen	spoken
broken	given	stolen
chosen	gotten	taken
driven	hidden	woken
eaten	ridden	woven
fallen	risen	written

More Irregular Past Participles

become	held	set
been	hit	shone
begun	hung	shot
bet	hurt	shown
blown	kept	shut
bought	known	slept
brought	laid	slid
built	lain	sold
burst	led	spent
caught	left	sprung
come	lent	stood
cost	let	stuck
cut	lit	sung
done	lost	sunk
drawn	made	swept
drunk	meant	sworn
fed	met	swum
felt	paid	swung
flown	read	taught
fought	run	thought
found	rung	thrown
gone	said	told
grown	sat	torn
had	seen	won
heard	sent	worn

© Shell Education

151921—The Everything Guide to Phonics

323

Suffixes

Inflectional Suffixes

ING (marks the progressive form)

Double the Consonant (one-syllable words that end with a single vowel followed by a single consonant other than W or X)

batting	jogging	skipping
begging	kidding	slamming
betting	knitting	slapping
blotting	knotting	slipping
bragging	logging	snapping
budding	mapping	snipping
canning	mobbing	sobbing
chatting	mopping	spotting
chipping	napping	stabbing
chopping	netting	starring
chugging	nodding	stepping
clapping	padding	stirring
clipping	patting	stopping
cropping	petting	strumming
dimming	pinning	swabbing
dipping	planning	swapping
dotting	plodding	swatting
dragging	plotting	swimming
dripping	plugging	tagging
dropping	popping	tapping
fanning	potting	thinning
fitting	propping	throbbing
flapping	quitting	tipping
flipping	robbing	trapping
flopping	rubbing	trimming
grabbing	running	tripping
grinning	scanning	trotting
gripping	scarring	tugging
hemming	shipping	wagging
hopping	shopping	whizzing
hugging	shrugging	winning
humming	sipping	wrapping
jamming	skimming	zipping

Double the Consonant (multisyllabic words with a stressed final syllable that ends with a single vowel followed by a single consonant other than W or X)

abhorring	embedding	patrolling
acquitting	emitting	permitting
admitting	equipping	preferring
allotting	excelling	propelling
beginning	expelling	rebelling
committing	forbidding	referring
compelling	forgetting	regretting
concurring	incurring	repelling
conferring	inferring	submitting
controlling	occurring	transferring
deferring	omitting	transmitting

Just Add ING (one-syllable and multisyllabic words that end with vowel-Y)

annoying	enjoying	preying
betraying	fraying	relaying
braying	graying	saying
cloying	laying	slaying
decaying	neighing	spaying
delaying	obeying	splaying
deploying	okaying	spraying
destroying	paying	staying
dismaying	playing	straying
displaying	portraying	swaying
employing	praying	volleying

Inflectional Suffixes

ING (marks the progressive form) *(cont.)*

Just Add ING (multisyllabic words with an unstressed final syllable that ends with a single vowel followed by a single consonant)

benefiting	editing	leveling
caroling	entering	limiting
considering	exhibiting	severing
crediting	exiting	suffering
developing	inhabiting	

Drop the E (one-syllable words that end with silent E)

baking	loving	skating
biting	making	sliding
blaming	mining	sloping
caring	moving	smiling
chasing	naming	staring
chiming	noting	storing
daring	owing	striking
diving	pasting	taking
driving	piling	taming
filing	placing	tasting
flaming	racing	trading
fuming	raising	tuning
grading	riding	using
hiking	saving	voting
hoping	scoring	wasting
icing	shaking	waving
liking	sharing	whining
lining	shaping	writing
living	shoving	

Drop the E (multisyllabic words that end with silent E)

acquiring	devising	polluting
adhering	diluting	preceding
admiring	disgracing	preparing
adoring	disguising	producing
advising	disputing	promoting
amazing	dividing	proposing
amusing	embracing	providing
arranging	engaging	provoking
arriving	engraving	receding
aspiring	escaping	reciting
behaving	exchanging	reclining
cascading	exciting	reducing
colliding	excluding	refining
combining	excreting	refusing
competing	excusing	replacing
completing	expiring	requiring
composing	exploding	restoring
computing	exposing	resuming
conceding	igniting	retiring
concluding	ignoring	revering
confiding	impeding	revising
confining	imploding	reviving
confusing	imploring	revoking
consoling	including	saluting
conspiring	inquiring	seceding
consuming	inspiring	secreting
creating	inviting	stampeding
debating	invoking	supposing
deciding	obliging	surprising
declaring	parading	surviving
declining	perfuming	uniting
deleting	perspiring	
depleting	persuading	

Suffixes

Inflectional Suffixes

ER (marks the comparative form)

Double the Consonant (one-syllable words that end with a single vowel followed by a single consonant)

bigger	flatter	sadder
fatter	hotter	thinner

Drop the E (one-syllable and multisyllabic words that end with silent E)

braver	gentler	safer
closer	larger	simpler
coarser	looser	wiser
fiercer	nicer	
finer	riper	

Change the Y to I (one-syllable and multisyllabic words that end with consonant-Y)

angrier	dirtier	juicier
bossier	drier	lazier
bumpier	earlier	luckier
busier	easier	naughtier
cloudier	fancier	noisier
clumsier	foggier	prettier
crazier	funnier	saltier
creamier	happier	sillier
crispier	heavier	skinnier
daintier	itchier	uglier

EST (marks the superlative form)

Double the Consonant (one-syllable words that end with a single vowel followed by a single consonant)

biggest	flattest	saddest
fattest	hottest	thinnest

Drop the E (one-syllable and multisyllabic words that end with silent E)

bravest	gentlest	safest
closest	largest	simplest
coarsest	loosest	wisest
fiercest	nicest	
finest	ripest	

Change the Y to I (one-syllable and multisyllabic words that end with consonant-Y)

angriest	dirtiest	juiciest
bossiest	driest	laziest
bumpiest	earliest	luckiest
busiest	easiest	naughtiest
cloudiest	fanciest	noisiest
clumsiest	foggiest	prettiest
craziest	funniest	saltiest
creamiest	happiest	silliest
crispiest	heaviest	skinniest
daintiest	itchiest	ugliest

Inflectional Suffixes

S (marks the plural form)

Add ES (words that end with CH or TCH)

arches	finches	ranches
batches	inches	riches
beaches	latches	roaches
benches	lunches	scratches
branches	matches	speeches
bunches	notches	stitches
catches	patches	switches
churches	peaches	trenches
coaches	pitches	watches
couches	pouches	witches
crutches	punches	wrenches

Add ES (some words that end with O)

heroes	tomatoes	vetoes
potatoes	torpedoes	

Add ES (words that end with S or SS)

actresses	crosses	kisses
atlases	dresses	losses
bonuses	gases	messes
bosses	glasses	misses
buses	guesses	passes
businesses	harnesses	princesses
classes	hostesses	tosses
compasses	irises	waitresses

Add ES (words that end with SH)

ashes	flashes	sashes
brushes	gashes	sinuses
bushes	geniuses	splashes
choruses	lashes	viruses
circuses	leashes	walruses
crashes	pushes	wishes
dishes	rashes	

Add ES (words that end with X)

axes	fixes	sixes
boxes	foxes	taxes
exes	mixes	waxes

Change F to VES (words that end with F or FE)

calves	leaves	thieves
dwarves	lives	wharves
elves	loaves	wives
halves	scarves	wolves
hooves	selves	
knives	shelves	

Change IS to ES (words that end with IS)

analyses	metamorphoses
axes	nemeses
bases	oases
crises	parentheses
diagnoses	prognoses
ellipses	synopses
emphases	syntheses
hypotheses	theses

Suffixes

Inflectional Suffixes

S (marks the plural form) *(cont.)*

Change UM to A (words that end with UM)

bacteria	media	strata
curricula	memoranda	
data	referenda	

Change US to I (words that end with US)

alumni	fungi	radii
cacti	loci	stimuli
foci	nuclei	syllabi

Change Y to I and Add ES (one-syllable and multisyllabic words that end with consonant-Y)

accessories	centuries	ferries
anniversaries	charities	flies
armies	cherries	flurries
arteries	cities	fries
babies	colonies	galleries
batteries	comedies	glossaries
berries	communities	groceries
bodies	companies	guppies
booties	copies	hobbies
bounties	counties	industries
buddies	countries	injuries
buggies	daddies	jellies
bullies	daisies	juries
bunnies	diaries	ladies
canaries	dictionaries	levies
candies	duties	lilies
capillaries	emergencies	mommies
categories	factories	mysteries
cavities	fairies	nineties
celebrities	families	parties
cemeteries	fantasies	pastries

Change Y to I and Add ES *(cont.)*

pennies	quarries	studies
pharmacies	rubies	supplies
policies	sixties	theories
ponies	skies	tragedies
posies	spies	treaties
puppies	stories	trophies
qualities	strategies	

Just Add S (one-syllable and multisyllabic words that end with vowel-Y)

alleys	jockeys	pulleys
arrays	joeys	quays
boys	journeys	rays
chimneys	joys	trays
curtseys	medleys	turkeys
days	monkeys	valleys
donkeys	ospreys	ways
galleys	plays	
gurneys	ploys	

Irregular Plural Nouns

buffalo	geese	people
children	lice	sheep
deer	men	shrimp
dice	mice	teeth
feet	moose	women
fish	oxen	

Suffixes

Inflectional Suffixes

S (marks the third-person singular form)

Change the Y to I and Add ES (one-syllable and multisyllabic words that end with consonant-Y)

applies	electrifies	pries
beautifies	empties	relies
belies	fortifies	replies
buries	fries	scurries
carries	horrifies	shies
certifies	hurries	solidifies
classifies	implies	spies
complies	magnifies	supplies
copies	marries	tries
cries	multiplies	verifies
defies	mystifies	worries
denies	occupies	
dries	pities	

Just Add S (one-syllable and multisyllabic words that end with vowel-Y)

annoys	frays	says
betrays	grays	slays
brays	lays	spays
cloys	neighs	splays
decays	obeys	sprays
delays	okays	stays
deploys	pays	strays
destroys	plays	sways
dismays	portrays	volleys
displays	prays	weighs
employs	preys	
enjoys	relays	

© Shell Education

151921—The Everything Guide to Phonics

329

References

Anderson, Richard C., Elfrieda H. Hiebert, Judith A. Scott, and Ian A. G. Wilkerson. 1985. *Becoming a Nation of Readers: The Report of the Commission on Reading*. National Academy of Education.

Archer, Anita L., and Charles A. Hughes. 2010. *Explicit Instruction: Effective and Efficient Teaching*. New York: Guilford.

Beck, Isabel L., and Mark E. Beck. 2013. *Making Sense of Phonics: The Hows and Whys, Second Edition*. New York: Guilford.

Blevins, Wiley. 2017. *A Fresh Look at Phonics, Grades K–2: Common Causes of Failure and 7 Ingredients for Success*. Thousand Oaks, CA: Corwin.

———. 2023. *Phonics from A to Z: A Practical Guide, Fourth Edition*. New York: Scholastic.

Burkins, Jan, and Kari Yates. 2021. *Shifting the Balance: 6 Ways to Bring the Science of Reading into the Balanced Literacy Classroom*. Portsmouth, NH: Stenhouse.

Cothran, Martin. 2014."This History of Phonics." Memoria Press. June 1, 2014. memoriapress.com/articles/history-phonics.

Cunningham, Anne E. 1990. "Explicit Versus Implicit Instruction in Phonemic Awareness." *Journal of Experimental Child Psychology* 50 (3): 429–444. doi.org/10.1016/0022-0965(90)90079-n.

Domaradzki, Lexie. 2021. "Literacy Routine Map." In *Literacy Instructional Routines to Support Foundational Skills Instruction*. Boise, ID: Idaho State Department of Education.

Duke, Nell K., and Kelly B. Cartwright. 2021. "The Science of Reading Progresses: Communicating Advances Beyond the Simple View of Reading" *Reading Research Quarterly* (Special Issue) 56 (S1): S25–S44. doi.org/10.1002/rrq.411.

Ehri, Linnea C. 2002. "Phases of Acquisition in Learning to Read Words and Implications for Teaching." *BJEP Monograph Series II: Part 1 Learning and Teaching Reading* 7–28. doi.org/10.53841/bpsmono.2002.cat527.3.

Ferlazzo, Larry. 2021. "The What, Why, and How of 'Interleaving.'" EdWeek (blog). May 30, 2021. edweek.org/teaching-learning/opinion-the-what-why-how-of-interleaving/2021/05.

Fox, Barbara J. 2012. *Word Identification Strategies, Fifth Edition*. Hoboken, NJ: Merrill Education/Prentice Hall.

Gillon, Gail T. 2018. *Phonological Awareness: From Research to Practice, Second Edition*. New York: Guilford.

Henbest, Victoria S., and Kenn Apel. 2017. "Effective Word Reading Instruction: What Does the Evidence Tell Us?" *Communication Disorders Quarterly* 39 (1): 304.

Hoover, Wesley A., and Philip B. Gough. 1990. "The Simple View of Reading." *Reading and Writing: An Interdisciplinary Journal* 2 (2): 127–160.

Jump, Jennifer, and Robin D. Johnson. 2023. *What the Science of Reading Says about Word Recognition.* Huntington Beach, CA: Shell Education.

Kilpatrick, David A. 2020. "How the Phonology of Speech Is Foundational for Instant Word Recognition." *Perspectives on Language and Literacy* Summer 2020: 11–15. literacyhow.org/wp-content/uploads/2020/09/The-Phonology-of-Speech-in-WR-Kilpatrick.pdf.

Meese, Ruth L. 2016. "We're Not in Kansas Anymore: The TOTO Strategy for Decoding Vowel Pairs." *The Reading Teacher* 69 (5): 549–552.

Mesmer, Heidi A. 2019. *Letter Lessons and First Words.* Portsmouth, NH: Heinemann.

Moats, Louisa Cook. 1999. *Teaching Reading Is Rocket Science: What Expert Teachers of Reading Should Know and Be Able to Do. Washington, DC: American Federation of Teachers.* eric.ed.gov/?id=ED445323.

———. 2020. *Speech to Print: Language Essentials for Teachers, Third Edition.* Baltimore, MD: Paul H. Brookes Publishing.

Murre, Jaap M.J., and Joeri Dros. 2015. "Replication and Analysis of Ebbinghaus' Forgetting Curve." *PLOS ONE.* July 6, 2015. doi.org/10.1371/journal.pone.0120644.

National Reading Panel. 2000. *Report of the National Reading Panel: Teaching Children to Read: An Evidence-Based Assessment of the Scientific Research Literature on Reading and Its Implications for Reading Instruction.* National Institute of Child Health and Human Development, National Institutes of Health.

Padak, Nancy, and Timothy Rasinski. 2008. "The Games Children Play." *The Reading Teacher* 62 (4): 363–365.

Petrigna, Luca, Ewan Thomas, Jessica Brusa, Federica Rizzo, Antonino Scardina, Claudia Galassi, Daniela Lo Verde, Giovanni Caramazza, and Marianna Bellafiore. 2022. "Does Learning Through Movement Improve Academic Performance in Primary Schoolchildren? A Systematic Review." *Frontiers in Pediatrics* 10: 841582. doi.org/10.3389/fped.2022.841582.

Reutzel, D. Ray. 2015. "Early Literacy Research: Findings Primary-Grade Teachers Will Want to Know." *The Reading Teacher* 69 (1): 14–24.

Share, David L. 1999. "Phonological Recoding and Orthographic Learning: A Direct Test of the Self-Teaching Hypothesis." *Journal of Experimental Child Psychology* 72 (2): 95–129. doi.org/10.1006/jecp.1998.2481.

Smith, Jodene L. 2023. *What the Science of Reading Says: Literacy Strategies for Early Childhood.* Huntington Beach, CA: Shell Education.

Sousa, David A. 2011. *How the Brain Learns, Fourth Edition.* Thousand Oaks, CA: Corwin.

Tunmer, Wiliam E., and Wesley A. Hoover. 2019. "The Cognitive Foundations of Learning to Read: A Framework for Preventing and Remediating Reading Difficulties." *Australian Journal of Learning Difficulties* 24 (1): 75–93. doi.org/10.1080/19404158.2019.1614081.

Digital Learning Resources

What's Included

Sound Cards
Connect sounds to spellings, and introduce articulation to encourage proper mouth positions when pronouncing phonemes.

Letter Cards
Model blending, segmenting, and dividing words into syllables with cards that are perfectly sized for use with pocket charts or small groups.

Sound Boxes
Focus attention on phonemic awareness by placing one counter per sound box for each sound or syllable in a word.

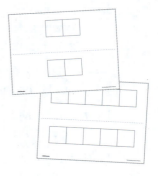

Basic Letter Tiles
Map sounds to letters, and promote decoding and encoding with tiles that are perfectly sized for use with sound boxes. Includes 52 letters and 5 counters.

Word Sort Templates
Create word-sort activities with charts that allow for sorting words into 2, 3, or 4 categories. Includes a template for cutting out words to use with the charts.

Intermediate Letter Tiles
Map sounds to letter teams, and promote decoding and encoding with tiles that are perfectly sized for use with sound boxes. Includes 10 counters.

Accessing the Digital Resources

The digital resources can be downloaded by following these steps:

1. Go to **www.tcmpub.com/digital**
2. Use the 13-digit ISBN number to redeem the digital resources.
3. Respond to the questions using the book.
4. Follow the prompts on the Content Cloud website to sign in or create a new account.
5. The content redeemed will appear on your My Content screen. Click on the product to look through the digital resources. All file resources are available for download. Select files can be previewed, opened, and shared. Any web-based content, such as videos, links, or interactive text, can be viewed and used in the browser but is not available for download.

For questions and assistance with your ISBN redemption, please contact Teacher Created Materials.

email: customerservice@tcmpub.com

phone: 800-858-7339

Notes

Notes

Notes